Wei-Bin Zhang

A Theory of International Trade

Capital, Knowledge, and Economic Structures

Springer

382
Z 63 t

Author

Dr. Wei-Bin Zhang
National University of Singapore
Department of Economics
10 Kent Ridge Crescent
Singapore 119260

Library of Congress Cataloging-in-Publication Data

Zhang, Wei-Bin, 1961-
   A theory of international trade : capital, knowledge, and economic structures / Wei-Bin Zhang.
      p. cm. -- (Lecture notes in economics and mathematical systems, ISSN 0075-8442 ; 482)
   Includes bibliographical references and index.
   ISBN 3540669175 (softcover : alk. paper)
   1. International trade--Econometric models. I. Title. II. Series.

   HF1379 .Z49 2000
   382--dc21

                                                              99-059378

ISSN 0075-8442
ISBN 3-540-66917-5 Springer-Verlag Berlin Heidelberg New York

Springer-Verlag is a company in the specialist publishing group BertelsmannSpringer
© Springer-Verlag Berlin Heidelberg 2000
Printed in Germany

Typesetting: Camera ready by author
Printed on acid-free paper   SPIN: 10734481   42/3143/du   543210

Acknowledgements

I completed this book at the Department of Economics, the National University of Singapore. I am grateful to an anonymous referee for valuable comments. I would like to thank Economics Editor Dr. Werner A. Müller and Economics Editorial Ruth Milewski for effective co-operation.

Chapters 2 to 11 are based on my published or unpublished manuscripts. Grateful acknowledgment is made to the following sources for the use of my published materials:

Chapter 2 for Zhang, W.B. (1994a) International Economic Journal;
Chapter 3 for Zhang, W.B. (1995b) International Economic Journal;
Chapter 4 for Zhang, W.B. (1995a) Economic Modelling;
Chapter 5 for Section 3.1 in Zhang, W.B. (1999a) and Zhang, W.B. (1994a);
Chapter 7 for Zhang, W.B. (1992b) Economic Letters;
Chapter 8 for Zhang, W.B. (1993a) International Review of Economics and Finance;
Chapter 9 for Zhang, W.B. (1995) A Two-Region Trade Equilibrium Model - Each Region with Two Classes and Two Sectors. Working Paper of CERUM, University of Umeå, CWP-1995:3.

Preface

Over more than two centuries the development of economic theory has created a wide array of different concepts, theories, and insights. My recent book *Capital and Knowledge* (Zhang, 1999a) shows how separate economic theories such as the Marxian economics, the Keynesian economics, the general equilibrium theory, and the neoclassical growth theory can be examined within a single theoretical framework. The *Capital and Knowledge* constructs an economic theory to account for the phenomena explained by the main economic theories (of national economies) in a unified manner. It tries to draw together the disparate branches of economics into a single organized system of knowledge.

This book is a part of my economic theory with endogenous population, capital, knowledge, preferences, sexual division of labor and consumption, institutions, economic structures and exchange values over time and space (Zhang, 1996a). As an extension of the *Capital and Knowledge*, which is focused on the dynamics of national economies, this book is to construct a theory of international trade. We are concerned with dynamic relations between international division of labor, division of consumption and determination of prices structure in global economy. We examine dynamic interdependence between capital accumulation, knowledge creation and utilization, economic growth, price structures and international trade patterns under free competition. Our theory is constructed on the basis of a few concepts within a compact framework. The comparative advantage of our theory is that in providing rich insights into complex of international trades it uses only a few concepts and simplified functional forms and accepts a few assumptions about behavior of consumers, producers and institutional structures.

This book constructs a theoretical framework which would permit valid generalizations from one special modeling structure to another, and would deepen our understanding of economic evolution. It is a part of my broad approach to revealing complex of economic evolution (Zhang, 1991c, 1999a, 1998a, 1999b, 2000). I wish that the reader might appreciate this book within the grand framework of economic analysis that I have made great efforts to construct.

Contents

1 Introduction 1
  1.1   The Ricardian Trade Theory 1
  1.2   The Neoclassical Theory 4
  1.3   The Heckscher-Ohlin Theory 7
  1.4   Trade Theory with Capital Accumulation 9
  1.5   Trade with Non-Constant Returns to Scale 11
  1.6   Trade Theory with Endogenous Technology 14
  1.7   The Structure of the Book 17

2 Global Growth and Trade Patterns 23
  2.1   The Trade Model with Capital Accumulation 24
  2.2   The Two-Country Economy 30
  2.3   Some Special Cases of the Two-Country Economy 34
  2.4   Discussing the Multi-Country Case 36
  Appendix 38
  A. 2.1 Equilibra and Stability in the Two-Country Economy 38

**3 Growth, Trade, and Wealth Distribution among
Groups** 41
  3.1   The Dynamic Trade Theory 43
  3.2   Equilibrium of the World Economy 45
  3.3   The Impact of the Propensity to Hold Wealth 49
  3.4   The Impact of Human Capital 51

**4 Trade, Time Distribution, and Sexual Division of
Labor** 53
  4.1   International Trade with Sexual Division of Labor 54
  4.2   Equilibrium of the Global Economy 58
  4.3   Time Allocation and Trade Patterns 61
  4.4   The Impact of the Wife's Human Capital 64
  4.5   Concluding Remarks 65

**5 Growth and Trade Patterns with National Public
Goods** 67
  5.1   The Trade Model with Public Goods 67

5.2   Equilibria of the Global Economy 71
5.3   The Impact of Changes in the Tax Rate 75
5.4   The Impact of Changes in the Population 77

6 Growth, Trade, and International Migration 80
6.1   The Growth Model with Trade and Migration 81
6.2   Equilibrium of the Global Economy 85
6.3   The Impact of Amenity on Trade and Migration 90
6.4   The Impact of Human Capital on Trade and Migration 93
6.5   Concluding Remarks 96

7 Trade with Endogenous Capital and Knowledge 97
7.1   The Model with Capital and Knowledge 98
7.2   The Dynamics of the Trade System 100
7.3   The Global Economy in the Autarky System 104
7.4   A Comparison of the Autarky and Trade Systems 106
7.5   Concluding Remarks 108

8 Global Economic Growth with Trade and Research 109
8.1   The Model with Trade and Research 110
8.2   The Dynamics of the Free Trade System 113
8.3   Equilibria and Stability Conditions 115
8.4   Does Free Trade Benefit the World Economy? 118
8.5   The Impact of Knowledge Accumulation Efficiency 121
8.6   Research, Knowledge, and Trade 122
       Appendix 122
       A. 8.1 Equilibra and Stability of the Autarky System 122

9 Trade Patterns in a Multi-Group and Multi-Sector
Global Economy 124
9.1   The Multi-Group and Multi-Sector Model 125
9.2   The Existence of Equilibrium 128
9.3   The Impact of Labor Force and Land 133
9.4   The Impact of Landlords' Propensity to Consume Foreign
       Goods 137
9.5   Concluding Remarks 138
       Appendix 138
       A. 9.1 Checking Lemma 9.3.2 138

10 Global Growth, Trade, and Economic Structures 140
10.1   The Growth Model with Trade and Structures 141
10.2   The Dynamic Properties of the System 144
10.3   The Savings Rates and the World Economy 148
       Appendix 153
       A. 10.1 Proving Proposition 10.2.1 153
       A. 10.2 Proving Proposition 10.2.2 156

11 A Multi-Sector Trade Model with Endogenous Knowledge 160

11.1 The Multi-Sector Model with Endogenous Knowledge 160

11.2 Equilibria and Stability 164

11.3 The Impact of Knowledge Accumulation Efficiency 166

11.4 The Impact of the Preference for Foreign Goods 168

Appendix 171

A. 11.1 Proving Proposition 11.2.1 171

A. 11.2 Proving Proposition 11.2.2 173

12 Further Issues on International Trade 175

Bibliography 180

Name Index 190

1 Introduction

This book is to construct a theory of international trade. We are concerned with dynamic relations between international division of labor, division of consumption and determination of prices structure in the global economy. Our main contributions are related to revealing dynamic interdependence between capital accumulation, knowledge creation and utilization, economic growth, price structures and international trade patterns under free competition. We build our theory in a compact theoretical framework with a few concepts. The comparative advantage of our theory is that it uses only a few concepts and simplified functional forms and accepts a few assumptions about behavior of consumers, producers and institutional structures, but it achieves rich conclusions and it is conceptually easy to extend and generalize the theory because of its consistency and simplicity. Before developing our trade theory, we review some main theories of international economics.

1.1 The Ricardian Trade Theory

Adam Smith (1776) held that a country could gain from free trade. He pointed out that if one country has an absolute advantage over the other in one production and the other country has an absolute advantage over the first in another production, both countries gain from trading. But Smith failed to create a convincing economic theory of international trade. It is generally agreed that David Ricardo is the creator of the classical theory of international trade, even though many concrete ideas about trade existed before his *Principles* (Ricardo, 1817, Morishima, 1989). The theories of comparative advantage and the gains from trade are usually connected with his name. The theory of comparative advantage or the theory of comparative costs is one of oldest theories of economics. In this theory the crucial variable used to explain international trade patterns is technology. The theory holds that a difference in comparative costs of production is the necessary condition for the existence of international trade. But this difference reflects a difference in techniques of production. According to this theory, technological differences between countries determine international division of labor and consumption and trade patterns. It holds that trade is beneficial to all participating countries. This conclusion is against the viewpoint about trade held by the doctrine of mercantilism. In mercantilism it is argued that the regulation and planning of economic activity are efficient means of fostering the goals of nation.

In order to illustrate the theory of comparative advantage, we consider an example constructed by Ricardo. We assume that the world consists of two countries (for instance, England and Portugal). There are two commodities (cloth and wine) and a single factor (labor) of production. Technologies of the two countries are fixed. Let us assume that the unit cost of production of each commodity (expressed in terms of labor) is constant. We consider a case in which each country is superior to the other one in production of one (and only one) commodity. For instance, England produces cloth in lower unit cost than Portugal and Portugal makes wine in lower unit cost than England. In this situation, international exchanges of commodities will occur under free trade conditions. It benefits both England and Portugal if the former is specified in the production of cloth and the latter in wine. This case is easy to understand. The Ricardian theory also shows that even if one country is superior to the other one in the production of two commodities, free international trade may still benefit the two countries. We may consider the following example to illustrate the point.

Let us assume that the unit costs of production of cloth and wine in terms of labor are respectively 4 and 8 in England; while they are 6 and 10 in Portugal. That is, England is superior to Portugal in the production of both commodities. It seems that there is no scope for international trade since England is superior in everything. But the theory predicts a different conclusion. It argues that the condition for international trade to take place is the existence of a difference between the comparative costs. Here, we define comparative costs as the ratio between the unit costs of the two commodities in the same countries. In our example comparative costs are $4/8 = 0.5$ and $6/10 = 0.6$ in England and Portugal respectively. It is straightforward to see that England has a relatively greater advantage in the production of cloth than wine: the ratio of production costs of cloth between England and Portugal is $4/6$; the ratio of production costs of wine is $8/10$. It can also seen that Portugal has a relatively smaller disadvantage in the production of wine. The Ricardian model predicts that if the terms of trade are greater than 0.5 and smaller than 0.6, British cloth will be exchanged for Portuguese wine to the benefit of both countries. For instance, if we fix the trade terms at 0.55 which means that 0.55 units of wine exchanges for one unit of cloth, then in free trade system in England one unit of cloth exchanges for 0.55 units of wine (rather than 0.5 as in isolated system) and in Portugal 0.55 (rather than 0.6) unit of wine exchanges for one unit of cloth. The model thus concludes that international trade is beneficial to both countries. It is easy to check that the terms of trade must be strictly located between the two comparative costs (i.e., between 0.5 and 0.6 in our example). It is direct to check that if the terms of trade were equal to either comparative cost, the concerned country would have no economic incentive to trade; if the terms of trade were outside the interval between the comparative costs, then some country will suffer a loss by engaging in international trade.

This theory may be represented in different ways. For instance, we may interpret the theory of comparative costs in terms of optimization. We refer the following example to Gandolfo (1994a). We consider a simple case in which the world economy consists of two countries and produces commodities. Here, we consider the benefits from international trade in terms of an increase in the quantity (rather than utility) of goods which can be obtained from the given amount of labor. Our optimal problem is to maximize each country's real income under constraints of the fixed labor and technology. We use p_x and p_y to denote the absolute prices of goods x and y (expressed in terms of some external unit of measurement, for instance, gold). Under the assumptions of free trade, perfect competition and zero-transportation cost, the domestic price ratio is equal between the two countries. The exchange ratio of the two goods, p_x / p_y, is taken as given. Let x_j and y_j denote respectively country j's outputs of goods x and y and N_j stand for country j's fixed labor force. Country j's optimal problem is defined by

$$Max\ Y_j = (\frac{p_x}{p_y})x_j + y_j,$$

subject to $\quad a_{1j}x_j + a_{2j}y_j \le N_j,\ \ x_j, y_j \ge 0,\ \ j = 1, 2 \qquad (1.1.1)$

in which Y_j, is country j's real national income measured in terms of good y and a_{1j} and a_{2j} are respectively country j's unit costs of production of goods x and y. The optimal problems defined by (1.1.1) can find an easy graphic solution. It is shown that international trade and international specification occur as a consequence of the maximization of the real national income of each country separately considered.

One of the attractive features of the Ricardian model is that its modeling structure allows virtually all the results obtained for the simple two-commodity and two-country case to be extended to many countries and many commodities, even though some new features appear in high dimensions (e.g., Jones and Neary, 1984). For example, when the global economy consists of many commodities but only two countries, commodities can be ranked by comparative costs in a chain of decreasing relative labor costs:

$$\frac{a_{21}}{a_{11}} > \frac{a_{22}}{a_{12}} > \cdots > \frac{a_{2j}}{a_{1j}} > \cdots > \frac{a_{2n}}{a_{1n}} \qquad (1.1.2)$$

in which a_{ij} is country i's labor requirement per unit output in sector j, $i = 1, 2$, $j = 1, 2, ..., n$. Demand conditions determine where the chain is broke. The comparative unit costs ensure that country 1 must export all commodities to the left of the break and import all those to the right, with at most one commodity produced in common.

This theory assumes that production costs are independent of factor prices and the composition of output. The model throws no light on issues related to the internal distribution of income since it assumes either a single mobile factor or multiple mobile factors which are used in equal proportions in all sectors. From this theory we can only determine the limits within which the terms of trade must lie. Since it lacks of consideration of demand sides, the theory cannot determine how and at what value the terms of trade are determined within the limits. This is a serious limitation of this theory because a trade theory should be able to explain the causes and directions of trade but also to determine the terms of trade.

1.2 The Neoclassical Theory

The Ricardian theory failed to determine the terms of trade, even though it can be used to determine the limits in which the terms of trade must lie. It was recognized long ago that in order to determine the terms of trade, it is necessary to build trade theory which not only takes account of the productive side but also the demand side (Negishi, 1972, Dixit and Norman, 1980, Jones, 1979). The neoclassical theory holds that the determinants of trade patterns are to be found simultaneously in the differences between the technologies, the factor endowments, and the tastes of different countries (Mill, 1848, Marshall, 1890). Preference accounts for the existence of international trade even if technologies and factor endowments were completely identical between countries.

The Marshallian offer curve has been often used to analyze problems such as the existence of equilibrium, the stability of equilibrium, the gains from trade, optimum tariffs and so on within static frameworks. For illustration, we show how Mill solved the trade equilibrium problem and how this problem can be solved with help of modern analytical tool. Mill introduced the equation of international demand, according to which the terms of trade are determined so as to equate the value of exports and the value of imports. He argued: "the exports and imports between the two countries (or, if we suppose more than two, between each country and the world) must in the aggregate pay for each other, and must therefore be exchanged for one another at such values as will be compatible with the equation of the international demand" (Mill, 1848: 596). Mill initiated the theory of reciprocal demand which is one of the earliest examples of general equilibrium analysis in trade theory. In Chapter 18, book 3 of his *Principles*, he showed the existence of trade equilibrium, using a simplified model and explicitly solving equations in the model numerically. He assumed that there exists only one factor of production and production is subjected to constant returns to scale and requires on the demand side as follows: "Let us therefore assume, that the influence of cheapness on demand conforms to some simple law, common to both countries and to both commodities. As the simplest and most convenient, let us suppose that in both countries any given increase of cheapness produces an exactly proportional increase of consumption; or, in other words, that the value expended in the commodity, the cost incurred for the sake of obtaining it, is always the same, whether that cost affords a greater or a smaller quantity of the commodity." (Mill, 1848: 598). As a numerical example, consider that the world economy consists of Germany and England and the economic system has two goods, cloth and linen. Let us assume that in Germany 10 yards of cloth was exchanged for 20 yards of linen and that England wants to sell $1,000,000$ yards of cloth to Germany. If Germany wants $800,000$ yards of cloth, this is equal to $1,600,000$ yards of linen at German exchange ratio. Since German expended value in cloth is constant, England will receive $1,600,000$ yards of linen in exchange of $1,000,000$ yards of cloth, replacing Germany supply of cloth entirely. Under the assumption mentioned above and some additional requirements, Mill explicitly solved the international exchange ratio of two commodities in terms of coefficients of production in two countries and by so doing showed the existence of trade equilibrium. Chipman pointed out that the case analyzed by Mill can be treated as a problem of non-linear programming and the existence of trade equilibrium can be proved by the existence theorem of a solution of non-linear programming (Chipman, 1965a, Negishi, 1972).

We now use analytical methods to prove the existence of trade equilibrium as showed by Mill (Negishi, 1972). This example also illustrates the difference between the Ricardian theory and the neoclassical theory. Let subscript indexes 1 and 2 represent respectively Germany and England. We denote the amount of cloth and linen produced by country j respectively y_{jc} and y_{jl} which are non-negative. If we denote the total amount of cloth (linen) produced in country j when the country is completely specified in producing cloth (linen) by a_{jc} (a_{jl}), the possible sets of y_{jc} and y_{jl} are given by

$$\frac{y_{jc}}{a_{jc}} + \frac{y_{jl}}{a_{jl}} \le 1, \quad y_{jc}, y_{jl} \ge 0, \quad j = 1, 2. \tag{1.2.1}$$

The above two equations mean that the demand for labor does not exceed the supply in each country. We denote respectively the prices of cloth and linen by p_c and p_l. At equilibrium country j 's production structure (y_{jc}, y_{jl}) should maximize

$$\frac{p_c}{p_l} y_{jc} + y_{jl}.$$

Multiplying (1.2.1) by a_{jc} ($j = 1, 2$) and adding the two equations, we get

$$y_c + \frac{a_{1c}}{a_{1l}} y_{1l} + \frac{a_{2c}}{a_{2l}} \le a_c$$

where

$$y_c \equiv y_{1c} + y_{2c}, \quad a_c \equiv a_{1c} + a_{2c}.$$

If we assume that Germany has the comparative advantage in linen, i.e., $a_{1c} / a_{1l} < a_{2c} / a_{2l}$, from the above inequality we get

$$\frac{y_c}{a_{1c}} + \frac{y_l}{a_{1l}} \le \frac{a_c}{a_{1c}} \tag{1.2.2}$$

where $y_l \equiv y_{1l} + y_{2l}$. Similarly multiplying (1.2.1) by a_{jl}, we get

$$\frac{y_c}{a_{2c}} + \frac{y_l}{a_{2l}} \le \frac{a_l}{a_{2l}} \tag{1.2.3}$$

where $a_l \equiv a_{1l} + a_{2l}$.

In order to describe the demand, let $x_c \, (\ge 0)$, $x_l \, (\ge 0)$ and $R \, (\ge 0)$ respectively stand for the demand for cloth, demand for linen, and income measured in terms of the factor of production. Maximizing the following utility

$$U = x_c x_l$$

subject to the budget constraint $p_c x_c + p_l x_l = R$ yields the demand functions

$$x_c = \frac{R}{2 p_c}, \quad x_l = \frac{R}{2 p_l}$$

which satisfy Mill's assumption. Since the two countries have an identical preference structure but different incomes, we have that country j's demand for cloth and linen, X_{jc} and X_{jl}, are given by

$$X_{jc} = \frac{R_j}{2 p_c}, \quad X_{jl} = \frac{R_j}{2 p_l}, \quad j = 1, 2 \tag{1.2.4}$$

where R_j is country j's income. Since demands for commodities cannot exceed supplies at the equilibrium of free international trade, we have

$$X_c \leq y_{1c} + y_{2c}, \quad X_l \leq y_{1l} + y_{2l} \tag{1.2.5}$$

where

$$X_c \equiv X_{1c} + X_{2c}, \quad X_l \equiv X_{1l} + X_{2l}.$$

Introduce the world utility function as

$$U = \log X_c + \log X_l.$$

We maximize this U subject to (1.2.1) and (1.2.5). The Lagrangean is given by

$$\log X_c + \log X_l + p_c(y_{1c} + y_{2c} - X_c) + p_l(y_{1l} + y_{2l} - X_l)$$

$$+ \sum_{j=1}^{2} w_j \left(\frac{y_{jc}}{a_{jc}} + \frac{y_{jl}}{a_{jl}} - 1 \right).$$

It is shown that the Lagrangean has a strictly positive saddle point at which (1.2.1) and (1.2.5) are satisfied with equality at the saddle point. In fact, this saddle point is an equilibrium of free international trade, with p_c / p_l, w_1 / p_l and w_2 / p_l respectively satisfying the price of cloth, the price of factor of production in Germany and in England. Since the world total income is equal to

$$p_c X_c + p_l X_1 = w_1 + w_2$$

we have $R_j = w_j$. By (1.2.4) we get X_{jc} and X_{jl} which is an optimal solution of the problem that country j maximizes its utility subject to its budget constraint with the given world prices.

1.3 The Heckscher-Ohlin Theory

The Ricardian model and Heckscher-Ohlin model are two basic models of trade and production. They provide the pillars upon which much of pure theory of international trade rests. The so-called Heckscher-Ohlin model has been one of the dominant models of comparative advantage in modern economics. The Heckscher-Ohlin theory emphasizes the differences between the factor endowments of different countries and differences between commodities in the intensities with which they use these factors. The basic model deals with a long-term general equilibrium in which the two factors are both mobile between sectors and the cause of trade is different countries having different relative factor endowments. This theory deals with the impact of trade on factor use and factor rewards. The theory is different from the Ricardian model which isolates differences in technology between countries as the basis for trade. In the Heckscher-Ohlin theory costs of production are endogenous in the sense that they are different in the trade and autarky situations, even when all countries have access to the same technology for producing each good. This model has been a main stream of international trade theory. According to Either (1974), this theory has four "core proportions". In the simple case of two-commodity and two-country world economy, we have these four propositions (which are of course held under certain conditions) as follows: (1) factor-price equalization theorem by Lerner (1952) and Samuelson (1948, 1949), stating that free trade in final goods alone brings about complete international equalization of factor prices; (2) Stolper-Samuelson theory by Stolper and Samuelson (1941), saying that an increase in the relative price of one commodity raises the real return of the factor used intensively in producing that commodity and lowers the real return of the other factor; (3) Rybczynski theorem by Rybczynski (1955), stating that if commodity prices are held fixed, an increase in the endowment of one factor causes a more than proportionate increase in the output of the commodity which uses that factor relatively intensively and an absolute decline in the output of the other commodity; and (4) Heckscher-Ohlin theorem by Heckscher (1919) and Ohlin (1933), stating that a country tends to have a bias towards producing and exporting the commodity which uses intensively the factor with which it is relatively well-endowed.

The Heckscher-Ohlin theory provides simple and intuitive insights into the relationships between commodity prices and factor prices, factor supplies and factor rewards, and factor endowments and the pattern of production and trade. Although the Heckscher-Ohlin model was the dominant framework for analyzing trade in the 1960s, it had neither succeeded in supplanting the Ricardian model nor had been replaced by the specific-factor trade models. Each theory has been refined within 'small scales'. Each theory is limited to a range of questions. It is argued that as far as general ideas are concerned, the Heckscher-Olin theory may be considered as a special case of the neoclassical theory mentioned before as it accepts all the logical promises of neoclassical methodology (e.g., Gandolfo, 1994a). The Heckscher-Olin theory may be seen as a special case of the neoclassical trade theory in which production technology and preferences are internationally identical. This loss of generality has long been held necessary in order to construct a clear picture of international trade patterns and division of labor and consumption. This book shows that it is possible to construct a compact trade theory without loss of the generality characterized of the neoclassical trade theory.

Ricardo's initial discussion of the concept of comparative advantage is limited to the case when factors of production are immobile internationally. His arguments about gains from trade between England and Portugal are valid only if English labor and/or Portuguese technology (or climate) are prevented from moving across national boundaries. The Heckscher-Ohlin theory is similarly limited to the study of how movements of commodities can substitute for international movements of productive factors. It is obvious that if technologies are everywhere identical and if production is sufficiently diversified, factor prices become equalized between countries. But if production functions differ between countries, no presumption as to factor equalization remains. Most of early contributions to trade theory deal with goods trade only and ignore international mobility of factors of production. For a long period of time since Ricardo, the classical mobility assumption had been well accepted. This assumption tells that all final goods are tradable between countries whereas primary inputs are non-tradable, though they are fully mobile between different sectors of the domestic economy. In reality, this classical assumption is invalid in many circumstances. For instance, many kinds of final 'goods', services, are not-trade and capitals are fully mobile between countries as well as within domestic economies. A great deal of works on trade theory has been concerned with examining the consequences of departures from these assumptions. There is an extensive literature on various aspects of international factor mobility (Jones and Kenen, 1984, Ethier and Svensson, 1986, Bhagwati, 1991, Wong, 1995). We will not review this literature.

1.4 Trade Theory with Capital Accumulation

It may be true to say that most of the pure theory of international trade emerged from Ricardo's *Principles*. The simple example of the exchange of cloth and wine between England and Portugal gives us a beautiful illustration of the concept of comparative advantage. The further development of the subject by Mill, Marshall and Edgeworth remained largely within the bounds set by Ricardo. Since then, there had been much attention focused on the determination of the terms of trade by reciprocal demand within frameworks of many goods, countries and factors under various forms of intervention. As mentioned by Findlay (1984), one topic that was almost entirely absent from the pure theory of international trade was any consideration of the connection between economic growth and international trade in classical literature of economic theory. Almost all of trade models developed before the 1960s are static in the sense that the supplies of factors of production are given and do not vary over time; the classical Ricardian theory of comparative advantage and the Heckscher-Ohlin theory are static since labor and capital stocks (or land) are assumed to be given and constant over time. Although Marshall held that it is important to study international trade in order to be clear of the causes which determine the economic progresses of nations, it has only been in the last three or four decades that trade theory has made some systematical treatment of endogenous capital accumulation or technological changes in the context of international economics.

The consideration of endogenous capital or technological change in trade theory was influenced by development of neoclassical growth theory with capital accumulation and growth theory with endogenous knowledge. This order of development of economic theory is reasonable as it is only after we are able to explain how national economies operate that we can effectively model international economies. When economists had no compact framework to explain national economies, it is hard to imagine how international economies could be analyzed comprehensively. A national economy may be perceived as a special case of the global economy in the sense that the global economy is national when it consists of identical multiple national economies. Since there was no compact framework of operations of national economies with endogenous capital and knowledge, it is reasonable to know that there was no compact framework to analyze international trade.

Trade models with capital movements are originated by MacDougall (1960) and Kemp (1961), even though these models were limited to static and one-commodity frameworks. A dynamic model, which takes account of accumulating capital stocks and of growing population within the Heckscher-Ohlin type of model is initially developed by Oniki and Uzawa and others, in terms of the two-country, two-good, two-factor model of trade. The Oniki-Uzawa model is developed within the framework of neoclassical growth theory. The model is primarily concerned with the process of world capital accumulation and distribution with demands and supplies as fast processes. The two-sector growth model has often been applied to analyze the interdependence between trade patterns and economic growth. These models are used to study the dynamics of capital accumulation and the various balance of payments accounts. There are different sets of assumptions made about the structure of trade. For instance, In the trade models by Oniki and Uzawa (1965) and Johnson (1971) free trade in both consumption and investment goods are allowed. This framework was extended by Zhang (1995a, 1996b, 1997, 1998b, 1998c). An alternative specification of trade structure in the growth framework allows for the existence of international financial markets and for free trade in consumption goods and securities, but not in investment goods (e.g., Fisher and Frenkel, 1972). This framework emphasizes the interaction of foreign borrowing, debt service, and domestic capital accumulation. The two-sector neoclassical growth theory was also applied to analyzing small open economies (Bardhan, 1965, Ryder, 1967, Bruce, 1977).

Eaton (1987) proposed a dynamic two-sector, three-factors model of international trade. The dynamic specification of the model is based on Samuelson's (1958) overlapping generations model. The dynamic model at each point of time t proposed by Eaton is identical to the three-factor, two-commodity model examined in a static context by Jones (1971), Samuelson (1971) and Mussa (1974). The model tries to extend the Heckscher-Ohlin theory to include endowments of factor as endogenous variables. In this model land and capital serve not only as factors of production but also as assets which individuals use to transfer income from working periods to retirement. The model shows that changes in the terms of trade and in the endowments of fixed factors do not necessarily have the same effects on factor prices and on the composition of output as they do in a static framework. Some results obtained from the specific-factors model about the relationships between commodity prices and factor prices, factor endowments and factor rewards, and factor endowments and the pattern of production are not held in the dynamic model. For instance, a permanent increase in the relative price of one commodity does not necessarily lower the steady-state income of the factor specific to the industry producing the other commodity.

Obstfeld (1981) examined the savings behavior of a small economy facing a certain world real interest rate. Obstfeld proposes a dynamic Heckscher-Ohlin model with internationally mobile capital and overlapping generations of infinitely-lived agents.

The model focuses on the effects of government debt and spending shocks. Devereux and Shi (1991) developed a trade model which includes intertemporal consumption-savings decisions with the use of recursive preferences. These preferences make it possible to analyze heterogeneity in a representative-agent infinite horizon model with well-defined steady states. The key factors driving the steady state are the convergence of national rates of time preference with one another and the monotonical relationship between consumption and the real interest rate at the steady state. This implies that each country's share of total world output depends only on its degree of impatience and not on country-specific factors. From this model it concludes that the more patient country has a higher steady-state consumption and will be a steady-state external creditor.

1.5 Trade with Non-Constant Returns to Scale

As shown in Zhang (1994c, 1999a), increasing returns to scale is a characteristic feature of many economic activities. It may come from population dynamics, knowledge creation and utilization, and institutional changes. But the history of economic analysis shows that it is not an easy matter to formally model non-constant return to scales within a competitive framework. In fact most of economic theories are developed under the assumption of constant returns to scale, even though economists have long ago recognized the significance of increasing returns to scale in production for determining international trade patterns. Nonetheless increasing returns had never played a central role in the trade theory until the recent developments of the new trade theory. The assumption that technology exhibits constant returns to scale has been accepted in most general equilibrium models. Most theoretical economists have been wary of modeling increasing returns. It is analytically difficult to handle with increasing returns within the framework of perfect competition. New modeling frameworks require in order to maintain the assumption of perfectly competitive behavior with increasing returns. Some years ago Chipman (1965b) pointed out two reasons for this omission. The first reason is that economies of scale tend to be ignored in theoretical models not so much on empirical grounds as for the simple reason that it is difficult to build a trade theory with increasing returns. This is indeed a poor reason; but no theoretical trade economist could avoid being criticized for neglecting one of the principle sources of international trade simply due to this reason. The second reason given by Chipman is that the presence of increasing returns in production leads to multiple equilibria. The existence of multiple trade patterns introduces an intrinsic arbitrariness into the determination of the international pattern of specification and trade. It is known that if there are multiple equilibria, comparative static analysis becomes invalid. It should be remarked that what Chipman had pointed out have been recently overcome by trade economists. Trade economists have proposed many theoretical trade models with increasing returns. They have overcome the theoretical difficulties involved in building such models and they have recently accepted the existence of multiple equilibria and instability as economists naturally accepted the existence of a unique equilibrium and stability in the 60s and 70s.

Adam Smith (1776) used the story of the pin factory to illustrate the idea that the conception of increasing returns to scale is central to the explanation of long-run growth. There is interdependence between the division of labor and learning by doing. As skill is increased, the worker will concentrate on a special task and thus further increase his skill. Smith examined the relationship between international division of labor and trade. Marshall was aware of the inevitably changing technological and social framework within which economies operated. He provided a vision of "organic growth" of economic systems. He considered individuals to respond to economic opportunities locally with partial adjustments occurring over time. Increasing return to scale economies were explicitly treated in his theoretical framework of partial analysis. He argued that returning to scale economies were due to technological changes and other social and economic factors. Marshall (1890) distinguished between internal and external scale economies and examined the possibility of multiple equilibria. He recognized possible technological and organizational sources of increasing returns to scale that are internal to establishments, business firms and industries. He noted a number of conditions, including greater possibilities for specialization in the provision of intermediate inputs, a finer division of labor, and the more rapid diffusion of innovation among specialized producers and workers. Marshall introduced the notion of an "external economy" to discuss the existence of the equilibrium of a decentralized price taking economy in the presence of aggregate increasing returns. He noted that an increase in trade represents a form of external economy when production knowledge cannot be kept secret. Marshall's argument shows that if knowledge is treated as an endogenous variable in economic growth, then the system may exhibit multiple equilibria and it is not necessary for equilibrium to be stable.

Classical trade theory does not neglect technology. Ricardo's doctrine of comparative costs presupposed that countries differed from one another in the productivity of labor in producing commodities. Although the Ricardian theory is not concerned with how technology itself may be affected by trade, the theory studies the consequence of technologies differing between countries. Marshall was concerned with trade and increasing returns. Issues related to gains from trade and other social welfare were well raised even in the classical tradition. For instance, Marshall discussed terms of trade effects, arguing that with increasing returns to scale a country may improve its terms of trade by expanding demand for its imports. Graham (1923) argued that economies of scale may cause a country to lose from trade. For instance, consider an economy in which there is a single production factor, labor, and equal prices of both goods. Also suppose that as a result of foreign trade a country shifts labor from the increasing returns to scale industry to the decreasing returns to scale industry. Then output per man falls in both industries, thereby reducing gross domestic product at constant prices. He held that when a country has a sector with increasing returns to scale and a sector with decreasing returns to scale it may lose from trade. He suggested that in this case a tariff is beneficial. Knight (1924) argued that Graham's analysis of the possible losses from trade is valid if the economies of scale are external to the firm and internal to the industry; but it is wrong if the economies of scale are internal to the firm. Ethier (1979, 1982b) explored the conditions under which

Graham's arguments hold: they depend on the nature of the increasing returns which are either national or international and the pattern of change in relative prices due to the transition from autarky to trade.

Economists have recognized long time ago that economies of scale provide an alternative to differences in technology or factor endowments as an explanation of international trade. But increasing returns as a cause of trade has received relatively little attention from formal trade theory. Ohlin (1933) pointed out that economies of scale serve as one explanation of foreign trade patterns. Since then, many trade theorists emphasized the role of monopolistic competition in differentiated products. In particular, there exist early attempts to extend trade theory on the basis of Chamberlin's *Monopolistic Competition* (Chamberlin, 1933). Explicit general-equilibrium analysis of trade based on external economies was initiated with Matthews (1949). Kemp and Negishi (1970) made an important contribution to the literature, showing that gains from trade are guaranteed if free trade leads to an expansion (noncontraction) of all increasing returns industries and nonexpansion of all decreasing returns industries. Eaton and Panagariya (1979) refined the Kemp-Negishi result. They proved that there are gains from trade as long as there exists an industry such that all industries with stronger degree of increasing returns (to weaker decreasing returns) do not contract in the move to free trade, and all industries with weaker increasing returns (or stronger decreasing returns) do not expand. In order to take account the relative importance of increases and decreases in the increasing returns to scale sectors, Markusen and Melvin (1984) defined a weighted average rule which applies under the assumption of convex production possibilities frontier and the absence of factor market distortions. But this rule is not valid when increasing returns lead to nonconvex production possibilities. Helpman and Krugman (1985) provided a rule that applies if aggregate factor usage is fixed between equilibria. Grinols (1992) develop a rule which applies to more general cases and does not require a convex production possibility frontier or fixed factor usage between equilibria. He develops a sufficient condition for gains from trade when some increasing returns industries expand and others contract. His conclusions do not depend on the restrictions that the production frontier must be convex, changes must satisfy a pre-specified hierarchical pattern, or that total factor supplies must be fixed between equilibria.

Krugman (1989, 1990) developed a trade model with a single scarce factor of production, labor, on the basis of the assumptions that scale economies are internal to firms and the market structure is one of Chamberlian monopolistic competition. His treatment of monopolistic competition was influenced by the model by Dixit and Stiglitz (1977). He produced trade between identical economies where comparative advantage is not the cause of trade, whether that comparative advantage comes from Ricardian or Heckscher-Ohlin factors. It is shown that trade may be a way of extending the market and allowing exploitation of scarce economies, with the effects of trade being similar to industrial, urban, or regional agglomeration. This trade model is better suited to explain intraindustry trade (i.e., trade in similar products) between advanced countries.

Much of the early attention in the literature of modeling two-way trade with increasing returns was placed on trade at the final product level, rather than trade in intermediate products. Ethier (1979, 1982a) emphasized that returns to specification and two-way trade in intermediate products imply external returns to scale that spill over between economies. It is argued that the spillover effects associated with international scale economies are an immediate result of the global and regional integration of industries subject to external static or dynamic scale effects. In Francois (1994), a dual model of trade under international returns economies is developed and applied to examine foreign investment, labor migration, and commercial policy. It is demonstrated that spillover effects associated with international scale economies are an immediate result of global and regional integration of industries, and have important implications for commercial policy. As far as economic modeling is concerned, the models with increasing returns mentioned above were limited to static frameworks. These works did not provide much indication as to what are the dynamic effects of international trade on growth, technological progress, and welfare.

The effects of increasing returns to scale on international trade have been one of the main topics in international trade theory for many years. A host of trade problems such as trade patterns, gains from trade, commercial policy, transaction corporations, direct foreign investment have been examined within economic systems with increasing returns. Yet, these concerns are mostly pursued under noncompetitive frameworks. There are many models in the theory of international trade in the presence of economies of scale and monopolistic competition. This book will not follow this tradition. We propose a theory of international trade in the presence of economies of scale and free competition.

1.6 Trade Theory with Endogenous Technology

Except population and institutions, knowledge is a significant source of returns to scale economies. Classical economists such as Smith, Marx, Marshall and Schumpeter, emphasized various aspects of knowledge in economic dynamics. But there were only a few formal economic models which deal with interdependence between economic growth and knowledge accumulation before the 1960s. Development of macroeconomics and theory of international trade are intimately connected. Neoclassical growth theory has been adopted to study relationships between trade and economic growth. But most of trade models with endogenous capital assume constant returns to scale production functions with inputs of capital and labor. Technological change is assumed to be exogenous or an ad hoc function of variables that can be analyzed separately from the basic factors of production function. The neoclassical growth theory developed in the 60s and 70s was crucially dependent on some exogenous parameters such as exogenous technological progress and an exogenous saving rate. However, it has been pointed out that the neoclassical growth theory cannot satisfactorily explain many empirical observations such as the diversity in per capita GNP growth rates across regions or countries. The neoclassical growth framework failed to provide a satisfactory framework for analyzing long-run growth. These models conclude that if countries with the same preference and technology will converge to identical levels of income and asymptotic growth rates.

In the 70s Arrow's learning by doing model (Arrow, 1962) and research models (Uzawa, 1965, Phelps, 1966) initiated a new trend of modeling interdependence between knowledge and economic growth. Although research on human capital (e.g., Becker, 1975) and technological change (e.g., Robson, 1980, Sato and Tsutui, 1984, Nelson and Winter 1982) caused attention from economists, it may be said that growth with endogenous knowledge was not a mainstream of theoretical economics in the 80s. Since Romer (1986) and Lucas (1988) published their works on knowledge-based growth models, there has been a continuously increasing literature in the new growth theory. In the new growth theory, knowledge accumulation plays an important role in generating endogenously determined and sustained growth (Zhang, 1990a, 1990c, 1993b, 1993c, Jensen, 1994, Valdés, 1999), even though most of the recent works in the new growth theory have neglected physical capital accumulation. Recently there have been a rapidly increasing number of publications in the theoretical economic literature concerning the relationship between knowledge accumulation and economic development (e.g., Aghion and Howitt, 1992, Zhang, 1996a, 1999a, Jensen and Wong, 1998, Maurer, 1998).

It would not be surprising to find that these knowledge-based economic frameworks have been extended to study small open economies or interactions of multiple countries. Trade economists have recently developed different trade models in which endogenous growth is generated either by the development of new varieties of intermediate or final goods or by the improvement of an existing set of goods with endogenous technologies (Grossman and Helpman, 1991, Ishikawa, 1992). These studies attempted to formalize equilibrium trade patterns with endogenous technological change and monopolistic competition. They often link trade theory with increasing-returns growth theory. Within such frameworks the dynamic interdependence between trade patterns, R&D efforts and various economic policies are well connected. With the development of models with endogenous long-run growth, economists now have formal techniques with which to explore the relationship between trade policy and long-run growth either with knowledge or with capital, but in most of them not both with capital and knowledge within the same framework. Exceptions can be found, for instance, in Zhang's trade models which include endogenous knowledge as well as capital (Zhang, 1991a, 1991b, 1992a, 1993a, 1994b).

Traditional trade theory failed to handle with issues of trade with increasing returns in a consistent way not because economists did not recognize the significance of increasing returns, but because free trade based on increasing returns is difficult to model formally under internationally and domestically perfect competition. It is not an easy matter to mathematically model trade with increasing returns. Theoretical economists engaged in trade theory did not show any possibility of formally explaining international trade based on increasing returns in a comprehensive framework. In fact, one of the main obstacles to formally model economies with non-constant returns is the problem of market structure. It is generally believed that increasing returns are inconsistent with perfect competition. But before the new trade theory became a dominant school, trade theorists interested in free economies constructed models consistent with the assumption of perfect competition. Faced with increasingly significance of endogenous technological changes in affecting trading patterns among economists, economists have recently produced the new trade theory. This theory produces many clear and simple mathematical models and provides insights into international trade based on increasing returns. These models explain trade in the presence of increasing returns and imperfect competition. The new trade theory is influenced by the developments in the theory of growth with endogenous knowledge and industrial organization. It highlights the roles of knowledge accumulation and international dissemination in explaining how trade structure and trade policy affects rates of growth. Specification and the rationalization at the immediate product level, along with related effects of trade, market integration, learning-by-doing, technical innovation, and other external returns have recently emerged as central issues in the new trade theory.

There are some models which deal with technology transfer via direct foreign investment in the theoretical literature on growth and international capital movements (e.g., Findlay, 1978, Zhang, 1989, Wang, 1990, Wang and Blomström, 1992). For instance, Findlay (1978) built a international growth model under the assumption about technology transfer that the rate of technological change in a less developed country will be an increasing function of the amount of foreign capital operating in the less developed country and the extent to which the technology in the advanced country exceeds that in the less developed one. Wang (1990) proposed a dynamic two-country model to examine the interactions among growth, technological change, and international capital movements. It includes capital accumulation and treats human capital as a country-specific variable. Perfect capital mobility links the two countries and human capital plays an important role in determining the effective rate of return for physical capital and affects the direction and magnitude of international capital movements. Rivera-Batiz and Romer (1991) developed a dynamic model with specification driven by R&D. Their model examines the effects of economic integration, though an increased flow of specified capital goods and of ideas, on economic growth rates. It demonstrates that to the extent that economic integration and other commercial policy changes increase the global resource or activity base over which external economies are generated, such integration may induce globally positive level and growth effects. Matsuyama (1991) developed a dynamic model to examine economic development under external economies and learning-by-doing effects. It is shown that free trade may lower the growth rate of low-income countries while accelerating the rate for high-income countries. These dynamic models exhibit instabilities and multiple equilibria. Hence, history as reflected in initial factor allocations, technology choices, and sectoral efficiency may be critical to the global economic development.

The new trade theory with endogenous knowledge has two main differences from the traditional trade theory. The first is that it is developed mainly under the assumption of imperfect competition. Although the significance of imperfect competition for the pure theory of international trade has been recognized and there are a number of macroeconomic models with imperfect competition as a crucial feature (e.g., Dixit and Stiglitz, 1977, Helpman and Krugman, 1985, Dixon and Rankin, 1994), most of these models are developed within a static framework with fixed factors of production. Like in the Dixit-Stiglitz model, many of these trade models assume monopolistic competition in which each good is produced by a separate firm and labor is the only factor of production. The new trade theory combines the trade models with imperfect competition and the growth models with endogenous knowledge. The second main difference between the traditional trade theory and the new trade theory is that most of the formal models in the new trade theory omits explicit treatment of physical capital. This lack of endogenous physical capital is not due to the fact that new trade theorists don't recognize the significance of physical accumulation. We mentioned that one of the reasons that traditional trade theorists did not make formal modeling of trade based on increasing returns is that they did not have some analytical frameworks to formally examine issues. It is due to a similar reason that trade in the presence of possible physical capital accumulation is not formally examined in the formal modeling of the new trade theory with endogenous knowledge. If endogenous physical capital accumulation is introduced into trade models in the new trade theory, it will be difficult to make models tractable. It is not surprising to know that the new trade theory omits formal treatment of endogenous physical capital. This book treats both physical capital accumulation and knowledge creation and utilization as endogenous variables within the framework recently proposed by Zhang (1999a).

1.7 The Structure of the Book

This book is to extend the dynamic theory of national economies recently proposed by Zhang (1999a) to include international trades. We are concerned with perfectly competitive international economies and our attention is focused on the 'real side' of international trade. We study trade and factor flows and their main interdependence with factors of production goods and factor prices. The allocation of resources and income distribution and their impact on economic welfare are investigated. Although this book does not follow any special school mentioned above, as become clear later on the main ideas of all these schools have strong influences on the development of the book. This book provides a single compact framework to deal with various problems which are solved by different theories of international trade. Although I do hesitate to call my theory 'more general' than the traditional theories of international trade under perfect competition, I show that the theoretical framework proposed in this book can cover many equilibrium as well as dynamic issues related to international trade. The remainder of this book is organized as follows.

Chapter 2 proposes a dynamic one-commodity and multiple-country trade model to examine trade patterns. We analyze trade issues within the framework of a simple international macroeconomic growth model with perfect capital mobility. We examine trade issues within a dynamic framework in a perfectly competitive trade system. In describing economic production, we follow the neoclassical trade framework. It is assumed that the countries produce a homogenous commodity. We attempt to make a contribution to the literature of international trade by proposing a dynamic trade model with capital growth under the assumption that the households make decisions on savings on the basis of their attitudes towards wealth at each point of time. That is, rather than using the concept of the subjective discount rate, we solve the problem of endogenous savings by treating wealth similarly to a consumption good in household decision making. This greatly reduces the complexity of the dynamic analysis of the two-country trade model with endogenous capital accumulation. This chapter is organized as follows. Section 2.1 develops the multi-country model with capital accumulation. Section 2.2 examines the dynamic properties of the two-country case. We prove the existence of equilibria in the system and explicitly provide stability conditions. It is shown that it is difficult to judge whether the system has a unique equilibrium and the dynamic model may be unstable. Section 2.3 studies trade patterns of the two-country system when the parameters are taken on some special values. Section 2.4 discusses the multi-country case.

Chapter 3 studies international trade and distribution of income and wealth among multiple groups of people in each country. The explanation of production and accumulation of national wealth and distribution of income and wealth is among the central tasks of economics. It is well known that Ricardo claimed that the division is the principal problem of political economy. The discovery of the laws which regulate distributive shares was considered as the principal problem in political economy. Marx considered the distribution of income between wages and other incomes as the key to explaining processes of capitalist systems. Marx's economics was based on the assumption that income distribution is determined according to groups. The understanding of dynamics of national growth and enlarged or reduced differences of living conditions and wealth among various groups of people is one of the essential aspects for understanding modern societies. But not to mention formal international trade theory, even in macroeconomics (of national economies) there are a few dynamic (mathematical) models with endogenous savings and income and wealth distribution. In this sense this chapter makes an original contribution to the literature of international trades with perfect competition. The objective of this chapter is to study the relationships between economic growth and free trade with multiple groups. The trade aspects of our model are based on the international macroeconomic one-sector growth model with perfect capital mobility developed in Chapter 2. A main difference between this chapter and the preceding one is that this chapter examines how free trade may affect people from different groups. This chapter classifies the population of each country into two groups. The two groups are assumed to have different human capital and utility functions. We are interested in how changes in the preferences and human capital of one group may affect the living conditions of all the groups in the world economy. For instance, we show that a change in one group's propensity to hold wealth may economically harm the other group in the same country, but it may benefit the groups in other countries in the free competitive world. This may similarly be the case for changes in human capital.

Chapter 4 explicitly introduces endogenous savings, time allocation and sexual division of labor into the trade model proposed in Chapters 2 and 3. Over the years there have been a number of attempts to modify neoclassical consumer theory to deal with economic issues about endogenous labor supply, family structure, working hours and the valuation of traveling time. For instance, there is an increasing amount of economic literature about the sexual division of labor, marriage and divorce, and decision-making about family size. There are also studies on the relationship between economic growth and the family distribution of income. There are studies of the female labor supply. Women choose levels of market time on the basis of wage rates and incomes. Lifetime variations in costs and opportunities - due to children, unemployment of the spouse, and general business cycle variations - influence the timing of female labor participation. There are studies on the relationship between home production and non-home production and time distribution. Possible sexual discrimination in labor markets has also attracted much attention from economists. But as far as I know, there is no formal dynamic economic model which deals with trade, growth and sexual division of labor. This chapter makes an initial attempt to introduce endogenous choice between working and leisure time of two sexes to neoclassical dynamic growth theory with international trade. This chapter is organized as follows. Sector 4.1 presents the basic model. Section 4.2 proves the existence of a unique equilibrium of the dynamic system. Section 4.3 examines how the factors of human capital levels of the two sexes and preference structures in the two countries determine economic conditions and trade patterns. Section 4.4 provides the effects of changes in the human capital level of female labor force in one country on the international economy. Section 4.5 concludes the chapter.

Chapter 5 is concerned with interdependence between growth and trade with national public goods. The previous chapters are concerned with international trade patterns and world economic growth without government intervention. But governments may intervene free economies in different ways. It is significant to examine how government's intervention may affect world trade. Chapter 5 proposes a two-country growth model with public sector attributes. The model describes a dynamic interaction between government policy, capital accumulation, national and international distribution of capital and labor, division of labor and capital distribution within each country. We analyze how differences in public policy, human capital and preference structures of the population may affect the global economy.

Chapter 6 is to address issues related to interdependence between migration, trade patterns and world economic growth. International migration is affected by many factors such as cost of transportation and communication and fast growth of international trade in goods and factor services. It is apparently not only economic factors that determine international migration patterns. Factors such as differences in social status, accessibility to friendship, climates and social environment in the home country and the foreign country are significant in affecting people's movement. It is necessary to examine migration issues within a framework that takes account of behavior of all the participants in the global economy. But it may be argued that only a few theoretical models with migration treat the world economy as a dynamic whole.

The purpose of this chapter is to address the issue of dynamic interdependence of economic growth and international migration within a compact framework. We develop a dynamic model with endogenous capital accumulation and international migration to gain insights into the important relationship between international migrants and economic growth of the world economy. As far as production and capital accumulation are concerned, the model in this chapter is developed within the framework represented in the preceding chapters. This chapter is organized as follows. Section 6.1 defines the model. Section 6.2 provides the conditions for existence of a unique equilibrium. Section 6.3 examines the impact of improvement in amenity levels that people of the migrating country obtain in the home and foreign countries on the world economic structure. Section 6.4 examines the impact of improvement in the level of human capital of people in the migrating country on the world economic structure. Section 6.5 concludes the chapter.

Chapter 7 proposes a global growth model with endogenous capital and knowledge. The previous chapters examine various aspects of international trades. We show how trade patterns are related to capital accumulation, preferences and sexual division of labor. But in all these models we assume that human capital is exogenously given. This chapter suggests a dynamic one-commodity and multiple-country trade model to examine interactions between savings rates, trade, knowledge utilization and creativity. This chapter considers knowledge as a public good in the sense that all countries access to knowledge and the utilization of knowledge by one country does not affect that by others. Due to cultural differences, educational systems and policies, knowledge utilization efficiency and creativity differ between countries. We formulate a model to show how the differences in savings rates, knowledge utilization efficiency and creativity may affect trade patterns. We show that free trade may benefit or harm any country in the world system, depending on the propensities to save and return to scales.

Chapter 8 is concerned with similar issues as in Chapter 7. But this chapter introduces research into the framework proposed in Chapter 7. Hence, there are two sources of knowledge accumulation, learning by doing and research. We are concerned with interdependence of capital and knowledge accumulation under government's intervention in research. In Chapter 7 we assume that knowledge accumulates through 'learning by doing' without any resources utilization. But knowledge creation and utilization need resources. To do research requires manpower as well as instruments. A fundamental character of modern industrial economies is the deliberate large-scale quest for knowledge. The number of workers who generate and manipulate knowledge and information has increasingly become a larger share of the working population. A common important economic question faced with modern economies is how to distribute national resources among knowledge creation, education and economic development. Although governments have played significant role in shaping development of science and technology, the question regarding the appropriate role for government in encouraging economic growth by supporting scientific research remains vexed. Economists have recently developed a number of models to investigate similar issues. But this chapter treats the problems in a way different from the current literature of international trade with endogenous technology and human capital and thus tends to make a contribution to the literature. This chapter is organized as follows. Sector 8.1 presents the basic model. Section 8.2 expresses the dynamics of the trade system in the term of knowledge and capital. Section 8.3 finds out conditions for existence of equilibria and for stability in the trade system. Section 8.4 examines the impact of trade upon knowledge accumulation and economic growth. Section 8.5 investigates the impact of changes in knowledge accumulation efficiency upon the trade system. Section 8.6 concludes the chapter. The appendix of this chapter provides the conditions for existence of equilibria and stability of the autarky system.

Chapter 9 addresses relations among growth, economic structure and trade patterns in a two-country world economy. The model is similar to the two-country, two-good, and two-factor neoclassical trade. Rather than classifying national product into investment and consumption commodities as in the Oniki-Uzawa model, we classify national product into commodity and services. It is assumed that each country supplies and consumes both commodity and services. The world trade pattern is determined not only by differences in technology and resources, but also by preference structures of countries in the trade system. When time and space are explicitly considered, services have their typical characteristics. In this chapter, it is assumed that services, such as hotels, restaurants, hospitals, education, transportation and communication systems, supplied by one country cannot be consumed by the other country. Any possible consumption by tourists is neglected in this chapter. As shown in this chapter, our dynamic multi-sector model is much more difficult to analyze and exhibits some complicated behavior which make it difficult to provide explicit conclusions under general conditions. The outline of this chapter is as follows. Sector 9.1 represents the basic model. Section 9.2 provides conditions for existence of equilibria and for stability. Section 9.3 examines effects of changes in country 1's savings rate on the world economy. Section 9.4 concludes the study. In the appendix, we prove the results in Section 9.2.

Chapter 10 is concerned with trade and economic structures with endogenous knowledge. We propose a dynamic two-country and multi-sector model with endogenous knowledge accumulation. The model describes a dynamic interdependence between knowledge utilization and creation, international division of labor, land rent and price structure over space under perfect competition. We examine how differences in knowledge utilization and creativity between the two countries may affect the economic geography. It is shown that the economic system may have either a unique or multiple equilibria and each equilibrium may be either stable or unstable, depending on knowledge utilization and creativity of the production sectors in the two countries. We also examine effects of changes in some parameters on the economic geography. Chapter 10 is organized as follows. Section 10.1 defines a two-country and multi-sector economic model with endogenous knowledge accumulation. Section 10.2 shows that the dynamic system may have either a unique or multiple equilibria and each equilibrium may be either stable or unstable, depending upon knowledge utilization and creativity of the different sectors.

Section 10.3 examines the effects of changes in knowledge accumulation efficiency upon the equilibrium economic geography. Section 10.4 studies the impact of changes in preferences on trade patterns. Section 10.5 concludes the chapter. The appendix proves the main results of Section 10.2.

Chapter 11 concludes this book, pointing out further possible extensions of this book and providing a broader vision of economic evolution than one actualized in this book.

2 Global Growth and Trade Patterns

As mentioned in Introduction, classical economists constructed different trade theories to explain why countries make trade. They argued that countries make trades due to various reasons under different conditions. They trade because they are different from each other. These differences may be either in real terms such as climates, technology and natural resources, or in monetary variables, such as prices, interest rates and wage rates. Classical economists proved that it does often benefit a nation to exchange desirable things which it cannot produce. Nations may benefit from trading as each of them may produce things it does relatively well.

The purpose of this chapter is to suggest a dynamic one-commodity and multiple-country trade model to examine interdependence between trades and global growth. We analyze trade issues within the framework of a simple international macroeconomic growth model with perfect capital mobility. This model is influenced by the neoclassical growth theory for national economies. The Solow-Swan model which was constructed under the influence of Harrod and Domar's works on economic growth opened a new way to modeling economic growth (Solow, 1956, Swan, 1956, Burmeister and Dobell, 1970, Zhang, 1990a, 1999a). The standard neoclassical growth model initiated a new course of development of economic growth theory by using the neoclassical production function and neoclassical production theory. It is known that since the publication of Oniki and Uzawa's paper on theory of trade and economic growth (Oniki and Uzawa, 1965), various trade models with endogenous capital have been proposed (e.g., Deardorff, 1973, Ruffin, 1979, Findlay, 1984, Smith, 1984, Frenkel and Razin, 1987, Eaton, 1987). In describing economic production, we follow the neoclassical trade framework. It is assumed that the countries produce a homogenous commodity (see, for instance, Wang, 1990, Ikeda and Ono, 1992).

Irrespective of analytical difficulties involved in analyzing two-country, dynamic-optimization models with capital accumulation, many efforts have been made to examine the impact of savings, technology and various policies upon trade patterns within this framework. For instance, Frenkel and Razin (1987) used a two-country and two-period model to analyze the effects of various fiscal policies, even though their model ignores capital accumulation. In Ikeda and Ono (1992), an optimal multi-country model was constructed to analyze dynamic trade patterns, even though the model ignores capital growth by assuming a constant capital supply. We attempt to make another contribution to the literature by proposing a dynamic trade model with capital growth under the assumption that the households make decisions on savings on the basis of their attitudes towards wealth at each point of time. That is, rather than using the concept of the subjective discount rate, we solve the problem of endogenous savings by treating wealth similarly to a consumption good in household decision making. This greatly reduces difficulties involved in the dynamic analysis of traditional two-country trade models with endogenous capital accumulation.

This chapter is organized as follows. Section 2.1 develops the multi-country model with capital accumulation. Section 2.2 examines the dynamic properties of the two-country case. We prove the existence of equilibria in the system and explicitly provide stability conditions. It is shown that it is difficult to judge whether the system has a unique equilibrium and the dynamic model may be unstable. Section 2.3 studies trade patterns of the two-country system when the parameters are taken on some special values. Section 2.4 discusses the multi-country case. It should be remarked that this chapter is based on Zhang (1994a).

2.1 The Trade Model with Capital Accumulation

Most aspects of our model are similar to the neo-classical one-sector growth model (Burmeister and Dobell, 1970, Zhang, 1990a, 1999a). It is assumed that there is only one (durable) good in the global economy under consideration. Households own assets of the economy and distribute their incomes to consume and save. Production sectors or firms use capital and labor. Exchanges take place in perfectly competitive markets. Production sectors sell their product to households or to other sectors and households sell their labor and assets to production sectors. Factor markets work well; factors are inelastically supplied and the available factors are fully utilized at every moment. Saving is undertaken only by households, which implies that all earnings of firms are distributed in the form of payments to factors of production. This assumption is retained throughout the book. We omit the possibility of hoarding of output in the form of non-productive inventories held by households. All savings volunteered by households are absorbed by firms. We require savings and investment to be equal at any point of time.

The system consists of multiple countries, indexed by $j = 1, ..., J$. Only one good is produced in the system. Perfect competition is assumed to prevail in good markets both within each country and between the countries, and commodities are traded without any barriers such as transport costs or tariffs. We assume that there is no migration between the countries and the labor markets are perfectly competitive within each country. Each country has a fixed labor force, N_j, ($j = 1, ..., J$). Let prices be measured in terms of the commodity and the price of the commodity be unity. We denote wage and interest rates by $w_j(t)$ and $r_j(t)$, respectively, in the

j th country. In the free trade system, the interest rate is identical throughout the world economy, i.e., $r(t) = r_j(t)$.

Behavior of producers

First, we describe behavior of the production sections. We use production functions to describe the physical facts of a given technology. A production function shows the terms on which services of productive input factors like human capital, machines, land and natural resources are transformed into output. It should be noted that properties of production functions have intimate relations with income distribution issues. Production inputs such as capital and labor cost production agents. In order to fully explain payments of all factor incomes, it is necessary to show how all factors are paid according to the production theory. Production is generally described as combination of multiple production factors such as natural resources, labor, knowledge, and capital. For simplicity this section assumes that there are only two productive factors, capital $K(t)$ and labor $N(t)$ at each point of time t. In this section the production process is described by some sufficiently smooth function $F(t) = F(K,N,t)$, where F is the output flow attainable with given amounts of $K(t)$ and $N(t)$ at time t. In $F(K,N,t)$, we use time t to generally illustrate exogenous conditions such as climates, technological conditions or institutional factors. Here, K and N are stocks of physical and human and capital; F describes the flow rate of asset services. The level of physical capital stocks K is measured in units of the output good itself. We assume that capital is malleable in the sense that one need distinguish neither its previous use nor the factor productions of its previous use. Malleable capital can be transferred quickly from a production process appropriate at one level of factor intensity to a different process appropriate to a different capital intensity. In this model labor is present and employed as a factor of production.

For simplicity of analysis, we specify the production functions as follows

$$F_j(t) = (K_j + E_j)^{\alpha_j} N_j^{\beta_j}, \quad \alpha_j + \beta_j = 1,$$
$$\alpha_j, \beta_j \geq 0, \quad j = 1, ..., J \tag{2.1.1}$$

where K_j are the capital stocks owned by country j, and $E_j > (<) \, 0$ are foreign capital stocks (home capital stocks located abroad).

According to the definition of E_j, we have the following accounting equation

$$\sum_{j=1}^{J} E_j = 0. \tag{2.1.2}$$

The marginal conditions are given by

$$r = \frac{\alpha_j F_j}{K_j + E_j}, \quad w_j = \frac{\beta_j F_j}{N_j}.$$ (2.1.3)

Behavior of consumers

How to model consumers' behavior in a dynamic system is a complicated issue. Consumers make decisions on choice of consumption levels of services and commodities as well as on how much to save (in terms of material and educational terms). There is no single purpose for people to make savings. Wealth may be accumulated for different reasons such as the capitalist spirit, old age consumption, providing education for children, power and social status (e.g., Ram, 1982, Modigliani, 1986, Gersovitz, 1988, Cole, Mailath and Postlewaite, 1992, Fershtman and Weiss, 1993). Those different reasons determine preference structures. In order to provide proper description of endogenous savings, we should know how individuals perceive the future. Different from the optimal growth theory in which the utility defined over future consumption streams is often used, we do not explicitly specify how consumers depreciate future utility resulted from consuming goods and services. We assume that we know the preference structure of consumers over goods and service consumption and wealth holding at the current state. Any specified attitude towards future consumption are reflected in the consumer's current preference structure over current consumption and saving structures. We assume that we can observe each consumer's preference structure over consumption levels of goods and services and current wealth, rather than an aggregated utility derived from consuming services and goods over the future. We don't consider it proper to add utility over time. Technically, we directly introduce wealth into temporary utility function.

We assume that households and firms are separate entities and that consumption is only undertaken by households and investment only by firms, consumers can allocate their current income $Y_j(t)$ and the past wealth to expenditure on goods and services $C_j(t)$ and savings $S_j(t)$. It should be noted that savings $S_j(t)$ may be negative in our general framework with multiple groups. We assume that the utility $U_j(t)$ that country j's consumers derive from consuming goods and holding wealth depends on the temporary levels of consumption $C_j(t)$ and wealth $K_j(t) + S_j(t) - \delta_k K_j(t)$, i.e.

$$U_j(t) = U(C_j, K_j + S_j - \delta_k K_j, t)$$

in which time t is used to generally illustrate exogenous conditions such as the consumer's age and preference change due to influences of fashions. Zhang (1992b) first used the above utility function. It implies that at each point of time the consumer has a preference described in the form of utility function over his current consumption and wealth. In this model, a consumer determines two variables, how much he consumes and how much he saves (when setting aside part of the current income $Y_j(t)$ into the 'saving account' or dissaves (when consuming some of the past savings). It is easy to explain $C_j(t)$ in $U_j(t)$. To explain $K_j(t) + S_j(t) - \delta_k K_j(t)$, we may consider a situation in which the consumer can change his savings, $p(t)K_j(t)$, with $p_j(t) = 1$, into 'money' at any point of time without any 'transaction cost' or time delay. In other words, the consumer perceives $K_j(t)$ in the same way as he can treat his salary income at each point of time. In fact, we may perceive that at each pay day the consumer "mixes" his current income $Y_j(t)$ and $K_j(t)$ and then decides how much he would spend on current consumption and how much he would put the total money in the saving account. In economics nothing should be free. Physical capital is subject to its laws of natural or social depreciation. Some one, for instance, the owner of physical capital, has to pay the depreciation. We assume that the consumer who owns the capital loses a fixed ratio δ_k of his past savings due to depreciation of physical capital. Hence, the consumer makes decision on $K_j(t) + S_j(t) - \delta_k K_j(t)$ at each point of time. Obviously, we take account of the consumer's attitudes towards the future by how the term $K_j(t) + S_j(t) - \delta_k K_j(t)$ enters the utility function as well as how the parameter t affects the consumer's utility function.

For simplicity, we specify country j's utility function as follows

$$U_j(t) = C^{\xi_j}(K + S - \delta_k K)^{\lambda_j}, \quad \xi_j, \lambda_j > 0 \tag{2.1.4}$$

in which the parameters ξ_j and λ_j are called respectively country j's propensity to consume goods and services and to own wealth. When $\lambda_j / \xi_j > \lambda_k / \xi_k$, we say that country j is more patient than country k.

In this chapter we fix the preference structure. It is quite reasonable to assume that one's attitude towards the future is dependent on factors such as capital gains, the stock of durables owned by oneself, income distribution and demographic factors. For instance, in the literature of consumption the well-studied permanent income hypothesis proposes that consumers' reaction to income changes depend on whether the income changes are regarded as 'transitory' or 'permanent'. This consideration may be taken into account in our analytical framework by assuming that the propensity ξ_j to consume goods and services is dependent on 'the average income' over a given period between time t to time $t - t_0$ where t_0 is the length of memory backwards in time

$$\xi_j(t) = G_j\{\int_{-t_0} Y_j(s)H_j(s)ds\}$$

where G_j is some given function and $H_j(t)$ is a function describing the 'weighted average' impact of income on the consumption propensity. As shown in Zhang (1999a) we may take account of preference changes by introducing possible dynamics of ξ_j by introducing, for instance

$$\frac{d\xi_j}{dt} = G(K,Y,C,\xi_j).$$

A well-used form of utility formulation is given in the traditional intertemporal framework. In the optimal growth theory, the economy maximizes

$$\int_0^\infty U_j[C_j(t),t]e^{-\rho t} dt$$

subject to the dynamic budget constraint of capital accumulation. The specified form means that the household's utility at time 0 is a weighted sum of all future flows of utility. The parameter, ρ (≥ 0), is defined as the rate of time preference. A positive value of ρ means that utilities are valued less than the later they are received. It should be remarked that Ramsey (1928) interpreted the agent as a social planner, rather than a household. The planner chose consumption and saving for the current and future generations.

In the above formula, there are two strict assumptions. The first is that utility is additional over time. Although we may add capital over time, it is a strict requirement to add utility over time. Intuitively it is not reasonable to add happiness over time. It is well known in utility theory that when we use utility function to describe consumer behavior an arbitrary increasing transformation of the function would result in identical maximization of the consumer at each point of time. Obviously, the above formulation will not result in an identical behavior if U_j is subjected to arbitrarily different increasing transformations at different times. The second implication of the above formation is that the parameter ρ is meaningless if utility is not additional over time. It is obvious that our formula does not involve these two issues. In our approach, we take account of social and cultural factors which affect saving behavior by the preference parameters at each point of time. As shown below, from operational point of view it is more convenient to use our formulation.

Accumulation of capital

The total net income Y_j of country j is given by

$$Y_j = rK_j + w_j N_j, \quad j = 1, ..., J.$$ (2.1.5)

From (2.1.3) and (2.1.5), we directly have

$$Y_j = F_j - rE_j, \quad j = 1, ..., J.$$ (2.1.6)

Households in each country have decision variables, C_j and S_j. The budget constraint is given by

$$C_j + S_j = Y_j, \quad j = 1, ..., J.$$ (2.1.7)

Substituting Y_j in (2.1.6) into (2.1.7) and then adding all the equations in (2.1.7), we obtain

$$C + S = F$$ (2.1.8)

where $C \equiv \sum_j C_j$ is the total consumption, $S \equiv \sum_j S_j$ is the total investment, $K \equiv \sum_j K_j$ is the total capital, and $F \equiv \sum_j F_j$ is the total output. This equation describes the balance of demand and supply in the world economy.

Country j's households maximize $U_j(t)$ in (2.1.4) subject to the budget constraint, (2.1.7). The optimal problem has the following unique solution

$$C_j = \xi_j \rho_j Y_j + (1 - \delta_k) \xi_j \rho_j K_j,$$
$$S_j = \lambda_j \rho_j Y_j - (1 - \delta_k) \xi_j \rho_j K_j$$ (2.1.9)

where

$$\rho_j \equiv \frac{1}{\xi_j + \lambda_j}.$$

We see that the consumption level of each country is positively dependent upon the net income and its capital stock; and the saving is positively dependent upon the net income but negatively upon its capital stocks.

The capital accumulation of country j is given by

$$\frac{dK_j}{dt} = S_j - \delta_k K_j.$$

Substituting S_j in (2.1.9) into the above equation yields

$$\frac{dK_j}{dt} = \lambda_j \rho_j Y_j - \delta_j K_j, \quad j = 1, 2, ..., J \tag{2.1.10}$$

where

$$\delta_j \equiv (1 - \delta_k)\xi_j \rho_j + \delta_k.$$

We have thus built the model which explains the endogenous accumulation of capital and the international distribution of capital in the world economy in which the domestic markets of each country are perfectly competitive, international product and capital markets are freely mobile and labor is internationally immobile. We now examine the properties of the system.

2.2 The Two-Country Economy

This section examines the behavior of the world economy when the system consists of two countries. First, we notice that when the system consists of only two countries, we have

$$E \equiv E_1 = -E_2.$$

When $E > (<)\ 0$, country 1 (2) uses country 2's (1's) capital.

From the condition that the world economy has an identical interest rate throughout, we get

$$\frac{\alpha_1 F_1}{K_1 + E} = \frac{\alpha_2 F_2}{K_2 - E}$$

From this equation and (2.1.3), we obtain

$$K_2 - E = \upsilon(K_1 + E)^\theta \tag{2.2.1}$$

in which

$$
\upsilon \equiv \left(\frac{\alpha_2}{\alpha_1} \right)^{1/\beta_2} \frac{N_2}{N_1^\theta}, \quad \theta \equiv \frac{\beta_1}{\beta_2} < 1.
$$

In remainder of this chapter, for convenience of discussion we require $\theta \leq 1$, i.e., $\beta_1 \leq \beta_2$. This requirement will not affect our discussion.

Introducing $x \equiv K_1 + E$, we may rewrite (2.2.1) as follows

$$
\Phi(x) \equiv x + \upsilon x^\theta - K = 0, \quad 0 < x < K. \tag{2.2.2}
$$

We now show that for any positive $K > 0$, the equation, $\Phi(x) = 0$ has a unique positive solution. It is easy to check that the function Φ has the following properties: $\Phi(0) < 0$, $\Phi(K) > 0$ and $d\Phi/dx > 0$ for all x. This implies that (2.2.2) has a unique positive solution

$$
x = \Lambda(K) > 0.
$$

For instance, in the case of $\upsilon = 1$, we have

$$
\Lambda(K) = \frac{K}{1 + \upsilon}.
$$

In the case of $\theta = 1/2$, we have

$$
x = \left\{ \left(\frac{\upsilon^2}{4} + K \right)^{1/2} - \frac{\upsilon}{2} \right\}^2.
$$

We thus solve E as a unique function of K_j as follows

$$
E = \Lambda(K) - K_1. \tag{2.2.3}
$$

Substituting (2.2.3) and r in (2.1.3) into (2.1.6) yields

$$
Y_j(K_1, K_2) = g_j(K_1, K_2), \quad j = 1, 2 \tag{2.2.4}
$$

where

$$g_1(K_1, K_2) \equiv \frac{\alpha_1 K_1 + \beta_1 \Lambda}{\Lambda^{\beta_1}} N_1^{\beta_1},$$

$$g_2(K_1, K_2) \equiv \frac{\alpha_2 K_2 + \beta_2 K - \beta_2 \Lambda}{(K - \Lambda)^{\beta_2}} N_2^{\beta_1}.$$

We thus can rewrite (2.1.7) as

$$\frac{dK_j}{dt} = \lambda_j \rho_j Y_j - \delta_j K_j, \quad j = 1, 2 \tag{2.2.5}$$

which consists of 2-dimensional differential equations.

Equilibrium of (2.2.5) is defined as a solution of the following two equations

$$\lambda_j \rho_j Y_j = \delta_j K_j, \quad j = 1, 2. \tag{2.2.6}$$

From (2.2.4) and (2.2.6), we directly solve K_j as functions of K as follows

$$K_1 = \frac{\beta_1 \Lambda}{\phi_1(\Lambda)}, \quad K_2 = \frac{\beta_2 \rho \Lambda^\theta}{\phi_2(\Lambda)} \tag{2.2.7}$$

in which

$$\phi_1(\Lambda) \equiv \frac{\delta_1 \Lambda^{\beta_1}}{\lambda_1 \rho_1 N_1^{\beta_1}} - \alpha_1, \quad \phi_2(\Lambda) \equiv \frac{\delta_2 \upsilon^{\beta_2} \Lambda^{\beta_1}}{\lambda_2 \rho_2 N_2^{\beta_2}} - \alpha_2. \tag{2.2.8}$$

As $K_j \geq 0$, $j = 1, 2$, it is necessary to require $\phi_j \geq 0$. Define

$$\Lambda_0 \equiv \min \{ \Lambda \,|\, \phi_j(\Lambda) = 0, \Lambda > 0, j = 1, 2 \}. \tag{2.2.9}$$

It is obvious that such a positive Λ_0 exists. As ϕ_j are increasing with respect to Λ, we see that Λ is meaningful only when $\Lambda > \Lambda_0$.

To guarantee $K \geq K_j$, $j = 1, 2$, where $K = \Lambda + \upsilon \Lambda^\theta$, we introduce

$$\Lambda_1 \equiv$$

$$\max\{\Lambda | \frac{\beta_1}{\phi_1(\Lambda)} = 1 + \upsilon\Lambda^{\theta-1}, \ \frac{\beta_2\upsilon\Lambda^{\theta-1}}{\phi_2(\Lambda)} = 1 + \upsilon\Lambda^{\theta-1}, \ \Lambda > \Lambda_0\}. \quad (2.2.10)$$

It is easy to show the existence of such a positive Λ_1.

Adding the two equations in (2.2.7) yields

$$\Phi^*(\Lambda) \equiv \frac{\beta_1}{\phi_1(\Lambda)} + \frac{\beta_2\upsilon\Lambda^{\theta-1}}{\phi_2(\Lambda)} - 1 - \upsilon\Lambda^{\theta-1} = 0 \quad (2.2.11)$$

where we use $K = K_1 + K_2$ and $K = \Lambda + \upsilon\Lambda^\theta$. As $\Phi^*(\Lambda_0) > 0$ and $\Phi^*(\Lambda_1) < 0$, we see that there is at least one positive $\Lambda_0 < \Lambda < \Lambda_1$ such that $\Phi^*(\Lambda) = 0$.

From (2.2.3) and (2.2.7), we have

$$E = \left\{1 - \frac{\beta_1}{\phi_1(\Lambda)}\right\}\Lambda.$$

The sign of $1 - \beta_1 / \phi_1(\Lambda)$ determines the direction of trade flow. As we cannot explicitly solve (2.2.11), it is not easy to explicitly interpret the economic meanings of the sign.

We have thus shown how to explicitly solve the equilibrium problem. The procedure is as follows: Λ by (2.2.11) $\to K_j$ by (2.2.7) $\to K = K_1 + K_2 \to Y_j$ by (2.2.4) $\to E$ by (2.2.3) $\to F_j$ by (2.1.1) $\to r$ and w_j by (2.2.3) $\to C_j$ and S_j by (2.2.9) $\to U_j$ by (2.1.4), $j = 1, 2$.

In the appendix of this chapter, we explicitly provide the conditions for the uniqueness of equilibrium and for stability. It is not easy to explicitly interpret the stability conditions because of the complicated expressions.

Summarizing the above discussion, we have the following lemma.

Lemma 2.2.1.

The two-country free trade system always has equilibria. In the case of $\theta = 1$, the system has a unique solution. In the case of $\theta < 1$, if $\Lambda_1 \leq \Lambda_2$, where Λ_2 is the solution of $1 - \theta = 1 / \phi_2(\Lambda)$, the system has a unique equilibrium. The stability condition is explicitly given in (2.A.1.8) in Appendix A.2.1.

As it is not easy to generally interpret the above conclusions, we will examine some special cases to illustrate the results.

2.3 Some Special Cases of the Two-Country Economy

This section examines the trade patterns when the parameters are taken on some special values. In this section, we always assume that the two country has an identical labor force, i.e., $N_1 = N_2$. As this section is mainly concerned with trade directions rather than trade volumes, it can be seen that this requirement is acceptable.

Case 1 Identical production function

First, we are concerned with the case that the two countries have identical production function, i.e., $\theta = 1$. From the appendix of this chapter, we know that the system has a unique equilibrium. From the definitions of $\phi_1(\Lambda)$ and $\phi_2(\Lambda)$) in (2.2.8), we see that if $\delta_1 / \lambda_1 \rho_1 > \delta_2 / \lambda_2 \rho_2$, i.e., $\xi_1 / \lambda_1 > \xi_2 / \lambda_2$, then

$$\phi_1(\Lambda) > \phi_2(\Lambda)$$

for any $\Lambda > \Lambda_0$. We require $\xi_1 / \lambda_1 > \xi_2 / \lambda_2$ in the following discussion.

On the other hand, in the case of $\theta = 1$ and $N_1 = N_2$, we can rewrite (2.2.11) as

$$\frac{1}{\phi_1(\Lambda)} + \frac{1}{\phi_2(\Lambda)} = \frac{2}{\beta} \tag{2.3.1}$$

where we use $\upsilon = 1$ and $\beta = \beta_1 = \beta_2$. From $\phi_1(\Lambda) > \phi_2(\Lambda)$ and (2.3.1), we have

$$\frac{2}{\phi_1(\Lambda)} < \frac{1}{\phi_1(\Lambda)} + \frac{1}{\phi_2(\Lambda)} = \frac{2}{\beta}.$$

Hence, we have $1 / \phi_1(\Lambda) < 1$. As $K_1 = \beta_1 \Lambda / \phi_1(\Lambda)$, we have $K_1 / \Lambda < 1$. With $\Lambda = K_1 + E$, we conclude that $E > 0$. In the case of $\theta = 1$ and $\upsilon = 1$, $\Lambda(K) = K / 2$, i.e., $K_1 + E = K / 2$. This implies that $K_1 < K_2$. As $S_j = \delta_k K_j$ at equilibrium, we have $S_1 < S_2$. From (2.2.1), we get $F_1 = F_2$ and $w_1 = w_2$. From (2.1.6) and $F_1 = F_2$, we have

$$Y_1 - Y_2 = - 2rE < 0. \tag{2.3.2}$$

We conclude that $Y_1 - Y_2$ is less than zero. From (2.1.7), $S_j = \delta K_j$ (2.2.6) and the definitions of δ_j, μ_j and υ_j, it is easy to check that

$$C_1 - C_2 = \left(K_1 - \frac{\delta_2 / \lambda_2 \rho_2}{\delta_1 / \lambda_1 \rho_1} K_2 \right) \frac{\delta_1}{\lambda_1 \rho_1} - \delta_k (K_1 - K_2) < 0 \tag{2.3.3}$$

where we use

$$\frac{\delta_2 / \lambda_2 \rho_2}{\delta_1 / \lambda_1 \rho_1} < 1, \quad \frac{\delta_1}{\lambda_1 \rho_1} > \delta_k .$$

Summarizing the above discussion, we have the following corollary.

Corollary 2.3.1.
Let $\theta = 1$, $N_1 = N_2$ and $\xi_1 / \lambda_1 > \xi_2 / \lambda_2$. Then, the system has a unique equilibrium at which $E > 0$, $K_1 < K_2$, $S_1 < S_2$, $F_1 = F_2$, $w_1 = w_2$, $Y_1 < Y_2$ and $C_1 < C_2$.

The condition, $\xi_1 / \lambda_1 > \xi_2 / \lambda_2$, implies that country 1 has lower propensity to hold wealth than country 2. The difference in preference determines that country 1 employs country 2's capital in economic production even though the two countries have identical production function and labor force. This result is well known in the literature of trade economics.

Case 2 Identical Preference
Let the two countries have an identical utility function, i.e., $\xi_1 = \xi_2$ and $\lambda_1 = \lambda_2$. We require $\theta < 1$, i.e., $\beta_1 < \beta_2$ and $\alpha_2 < \alpha_1$. From the definition of υ and (2.2.8), we have: $\phi_2(\Lambda) = \alpha_2 \phi_1(\Lambda) / \alpha_1$ for any $\Lambda > \Lambda_0$. Using this relation and (2.2.11), we have

$$1 + \upsilon \Lambda^{\theta-1} = \frac{\beta_1}{\phi_1(\Lambda)} + \frac{\beta_2 \upsilon \Lambda^{\theta-1}}{\phi_2(\Lambda)} = \left\{ 1 + \frac{\alpha_1 \beta_2 \upsilon \Lambda^{\theta-1}}{\alpha_2 \beta_1 \phi_2(\Lambda)} \right\} \frac{\beta_1}{\phi_1(\Lambda)}$$

$$> \left(1 + \upsilon \Lambda^{\theta-1} \right) \frac{\beta_1}{\phi_1(\Lambda)}. \tag{2.3.4}$$

From (2.3.4), we directly have $1 > \beta_1 / \phi_1(\Lambda)$. We thus have $K_1 / \Lambda > 1$, i.e., $E < 0$. Country 1's capital is employed by country 2.

Corollary 2. 3.2.
Let $\theta < 1$ and $\xi_1 / \lambda_1 = \xi_2 / \lambda_2$. Then, the system has a unique equilibrium at which at which $E > 0$.

As $\theta < 1$ implies that the marginal productivity of capital in country 1 is higher than that in country 2, the conclusion is reasonable under the condition that the two countries have identical preferences and labor forces.

Similarly, we may examine other cases. For instance, it is easy to check that if $\theta < 1$ and $\xi_1 / \lambda_1 > \xi_2 / \lambda_2$, then $E < 0$. But it is difficult to determine the sign of E in the case of $\theta > 1$ and $\xi_1 / \lambda_1 > \xi_2 / \lambda_2$. The above discussion implies that trade patterns are determined by complicated combinations of preferences and production functions of various countries. It is difficult to get general explicit conclusions even when we use simple production and utility functions.

2.4 Discussing the Multi-Country Case

This section shows that we may analyze the multi-country world economy similarly to the case in Section 2.2. First, we use the condition in (2.1.3) that countries in the world economy have an identical interest rate to obtain the following relations

$$K_j + E_j = \upsilon_j (K_1 + E_1)^{\theta_j}, \quad j = 2, ..., J \tag{2.4.1}$$

in which

$$\upsilon_j \equiv \left(\frac{\alpha_j}{\alpha_1} \right)^{1/\beta_j} \frac{N_j}{N_1^{\theta_j}}, \quad \theta_j \equiv \frac{\beta_1}{\beta_j}.$$

Summing the equations in (2.4.1) and using (2.1.2), we have

Summing the equations in (2.4.1) and using (2.1.2), we have

$$\Phi(x) \equiv \sum_j \upsilon_j x^{\theta_j} - K = 0, \quad 0 < x < K \tag{2.4.2}$$

where $x \equiv K_1 + E_1$ and $\theta_1 = \upsilon_1 = 1$. We now show that for any positive $K > 0$, the equation, $\Phi(x) = 0$ has a unique positive solution. It is easy to check that the function Φ has the following properties: $\Phi(0) < 0$, $\Phi(K) > 0$ and $d\Phi / dx > 0$ for all x. This implies that (2.4.2) has a unique positive solution, $x = \Lambda(K) > 0$. We thus solve E_j as functions of K_j as follows

$$E_j = \Lambda_j(K) - K_j \tag{2.4.3}$$

in which

$$\Lambda_j(\Lambda) \equiv \upsilon_j \Lambda^{\theta_j}, \quad j = 1, ..., J. \tag{2.4.4}$$

This implies that for any given capital vector $\{K_j\}$, the foreign capital vector $\{E_j\}$ is uniquely determined as functions of $\{K_j\}$.

Substituting r in (2.1.3) and (2.4.3) into (2.1.6), we see that the net income, $Y_j(t)$, of country j is solved as functions of K_j as follows

$$Y_j(K, K_j) = \frac{\alpha_j K_j + \beta_j \Lambda_j}{\Lambda^{\beta_j}} N_j^{\beta_j}. \tag{2.4.5}$$

We thus can rewrite (2.1.7) as

$$\frac{dK_j}{dt} = \lambda_j \rho_j Y_j(K, K_j) - \delta_j K_j, \quad j = 1, ..., J \tag{2.4.6}$$

which consists of J-dimensional differential equations. Equilibrium is given by

$$\lambda_j \rho_j Y_j = \delta_j K_j. \tag{2.4.7}$$

From (2.4.6) and (2.4.7), we directly solve K_j as functions of Λ, i.e., $K_j = \phi_j(K)$. The world capital stock is determined by the equation

$$K = \sum_j \phi_j(K).$$

Although we can analyze the properties of the dynamic system as in Section 2.2, it is difficult to explicitly interpret the results.

Appendix

A.2.1 Equilibria and Stability in the Two-Country Economy

The appendix provides the conditions for the existence of a unique equilibrium and for stability of the two-country free trade system. Taking derivatives of the function $\Phi^*(\Lambda)$ with respect to Λ yields

$$\Phi^{*\prime} = -\frac{\beta_1\phi_1{}'}{\phi_1^2} + \frac{(\theta-1)\beta_2\upsilon\Lambda^{\theta-2}}{\phi_2} - \frac{\beta_2\upsilon\Lambda^{\theta-1}\phi_2{}'}{\phi_2^2} - (\theta-1)\upsilon\Lambda^{\theta-2}$$

$$(2.A.1.1)$$

in which

$$\phi_1{}' = \frac{\beta_1\delta_1\Lambda^{\beta_1-1}}{\lambda_1\rho_1 N_1^{\beta_1}} > 0, \quad \phi_2{}' \equiv \frac{\beta_2\delta_2\upsilon^{\beta_2}\Lambda^{\beta_1-1}}{\lambda_2\rho_2 N_2^{\beta_2}} > 0. \qquad (2.A.1.2)$$

If $\Phi^{*\prime} < 0$ for any $\Lambda > \Lambda_0$, then $\Phi^{*\prime}(\Lambda) = 0$ has a unique solution. From (2.A.1.1), we see that in the case of $\theta = 1$, the system has a unique equilibrium. If $\Phi^{*\prime} > 0$, the equation may have multiple solutions.

Using $\phi_2 = \Lambda\phi_2{}'/\beta_2 - \alpha_2$ and $\theta = \beta_1/\beta_2$, we have

$$\Phi^{*\prime} = -\frac{\beta_1\phi_1{}'}{\phi_1^2} + \frac{\theta - 1 + (\beta_2 - \beta_1)\Lambda\phi_2{}' - \beta_2\Lambda\phi_2{}'/\phi_2}{\phi_2}\upsilon\Lambda^{\theta-2}.$$

$$(2.A.1.3)$$

From this, we see that if $\beta_2 - \beta_1 < \beta_2 / \phi_2$, then $\Phi^{*\prime} < 0$. This implies that if the equation has any solution in the domain (Λ_0, Λ_2), then $\Phi^* = 0$ has a unique solution in the domain. But if the inequality is not held, $\Phi^{*\prime}$ may be positive.

We now examine the stability of equilibria. From (2.2.4) and (2.2.5), we calculate

$$\frac{\partial Y_1}{\partial K_1} = \frac{\alpha_1 + \beta_1 \Lambda'}{\alpha_1 K_1 + \beta_1 \Lambda} g_1 - \frac{\beta_1 \Lambda'}{\Lambda} g_1,$$

$$\frac{\partial Y_2}{\partial K_2} = \frac{1 - \beta_2 \Lambda'}{\alpha_2 K_2 + \beta_2 K - \beta_2 \Lambda} g_2 - \frac{\beta_2 (1 - \Lambda')}{K - \Lambda} g_2,$$

$$\frac{\partial Y_1}{\partial K_2} = \frac{\partial Y_1}{\partial K_1} - \frac{\alpha_1 g_1}{\alpha_1 K_1 + \beta_1 \Lambda},$$

$$\frac{\partial Y_2}{\partial K_1} = \frac{\partial Y_2}{\partial K_2} - \frac{\alpha_2 g_2}{\alpha_2 K_2 + \beta_2 K - \beta_2 \Lambda} \tag{2.A.1.4}$$

in which $\Lambda' \equiv d\Lambda / dK$. From $\Lambda + \upsilon \Lambda^\theta = K$, we see that $\Lambda' < 1$. Two eigenvalues, f_1 and f_2, are given by

$$f_{1,2} = \frac{\eta_1}{2} \pm \eta_2^{1/2} \tag{2.A.1.5}$$

where

$$\eta_1 \equiv \lambda_1 \rho_1 \frac{\partial Y_1}{\partial K_1} + \lambda_2 \rho_2 \frac{\partial Y_2}{\partial K_2} - \delta_1 - \delta_2,$$

$$\eta_2 \equiv \frac{\eta_1^2}{4} + \lambda_1 \rho_1 \lambda_2 \rho_2 \frac{\partial Y_1}{\partial K_2} \frac{\partial Y_2}{\partial K_1}. \tag{2.A.1.6}$$

The necessary and sufficient condition for equilibrium to be stable is that $\eta_1 < 0$ and $4\eta_2 \le \eta_1^2$.

By (2.A.1.4) and (2.A.1.5), we have

$$\lambda_1 \rho_1 \frac{\partial Y_1}{\partial K_1} - \delta_1 = \frac{\alpha_1 \Lambda' K_1 (\Lambda - K_1) - \Lambda^2}{(\alpha_1 K_1 + \beta_1 \Lambda) K_1 \Lambda} \lambda_1 \rho_1 \beta_1 g_1,$$

$$\lambda_2 \rho_2 \frac{\partial Y_2}{\partial K_2} - \delta_2 = \rho_2 \beta_2 g_2 \lambda_2$$

$$\frac{(K_2 - \Lambda' K_2 - K + \Lambda)(K - \Lambda) - (\alpha_2 K_2 + \beta_2 K - \beta_2 \Lambda)(1 - \Lambda') K_2}{(\alpha_2 K_2 + \beta_2 K - \beta_2 \Lambda)(K - \Lambda) K_2}.$$

$$(2.A.1.7)$$

As Λ and $\Lambda - K_1$ are, respectively, the capital stock and foreign capital employed by country 1, we see that it is reasonable to have

$$\alpha_1 \Lambda' K_1 (\Lambda - K_1) - \Lambda^2 > 0.$$

This implies $\lambda_1 \rho_1 \partial Y_1 / \partial K_1 - \delta_1 < 0$. Similarly, we may have $\lambda_2 \rho_2 \partial Y_2 / \partial K_2 - \delta_2 < 0$. Accordingly, it is acceptable to have $\eta_1 < 0$.

The condition $4\eta_2 \le \eta_1^2$ can be rewritten as follows

$$\left(\frac{\partial Y_1}{\partial K_1} + \delta_k - \frac{\alpha_1 g_1}{\alpha_1 K_1 + \beta_1 \Lambda} \right) \left(\frac{\partial Y_2}{\partial K_2} + \delta_k - \frac{\alpha_2 g_2}{\alpha_2 K_2 + \beta_2 K - \beta_2 \Lambda} \right)$$

$$\le \left(\frac{\partial Y_1}{\partial K_1} - \frac{\delta_1}{\lambda_1 \rho_1} \right) \left(\frac{\partial Y_2}{\partial K_2} - \frac{\delta_2}{\lambda_2 \rho_2} \right).$$

$$(2.A.1.8)$$

It is difficult to explicitly interpret this condition.

3 Growth, Trade, and Wealth Distribution Among Groups

The previous chapter studied a global free-trade economy consisting multiple countries. As in most of formal trade models we assumed that there was a single group of people in each country. We examined interactions between preferences, labor force, capital accumulation and trade patterns. But in reality an economy consists of multiple groups of people. It is reasonable to question what economic impact free trade may have on different groups of people. Does free trade benefit all the groups, or benefit some groups or harm other groups, or harm all the groups in a special national economy? This chapter will study international trade and distribution of income and wealth among multiple groups of people in each country. We are interested in the way in which long-term global economic growth is affected by such factors. This chapter is based on my previous work (Zhang, 1995b).

The explanation of production and accumulation of national wealth and distribution of income and wealth is among the central tasks of economics. It is well known that Ricardo held that the discovery of the laws that regulate distributive shares was the principal problem in political economy. Marx considered the distribution of income between wages and other incomes as the key to explaining processes of capitalist systems. Marx's economics was based on the assumption that income distribution is determined according to groups. Marxian economics groups the population into capitalists and workers. The group division plays a key role in the determination of the real wage and the determination of capital accumulation. The issues about growth and distribution were certainly the main concerns of classical economists, such as Ricardo and Marx. But not to mention formal international trade theory, even in macroeconomics (of national economies) there are only a few dynamic (mathematical) models with endogenous savings and income and wealth distribution. It may be argued that important issues related to income and wealth distribution among groups have been largely neglected in the contemporary literature of economic theory.

It may be argued that the understanding of dynamics of national growth and enlarged or reduced differences of living conditions and wealth among various groups of people is one of the essential aspects for understanding modern societies. Despite impressive efforts of economists, it has become clear that it is not easy to analyze dynamic trade patterns in a formal manner. Interactions between capital accumulation, knowledge creation, knowledge utilization, economic structures, preference structures and trade patterns consist of nonlinear dynamic systems with considerable dimensions (Zhang, 1999a). Economists have recently made great efforts to examine dynamic interactions between trade patterns and economic development. But issues related to possible impact of trade within a multi-group framework remain to be investigated. For instance, it is difficult to find convincing answers about questions such as how differences in preferences of different groups of people affect patterns of trade and under what conditions free trade benefit economies of the global system. Although economic benefits and conflicts between nations have been examined using dynamic models in the literature of trade theory (e.g., Jones, 1971, Ruffin, 1979, Bhagwati and Srinivasan, 1983, Findlay, 1984, Eaton, 1987), issues concerning the effects of trade on different groups from the same country are not well addressed. It may be argued that the issues related to income and wealth distributions among different groups of people are important. For instance, it is important to know how a given national trade policy may affect economic conditions of different people in a country. It is also important to examine how changes in preferences, for example, of a country's educated people affect the economic conditions of other groups of people in the same country in a free trade context. When one country opens a given (for instance, rice) market to the world, the people engaged in that profession may be affected differently from the rest of the population.

The objective of this chapter is to study the relationships between economic growth and free trade with multiple groups. The trade aspects of our model are based on the international trade model developed in Chapter 2. A main difference between this chapter and the preceding one is that this chapter examines how free trade may affect different people from the same national economy. This chapter classifies the population of each country into two groups. The two groups are assumed to have different human capital and utility functions. We are interested in how changes in the preferences and human capital of one group may affect the living conditions of all the groups in the world economy. For instance, we show that a change in one group's propensity to hold wealth may economically harm the other group in the same country, but it may benefit the groups in other countries in the free competitive world. This may similarly be the case for changes in human capital.

It should be remarked that except the neoclassical growth theory and the neoclassical trade theory, this chapter is influenced by the post-Keynesian theory of growth and distribution (Panico and Salvadori, 1993). Kaldor initiated the formal presentation of two-class economic growth theory (Kaldor, 1955, 1956, 1961). In his 1955 paper Kaldor mentioned that this theory was not developed by Keynes even though it has been called 'Keynesian'. Kaldor tried to provide a solution to Harrod's problem on the convergence of the 'warranted' growth rate to the 'natural' growth rate. In 1962, Pasinetti reformulated the Kaldor model and introduced explicitly the assumption of steady growth. He also suggested a change in the saving function of workers and set the interest rate equal to the profit rate. After the publication of these seminal works, many papers about the topic have been published (e.g., Kaldor and Mirrlees, 1962, Samuelson and Modigliani, 1966, Chiang, 1973, Pasinetti, 1974, Marglin, 1984, Salvadori, 1991). The key feature of this theory is that it groups the population into different groups, whose consumption and saving behavior are homogenous within each group and are different among groups. This theory shows how each group may play a different role in the process of national capital accumulation. Like in the Ricardian and Marxian theories, this theory concerns the problem of distribution among different groups since it is believed that the theory of distribution plays the key role in explaining the whole mechanism of the dynamic economy. The theory is supposed to find out endogenous forces of economic dynamics which govern the rate of growth, the role of taxation, and so on. The post-Keynesian growth is different from the neo-classical growth theory in that the latter treats the problem of distribution merely as one aspect of the general pricing process.

3.1 The Dynamic Trade Model

Most parts of the model in this chapter are the same as the trade model in Chapter 2. The system has two countries, indexed by $j = 1, 2$, and produces one good. Similarly to the multi-group models in Zhang (1995b, 1999a), the population of each country is classed into two groups, indexed by group 1 and group 2, respectively. To describe the model, we introduce the following indexes

N_{jk} — the fixed population of group k in country j, $k = 1, 2$;

$K_{jk}(t)$ — the capital stocks owned by group k in country j, at time t;

$E(t) > (<) 0$ — country 2's (1's) capital stocks employed by country 1 (2);

$F_j(t)$ — country j's output;

$C_{jk}(t)$ — the consumption level of group k in country j;

$S_{jk}(t)$ — the savings made by group k in country j;

$w_{jk}(t)$ — the wage rate of group k in country j; and

$r(t)$ — the rate of interest.

Country j's total capital stock $K_j(t)$, the world's capital stocks $K(t)$, country j's qualified labor force N_j, and the world's qualified labor force N are given by

$$K_j = K_{j1} + K_{j2}, \quad K = K_1 + K_2, \quad N_j = z_{j1}N_{j1} + z_{j2}N_{j2},$$
$$N = N_1 + N_2 \tag{3.1.1}$$

where z_{jk} is the human capital of group k in country j, $k = 1, 2$. The parameter z_{jk} measures the productivity of group k in country j.

The production functions of the two countries are specified as follows

$$F_1(t) = (K_1 + E)^{\alpha_1} N_1^{\beta_1}, \quad F_2(t) = (K_2 - E)^{\alpha_2} N_2^{\beta_2},$$
$$\alpha_j + \beta_j = 1, \quad \alpha_j, \beta_j > 0, \quad j = 1, 2 \tag{3.1.2}$$

where $K_1 + E$ and $K_2 - E$ are the capital stocks employed by countries 1 and 2, respectively. For simplicity, we require $\alpha = \alpha_1 = \alpha_2$ and $\beta = \beta_1 = \beta_2$. The marginal conditions are given by

$$r = \frac{\alpha F_1}{K_1 + E} = \frac{\alpha F_2}{K_2 - E}, \quad w_{jk} = \frac{\beta z_{jk} F_j}{N_j}. \tag{3.1.3}$$

It is assumed that the utility level $U_{jk}(t)$ of group k in country j is dependent on its temporary consumption level $C_{jk}(t)$ and total wealth, $K_{jk}(t) + S_{jk}(t) - \delta_k K_{jk}(t)$, where δ_k is the fixed depreciation rate of capital. For simplicity, the utility functions $U_{jk}(t)$ are specified as follows

$$U_{jk}(t) = C_{jk}^{\xi_{jk}}(K_{jk} + S_{jk} - \delta_j K_{jk})^{\lambda_{jk}},$$
$$\xi_{jk} + \lambda_{jk} = 1, \quad \xi_{jk}, \lambda_{jk} > 0, \quad j, k = 1, 2. \tag{3.1.4}$$

Here, we call ξ_{jk} and λ_{jk} group jk's propensities to consume goods and to hold wealth, respectively. We interpret U_{jk} as in Chapter 2.

The net income Y_{jk} of group k in country j is given by

$$Y_{jk} = rK_{jk} + w_{jk} N_{jk}. \tag{3.1.5}$$

Households in each country have two decision variables, C_{jk} and S_{jk}. The budget constraints are given by

$$C_{jk} + S_{jk} = Y_{jk}, \quad j, k = 1, 2. \tag{3.1.6}$$

Country j's households maximize $U_j(t)$ in (3.1.4) subject to the budget constraint, (3.1.6). The optimal problem has the following unique solution

$$C_{jk} = \xi_{jk} Y_{jk} + (1 - \delta_k) \xi_{jk} K_{jk}, \quad S_{jk} = \lambda_{jk} Y_{jk} - (1 - \delta_k) \xi_{jk} K_{jk},$$
$$j, k = 1, 2. \tag{3.1.7}$$

We see that the consumption level of each country is positively dependent on the net income and its capital stock; and the investment is positively related to the net income but negatively dependent upon its capital stocks.

The capital accumulation of group k in country j is given by

$$\frac{dK_{jk}}{dt} = S_{jk} - \delta_k K_{jk}. \tag{3.1.8}$$

Substituting S_{jk} in (3.1.7) into the above equations yields

$$\frac{dK_{jk}}{dt} = \lambda_{jk} Y_{jk} - \delta_{jk} K_{jk} \tag{3.1.9}$$

where $\delta_{jk} \equiv \xi_{jk} + \delta_k \lambda_{jk}$.

As the product is either consumed or invested, we have

$$\sum_{jk} (C_{jk} + S_{jk}) = F_1 + F_2. \tag{3.1.10}$$

We have thus built the model. The system consists of 30 endogenous variables, K_{jk}, C_{jk}, S_{jk}, Y_{jk}, w_{jk}, U_{jk} ($j, k = 1, 2$), K_1, K_2, F_1, F_2, E, and r. It also contains the same number of independent equations. We now show that the system has solutions.

3.2 Equilibrium of the World Economy

This section examines dynamic properties of the economic system. From (3.1.9), we see that in order to write the dynamics in terms of $K_{jk}(t)$, it is sufficient to represent $Y_{jk}(t)$ as functions of $K_{jk}(t)$ at any point of time.

First, by (3.1.2) and

$$r = \frac{\alpha F_1}{K_1 + E} = \frac{\alpha F_2}{K_2 - E}$$

in (3.1.3), E is solved as a function of K_1 and K_2 as follows:

$$E(t) = \frac{N_1 K_2 - N_2 K_1}{N}. \tag{3.2.1}$$

Substituting (3.1.3), (3.1.2) and (3.2.1) into (3.1.5), we get

$$Y_{jk} = \frac{\alpha N K_{jk} / K + \beta z_{jk} N_{jk}}{N^\alpha} K^\alpha. \tag{3.2.2}$$

The above four equations determine Y_{jk} as functions of K_{jk}. By (3.2.2) and (3.1.9), the dynamics of the four variables $K_{jk}(t)$ are determined by the following four-dimensional autonomous differential equations

$$\frac{dK_{jk}}{dt} = \lambda_{jk} Y_{jk}(\{K_{jk}\}) - \delta_{jk} K_{jk}. \tag{3.2.3}$$

Summarizing the above discussion, we obtain the following lemma.

Lemma 3.2.1.
The dynamics of the economic system are determined by the four-dimensional differential equations, (3.2.3). The values of all other variables at any point of time are directly given by the following procedure: K_{jk} by (3.2.3) $\rightarrow$ $K_j = K_{j1} + K_{j2} \rightarrow E$ by (3.2.1) $\rightarrow Y_{jk}$ by (3.2.2) $\rightarrow F_j$ by (3.1.2) $\rightarrow r$ and w_{jk} by (3.1.3) $\rightarrow S_{jk}$ and C_{jk} by (3.1.7) $\rightarrow U_{jk}$ by (3.1.4).

The dynamic structure of the economic system is explicitly determined by the above lemma. By (3.2.2) and (3.2.3), equilibrium is given as a solution of the following equations

$$\frac{\alpha N K_{jk} / K + \beta z_{jk} N_{jk}}{N^\alpha} K^\alpha = \frac{\delta_{jk} K_{jk}}{\lambda_{jk}}. \tag{3.2.4}$$

By (3.2.4), we solve K_{jk} as functions of K as follows

$$K_{jk} = \frac{\beta z_{jk} N_{jk} K}{(\delta_{jk} K^{\beta} / \lambda_{jk} N^{\beta} - \alpha) N}. \qquad (3.2.5)$$

Since $K_{jk} \geq 0$ have to be satisfied, by (3.2.9) it is necessary to require

$$K \geq K_0 \equiv \min\left\{ \left(\frac{\alpha \lambda_{jk}}{\delta_{jk}} \right)^{1/\beta} N, \, j, \, k = 1, 2 \right\} > 0. \qquad (3.2.6)$$

Adding the above four equations and using $\sum_{jk} K_{jk} = K$, we have

$$\Phi(K) \equiv \frac{N}{\beta} - \sum_{jk} \frac{z_{jk} N_{jk}}{\delta_{jk} K^{\beta} / \lambda_{jk} N^{\beta} - \alpha}. \qquad (3.2.7)$$

Since $\Phi(K_0) < 0$, $\Phi(+\infty) > 0$ and $\Phi' > 0$ for $K_0 < K < +\infty$, the equation, $\Phi(K) = 0$, $K_0 < K < +\infty$, has a unique solution. The world capital stocks K are thus uniquely determined. By (3.2.5), the capital stocks K_{jk} of the two groups in the two countries are uniquely determined. By the procedure in lemma 3.2.1, the equilibrium values of the other variables are uniquely determined. The following proposition is held.

Proposition 3.2.1.
The dynamic system has a unique equilibrium.

Since the dynamic system is four-dimensional, it is not easy to provide stability conditions. It should be noted that the stability conditions for the case in which the two groups in each country have identical preferences and an equal level of human capital (i.e., $\xi_{j1} = \xi_{j2}$ and $z_{j1} = z_{j2}$) are provided in Chapter 2. We know that the equilibrium in this special case may be either stable or unstable.

We now examine the equilibrium trade pattern. By (3.2.1), (3.1.1) and (3.2.5), we have

$$E = \frac{\beta N_1 N_2 K}{N^2}$$

$$\left\{ \sum_k \frac{z_{2k} N_{2k}}{(\delta_{2k} K^{\beta} / \lambda_{2k} N^{\beta} - \alpha) N_2} - \frac{z_{1k} N_{1k}}{(\delta_{1k} K^{\beta} / \lambda_{1k} N^{\beta} - \alpha) N_1} \right\}. \qquad (3.2.8)$$

As it is not easy to explicitly interpret the above condition, we examine some special cases. It can be seen that E is positive (negative) if

$$\frac{z_{2k}N_{2k}}{(\delta_{2k}K^\beta / \lambda_{2k}N^\beta - \alpha)N_2} > (<) \frac{z_{1k}N_{1k}}{(\delta_{1k}K^\beta / \lambda_{1k}N^\beta - \alpha)N_1},$$
$$k = 1, 2. \qquad (3.2.9)$$

In the case of $z_{2k}N_{2k} = z_{1k}N_{1k}$, E is positive (negative) if $\delta_{2k} / \lambda_{2k} < (>) \delta_{1k} / \lambda_{1k}$, i.e., $1 / \lambda_{2k} < (>) 1 / \lambda_{1k}$. We may thus conclude that in the case in which the qualified labor force of group k ($k = 1$ and 2) in country 2 is equal to that of group k in country 1, then if group k in country 2 has higher (lower) propensities to hold wealth than in country 1, country 1 (2) will utilize some of country 2's (1's) capital stocks.

In the case of $\lambda_{2k} = \lambda_{1k}$, $k = 1, 2$, E is positive (negative) if $z_{2k}N_{2k} > (<) z_{1k}N_{1k}$. In the case in which the preferences of group k ($k = 1$ and 2) in country 2 are identical to those of group k in country 1, then if group k in country 2 has more (less) qualified labor force than in country 1, country 1 (2) will utilize some of country 2's (1's) capital stocks. It is difficult to interpret other cases. From the above discussion, it can be seen that the trade pattern is determined by differences in human capital and propensities to hold wealth between the two countries.

For convenience of discussion, in the remainder of this section it is assumed that the populations of the four groups are identical, i.e., $N_{jh} = N_{jh}$. By (3.2.5), the ratios of the capital stocks per capita between group jk and group ih are given by

$$\frac{K_{jk}}{K_{ih}} = \frac{\delta_{ih}K^\beta / \lambda_{ih}N^\beta - \alpha}{\delta_{jk}K^\beta / \lambda_{jk}N^\beta - \alpha} \frac{z_{jk}}{z_{ih}}, \quad k = 1, 2. \qquad (3.2.10)$$

We have that $K_{jk} > (<) K_{ih}$ if $z_{jk} > (<) z_{ih}$ and $\lambda_{jk} > (<) \lambda_{ih}$. That is, in the free trade world economy the level of capital stocks owned by group jk is higher (lower) than that owned by group ih if group jk has a higher level of human capital and a higher propensity to hold wealth than group ih.

By $\lambda_{jk}Y_{jk} = \delta_{jk}K_{jk}$ and (3.1.7), we obtain

$$\frac{Y_{jk}}{Y_{ih}} = \frac{\delta_{jk}\lambda_{ih}K_{jk}}{\lambda_{jk}\delta_{ih}K_{ih}}, \quad \frac{C_{jk}}{C_{ih}} = \frac{\xi_{jk}\lambda_{ih}K_{jk}}{\lambda_{jk}\xi_{ih}K_{ih}}. \tag{3.2.11}$$

By (3.2.10) and (3.2.11), we see directly that $Y_{jk} > (<) Y_{ih}$ if $z_{jk} > (<) z_{ih}$ and $\lambda_{jk} > (<) \lambda_{ih}$. In the case of $\delta_k = 0$, we have: $C_{jk} > (<) C_{ih}$ if $z_{jk} > (<) z_{ih}$ and $\lambda_{jk} > (<) \lambda_{ih}$. In other cases, it is difficult to explicitly judge the signs of $Y_{jk} - Y_{ih}$ and $C_{jk} - C_{ih}$. It is easy to interpret these conclusions.

3.3 The Impact of the Propensity to Hold Wealth

This section examines the effects of changes in the propensities λ_{jk} to hold wealth on the world economy. It is obviously sufficient to be concerned with λ_{11} alone. It should be noted that as $\xi_{11} + \lambda_{11} = 1$, we have $d\xi_{11} = - d\lambda_{11}$.

Taking derivatives of (3.2.7) with respect to λ_{11} yields

$$\Phi_0 \frac{dK}{d\lambda_{11}} = \frac{z_{11}N_{11}K^\beta}{(\delta_{11}K^\beta / \lambda_{11}N^\beta - \alpha)^2 \lambda_{11}^2 N^\beta} > 0 \tag{3.3.1}$$

where

$$\Phi_0 \equiv \sum_{jk} \frac{\beta\delta_{jk}z_{jk}N_{jk}}{(\delta_{jk}K^\beta / \lambda_{jk}N^\beta - \alpha)^2 \lambda_{jk}K^\alpha N^\beta} > 0. \tag{3.3.2}$$

As group 11's propensity to hold wealth is increased, the world's capital stocks are increased.

By (3.2.5), the effects on the four groups' capital stocks are given by

$$\frac{(\delta_{11}K^\beta - \alpha\lambda_{11}N^\beta)K}{K_{11}}\frac{dK_{11}}{d\lambda_{11}} = \alpha(\delta_{11}K^\beta - \lambda_{11}N^\beta)\frac{dK}{d\lambda_{11}} + \frac{K^{\beta+1}}{\lambda_{11}},$$

$$\frac{(\delta_{jk}K^\beta - \alpha\lambda_{jk}N^\beta)K}{K_{jk}}\frac{dK_{jk}}{d\lambda_{11}} = \alpha(\delta_{jk}K^\beta - \lambda_{jk}N^\beta)\frac{dK}{d\lambda_{11}},$$

$$jk \neq 11 \tag{3.3.3}$$

where $\delta_{11}K^{\beta} - \alpha\lambda_{11}N^{\beta} > 0$ and $\delta_{jk}K^{\beta} - \alpha\lambda_{jk}N^{\beta} > 0$. The sign of $dK_{11} / d\lambda_{11}$ is positive if $\delta_{11}K^{\beta} > \lambda_{11}N^{\beta}$. In the case of $\delta_{11}K^{\beta} < \lambda_{11}N^{\beta}$, it is not easy to explicitly determine the sign of $dK_{11} / d\lambda_{11}$.

The sign of $dK_{jk} / d\lambda_{11}$ is the same as that of $\delta_{jk}K^{\beta} - \lambda_{jk}N^{\beta} > 0$. Accordingly, an increase in group 11's propensity to hold wealth may reduce the capital stocks of other group(s). To see this accurately, let us assume that the preferences are different between any two groups. Let ih and pq denote the groups that have the lowest and highest propensity to hold wealth, respectively, i.e.

$$\frac{\delta_{ih}}{\lambda_{ih}} = \max\{\frac{\delta_{jk}}{\lambda_{jk}}, \text{ for all } jk\}, \quad \frac{\delta_{pq}}{\lambda_{pq}} = \min\{\frac{\delta_{jk}}{\lambda_{jk}}, \text{ for all } jk\}.$$

$$(3.3.4)$$

By (3.2.7), we have

$$\frac{N}{\beta} = \sum_{jk} \frac{z_{jk}N_{jk}}{\delta_{jk}K^{\beta}/\lambda_{jk}N^{\beta} - \alpha} > \frac{N}{\delta_{ih}K^{\beta}/\lambda_{ih}N^{\beta} - \alpha},$$

$$\frac{N}{\beta} = \sum_{jk} \frac{z_{jk}N_{jk}}{\delta_{jk}K^{\beta}/\lambda_{jk}N^{\beta} - \alpha} < \frac{N}{\delta_{pq}K^{\beta}/\lambda_{pq}N^{\beta} - \alpha}. \qquad (3.3.5)$$

By (3.3.5) and $\alpha + \beta = 1$, we have: $\delta_{ih}K^{\beta}/\lambda_{ih}N^{\beta} > 1$ and $\delta_{pq}K^{\beta}/\lambda_{pq}N^{\beta} < 1$. If group 11 has the lowest propensity to hold wealth, i.e., $ih = 11$, then $dK_{11}/d\lambda_{11} > 0$ and $dK_{pq}/d\lambda_{11} < 0$. That is, an increase in group 11's propensity to hold wealth enlarges group 11's capital stocks but reduces group pq's capital stocks. The effects on the other two groups may be either positive or negative. If group 11 has the highest propensity to hold wealth, i.e., $pq = 11$, then the effects on K_{11} and the other groups' capital stocks may be either positive or negative but group ih's capital stocks are certainly increased, i.e., $dK_{ih}/d\lambda_{11} > 0$. If $ih \neq 11$ and $pq \neq 11$, then $dK_{ih}/d\lambda_{11} > 0$, $dK_{pq}/d\lambda_{11} < 0$, and $dK_{11}/d\lambda_{11}$ and the impact on the other group's capital stocks may be either positive or negative. From this discussion, we see that the effects of changes in propensities to hold wealth are dependent on the comparative preference structures of the four groups. Each group's capital stocks may be either increased or decreased by changes in any group's propensity to hold wealth.

From $Y_{jk} = \delta_{jk} K_{jk} / \lambda_{jk}$ and $C_{jk} = \xi_{jk} K_{jk} / \lambda_{jk}$, we have

$$\frac{1}{C_{11}} \frac{dC_{11}}{d\lambda_{11}} = \frac{1}{K_{11}} \frac{dK_{11}}{d\lambda_{11}} - \frac{1}{\lambda_{11}\xi_{11}}, \quad \frac{1}{Y_{11}} \frac{dY_{11}}{d\lambda_{11}} = \frac{1}{K_{11}} \frac{dK_{11}}{d\lambda_{11}} - \frac{1}{\delta_{11}\lambda_{11}},$$

$$\frac{1}{C_{jk}} \frac{dC_{jk}}{d\lambda_{11}} = \frac{1}{Y_{jk}} \frac{dY_{jk}}{d\lambda_{11}} = \frac{1}{K_{jk}} \frac{dK_{jk}}{d\lambda_{11}} \qquad (3.3.6)$$

where $jk \neq 11$. Taking derivatives of (3.2.1) with respect to λ_{11} yields

$$N \frac{dE}{d\lambda_{11}} = N_1 \frac{dK_2}{d\lambda_{11}} - N_2 \frac{dK_1}{d\lambda_{11}}. \qquad (3.3.7)$$

It is not difficult to see that a change in group 11's propensity to hold wealth may either increase or reduce the trade gap between the two countries. By (3.1.2) and (3.1.3), we directly get $dF_j / d\lambda_{11}$, $dr / d\lambda_{11}$ and $dw_{jk} / d\lambda_{11}$. As it is difficult to explicitly interpret the results, we omit the representation.

3.4. The Impact of Human Capital

This section examines effects of changes in group 11's human capital z_{11} on the world economy. By (3.2.7), we get

$$\Phi_0 \frac{dK}{dz_{11}} = \frac{(\lambda_{11} N^\beta - \delta_{11} K^\beta) N_{11}}{(\delta_{11} K^\beta - \alpha\lambda_{11} N^\beta)\beta} + \frac{N_{11}}{N} \qquad (3.4.1)$$

where $\Phi_0 > 0$ is defined by (3.3.2). In the case of $\lambda_{11} N^\beta \geq \delta_{11} K^\beta$, an improvement in group 11's human capital increases the world capital stocks. If $\lambda_{11} N^\beta < \delta_{11} K^\beta$, the impact on K is ambiguous. As the equilibrium value K is not explicitly solved, it is not easy to interpret the condition $\lambda_{11} N^\beta \geq \delta_{11} K^\beta$.

Taking derivatives of (3.2.5) with respect to z_{11}, we obtain

$$\frac{\delta_{11} K^\beta - \alpha\lambda_{11} N^\beta}{K_{11}} \frac{dK_{11}}{dz_{11}} = \frac{\delta_{11} K^\beta - \alpha\lambda_{11} N^\beta}{z_{11}}$$

$$+ \alpha(\delta_{11} K^{\beta} - \lambda_{11} N^{\beta}) \left(\frac{1}{K} \frac{dK}{dz_{11}} - \frac{\delta_{11} K^{\beta} N_{11}}{N} \right),$$

$$\frac{(\delta_{jk} K^{\beta} - \alpha \lambda_{jk} N^{\beta}) K}{\alpha K_{jk}} \frac{dK_{jk}}{dz_{11}} =$$

$$(\delta_{jk} K^{\beta} - \lambda_{jk} N^{\beta}) \left(\frac{dK}{dz_{11}} - \frac{\delta_{jk} K^{\beta+1} N_{11}}{N} \right), \quad jk \neq 11. \tag{3.4.2}$$

It is easy to check that in the case in which the four groups have identical preferences, i.e., $\lambda = \lambda_{jk}$ ($\xi = \xi_{jk}$ and $\delta = \delta_{jk}$) for all j, k. By (3.2.7) and (3.3.5), we have

$$K^{\beta} = \frac{\lambda N^{\beta}}{\delta}, \quad K_{jk} = \left(\frac{\lambda}{\delta} \right)^{1/\beta} z_{jk} N_{jk} .$$

By these equations, we get

$$\frac{dK}{dz_{11}} = \left(\frac{\lambda}{\delta} \right)^{1/\beta} N_{11} > 0, \quad \frac{dK_{11}}{dz_{11}} = \frac{N_{11}}{z_{11}} > 0, \quad \frac{dK_{jk}}{dz_{11}} = 0 .$$

That is, an improvement of group 11's human capital enlarges group 11's capital stocks and the world's capital stocks, but has no impact on the capital stocks of the other three groups.

Taking derivatives of $Y_{jk} = \delta_{jk} K_{jk} / \lambda_{jk}$ and $C_{jk} = \xi_{jk} K_{jk} / \lambda_{jk}$ with respect to z_{11} respectively, we obtain

$$\frac{1}{C_{jk}} \frac{dC_{jk}}{dz_{11}} = \frac{1}{Y_{jk}} \frac{dY_{jk}}{dz_{11}} = \frac{1}{K_{jk}} \frac{dK_{jk}}{dz_{11}} \tag{3.4.3}$$

for all j, k. The sign of dC_{jk} / dz_{11} and dY_{jk} / dz_{11} is the same as that of dK_{jk} / dz_{11}.

4 Trade, Time Distribution, and Sexual Division of Labor

Issues related to international trades are not only one of the main concerns of professional economists, but also a main concern of politicians and the public in general. Various models were proposed to explain why nations trade and how trade patterns are determined. Different economists emphasize various factors, such as differences in national resources, capital accumulation and technology, in explaining trade issues. In Chapter 3, we studied global growth and trade patterns when each country's labor force is classified into two groups. The concern of this chapter is still to extend the model developed in Chapter 2. The main difference of this chapter from Chapter 2 is related to behavior of households of different countries. We explicitly introduce endogenous savings, time allocation and sexual division of labor in our model.

Over the years there have been a number of attempts to modify neoclassical consumer theory to deal with economic issues about endogenous labor supply, family structure, working hours and the valuation of traveling time (Becker, 1965, 1976, Mills and Hamilton, 1985, Folbre, 1986, Chiappori, 1988, 1992, Ashenfelter and Layard, 1992, Persson and Jonung, 1997, 1998). For instance, there is an increasing amount of economic literature about sexual division of labor, marriage and divorce, and decision-makings about family size. It has been argued that the increasing returns from human capital accumulation represent a powerful force creating a division of labor in the allocation of time between the male and female population (e.g., Becker, 1985). There are also studies on the relationship between economic growth and the family distribution of income (e.g., Fei, Ranis and Kuo, 1978). There are studies of the female labor supply. Women choose levels of market time on the basis of wage rates and incomes. Lifetime variations in costs and opportunities - due to children, unemployment of the spouse, and general business cycle variations - influence the timing of female labor participation (e.g., Mincer, 1962, Smith, 1977, Heckman and Macurdy, 1980). There are studies on relationships between home production and non-home production and time distribution (e.g., Lancaster, 1966, 1971). Possible sexual discrimination in labor markets has also attracted the attention from economists (e.g., Becker, 1957, Cain, 1986, Lazear and Rosen, 1990). The gains from marriage may be reduced as people become rich and educated. The growth in the female population's earning power may raise the forgone value of their time spent at child care, education and other household activities, which may reduce the demand for children and encourage a substitution away from parental activities. Divorce rates, fertility, and labor participation rates may interact in much more complicated ways. Decision making about on family size is extremely complicated (e.g., Becker, 1976, 1981, Weiss and Willis, 1985).

This chapter makes an initial attempt to introduce endogenous choice between working and leisure time of two sexes to the neoclassical dynamic growth theory with international trade. This chapter is organized as follows. Sector 4.1 presents the basic model. Section 4.2 proves the existence of a unique equilibrium of the dynamic system. Section 4.3 examines how the factors of human capital levels of the two sexes and preference structures in the two countries determine economic conditions and trade patterns. Section 4.4 provides the effects of changes in the human capital level of female labor force on the international economy. Section 4.5 concludes the chapter.

4.1 International Trade with Sexual Division of Labor

The model in this chapter is similar to the two-country one-sector model proposed in Chapter 2. The system consists of two countries, indexed by $j = 1, 2$. For simplicity, we assume that country j has N identical families. Each family consists of four members - father, mother, son and daughter. The total population of country j is equal to $4N$. It is assumed that only the adults may work. The young people get educated before they get married and joint the labor market. We assume that the husband and wife pass away at the same time. When the parents pass away, the son and the daughter respectively find their marriage partner and get married. The properties left by the parents are shared equally among the male and female children. The children are educated so that they have the same human capital as their parents. When a new family is formed, the young couple joins the labor market and has two children. As all the families are identical, the family structure is invariant over time under these assumptions. There is sexual division of labor in the family. The children consume goods and accumulate knowledge through education. The parents do home work and find job for family's living.

The industrial product is selected to serve numeaire. We introduce the following variables:

m — subscript indexes for sex; $m = 1$, male, $m = 2$, female;

$N_j(t)$ — the total labor supply in country j at time t;

$N_{jm}(t)$ the total labor supply of sex m in country j;

$T_{jm}(t)$ and $T_{jm}^h(t)$ — the working and leisure time of sex m in country j, respectively;

$K_j(t)$ — the capital stocks owned by country j;

$E(t) > (<) 0$ — country 2 's (country 1 's) capital stocks employed by country 1 (2);

$F_j(t)$ — country j 's output;

$w_{jm}(t)$ — the wage rate per unity of working time of sex m in country j; and

$r(t)$ — the rate of interest rate, internationally identical.

The labor supplies $N_{jm}(t)$ and $N_j(t)$ are defined as follows

$$N_{jm} = z_{jm}T_{jm}(t)N, \quad N_j(t) = N_{j1}(t) + N_{j2}(t), \quad j, m = 1, 2 \qquad (4.1.1)$$

where z_{jm} are human capital index of country j 's sex m. For simplicity of analysis, we assume that the labor supply of each sex is linearly related to its working time. Although it is reasonable to assume that the labor supply may exhibit certain nonlinear relationship with working time (for instance, over-working may reduce productivity per unity of time), this chapter is only concerned with the above forms. In this study, the human capital indexes z_{jm} are assumed to be constant.

Production functions of the two countries are specified as follows

$$F_1(t) = (K_1 + E)^\alpha N_1^\beta, \quad F_2(t) = (K_2 - E)^\alpha N_2^\beta,$$
$$\alpha + \beta = 1, \quad \alpha, \beta > 0 \qquad (4.1.2)$$

where $K_1 + E$ and $K_2 - E$ are capital stocks employed by countries 1 and 2, respectively.

The marginal conditions are given by

$$r = \frac{\alpha F_1}{K_1 + E} = \frac{\alpha F_2}{K_2 - E}, \quad w_{jm} = \frac{\beta z_{jm} F_j}{N_j}. \qquad (4.1.3)$$

By (4.1.2) and (4.1.3), we have

$$\frac{N_1}{N_2} = \frac{K_1 + E}{K_2 - E}, \quad \frac{w_{j1}}{w_{j2}} = \frac{z_{j1}}{z_{j2}}. \qquad (4.1.4)$$

The ratio of the wage rates between the husband and the wife in each country is only dependent on the ratio of their productivity per unity of time. The ratio of the total labor supplies between the two countries is equal to the ratio of the capital stocks employed by the production sectors.

We assume that utility level U_j of a typical household of country j is dependent on the temporary consumption level $C_j(t)$, husband's and wife's leisure time (time at home), $T_{j1}^h(t)$ and $T_{j2}^h(t)$, and the household's wealth, $K_j(t) + S_j(t) - \delta_k K_j(t)$, where $S_j(t)$ are country j's savings at time t and δ_k is the fixed depreciation rate of capital. We specify the utility functions as follows

$$U(t) = T_{j1}^{h\sigma_{j1}} T_{j2}^{h\sigma_{j2}} C_j^{\xi_j} (K_j + S_j - \delta_k K_j)^{\lambda_j},$$
$$\sigma_{j1}, \sigma_{j2}, \xi_j, \lambda_j > 0, \quad j = 1, 2 \qquad (4.1.5)$$

where the parameters, $\sigma_{j1}, \sigma_{j2}, \xi_j, \lambda_j$, are respectively the father's and mother's propensities to use leisure time, the family's propensities to consume goods and the family's propensity to hold wealth in country j.

Let T_0 denote the total available time. The time constraint requires that the amounts of time allocated to each specific use add up to the time available

$$T_{jm} + T_{jm}^h = T_0, \quad j, m = 1, 2. \qquad (4.1.6)$$

The total net income Y_j of country j is given by

$$Y_j = rK_j + w_{j1}T_{j1}N + w_{j2}T_{j2}N, \quad j = 1, 2. \qquad (4.1.7)$$

The net income of country j is equal to the sum of the interest payment for the country's capital stocks and the labor force's total wage incomes. From (4.1.3) and (4.1.7), we have

$$Y_1 = F_1 - rE, \quad Y_2 = F_2 + rE \qquad (4.1.8)$$

where $\alpha + \beta = 1$ is used. The above equations state that a country's net income is equal to the total output minus the interest payment for foreign capital.

A household in each country makes decisions on values of the four variables, T_{j1}^h, T_{j2}^h, C_j and S_j. Country j's budget constrain is given by

$$C_j + S_j = Y_j, \quad j = 1, 2. \tag{4.1.9}$$

By (4.1.6), (4.1.7) and (4.1.9), we rewrite the budget constrains as follows

$$C_j + S_j + w_{j1}T_{j1}^h N + w_{j2}T_{j2}^h N = w_{j1}T_0 N + w_{j2}T_0 N + rK_j. \tag{4.1.10}$$

Maximizing U_j in (4.1.5) subject to (4.1.10) yields

$$T_{jm}^h = \frac{\sigma_{jm}\Omega_j}{w_{jm}N}, \quad C_j = {}_j\Omega_j, \quad S_j = \lambda_j\Omega_j - (1 - \delta_k)K_j,$$

$$j, m = 1, 2 \tag{4.1.11}$$

where

$$\Omega_j \equiv {}_j(w_{j1}T_0 N + w_{j2}T_0 N + rK_j + K_j - \delta_k K_j),$$

$$\rho_j \equiv \frac{1}{\sigma_j + \xi_j + \lambda_j}, \quad \sigma_j \equiv \sigma_{j1} + \sigma_{j2}. \tag{4.1.12}$$

From (4.1.6) and (4.1.12), the ratio of time at home between the husband and wife in country j is given by

$$\frac{T_{j1}^h}{T_{j2}^h} = \frac{\sigma_{j1}z_{j2}}{\sigma_{j2}z_{j1}} \tag{4.1.13}$$

where $\sigma_{j1} / \sigma_{j2}$ and z_{j2} / z_{j1} are, respectively, the ratio of husband's and wife's propensity to consume leisure time and the ratio of productivity between wife and husband. It can be seen that the ratio of husband and wife's time distribution is only dependent on their comparative propensities to stay at home (for family's service production) and comparative advantages in working outside home. If the husband and the wife have equal levels of the propensities to stay at home and productivity, then their time distribution is identical. If the husband's propensity to stay at home is lower than that of the wife's and the husband's productivity is higher than the wife's productivity, then the husband works longer hours outside home than the wife.

The ratio of time at home between the same sex of the two countries are given by

$$\frac{T_{1m}^h}{T_{2m}^h} = \frac{\sigma_{1m} z_{2m} N_2 \Omega_1}{\sigma_{2m} z_{1m} N_1 \Omega_2}. \tag{4.1.14}$$

As the ratio Ω_1 / Ω_2 is time-dependent, it is difficult to explicitly judge the time allocation difference between two groups of the same sex.

According to the definitions of S_j, country j's capital accumulation is given by

$$\frac{dK_j}{dt} = \lambda_j \Omega_j - K_j, \quad j = 1, 2. \tag{4.1.15}$$

As the product is either consumed or invested, we have

$$C_1 + S_1 + C_2 + S_2 = F_1 + F_2. \tag{4.1.16}$$

We have thus built the model with endogenous accumulation of capital and international distribution of capital in a world economy. The system has 26 variables, $K_j, F_j, C_j, S_j, T_{jm}^h, T_{jm}, Y_j, U_j, w_{jm}, j, m = 1, 2, r$, and E.

4.2 Equilibrium of the Global Economy

This section proves that the dynamic trade system has a unique equilibrium. By (4.1.15), at equilibrium we have the following equations

$$\lambda_j \Omega_j = K_j, \quad j = 1, 2. \tag{4.2.1}$$

Substituting (4.2.1) into (4.1.11) yields

$$T_{jm}^h = \frac{\sigma_{jm} K_j}{\lambda_j w_{jm} N}, \quad C_j = \frac{\xi_j K_j}{\lambda_j}, \quad S_j = \delta_k K_j, \quad j, m = 1, 2. \tag{4.2.2}$$

From (4.2.2), (4.1.1) and (4.1.9), we get

$$Y_j = \delta_j K_j \tag{4.2.3}$$

where $\delta_j \equiv \xi_j / \lambda_j + \delta_k$. By (4.1.4), (4.1.6) and (4.1.1), we solve

$$E = \frac{T_1 K_2 - T_2 K_1}{T}, \quad K_1 + E = \frac{T_1 K}{T}, \quad K_2 - E = \frac{T_2 K}{T} \qquad (4.2.4)$$

where

$$K \equiv K_1 + K_2, \quad T_j \equiv z_{j1} T_{j1} + z_{j2} T_{j2}, \quad T \equiv T_1 + T_2 . \qquad (4.2.5)$$

By (4.1.3) and (4.2.4), we have

$$r = \alpha N^\beta \left(\frac{T}{K}\right)^\beta, \quad \frac{w_{jk}}{z_{jk}} = \left(\frac{K}{T}\right)^\alpha \frac{\beta}{N^\alpha}. \qquad (4.2.6)$$

From (4.1.12) and (4.2.1), we obtain

$$w_{j1} T_0 N + w_{j2} T_0 N + r K_j = a_j K_j, \quad a_j \equiv \frac{\sigma_j + \xi_j + \delta_k \lambda_j}{\lambda_j}. \qquad (4.2.7)$$

Substituting (4.2.6) into (4.2.7) yields

$$\left(z_j + \frac{\alpha K_j T}{K}\right)\left(\frac{K}{T}\right)^\alpha N^\beta = a_j K_j \qquad (4.2.8)$$

where $z_j \equiv (z_{j1} + z_{j2})\beta T_0$. Dividing the first equation by the second one in (4.2.8) yields

$$T = \frac{a_2 z_1 - a_1 z_2 \Lambda}{(a_1 - a_2)\alpha \Lambda}(1 + \Lambda) \qquad (4.2.9)$$

where $\Lambda \equiv K_1 / K_2$. In the case of $a_1 = a_2$, $\Lambda = z_1 / z_2$. It should be remarked that in the case of $a_1 = a_2$, T is determined by (4.2.13) given below. The other variables for the case of $a_1 = a_2$ are determined similarly as in the case of $a_1 \neq a_2$.

In the remainder of this section, $a_1 \neq a_2$ is required. From $T_{jm} + T_{jm}^h = T_0$, (4.2.2) and (4.2.6), we get

$$z_{jm}T_0 - z_{jm}T_{jm} = \left(\frac{T}{K}\right)^\alpha \frac{\sigma_{jm}K_j}{\beta\lambda_j N^\beta}, \quad j, m = 1, 2.$$

(4.2.10)

Adding the four equations in (4.2.10) yields

$$z - T = \left(\frac{\sigma_1 K_1}{\lambda_1} + \frac{\sigma_2 K_2}{\lambda_2}\right)\left(\frac{T}{K}\right)^\alpha \frac{1}{\beta N^\beta}$$

(4.2.11)

where

$$z \equiv (z_{11} + z_{12} + z_{21} + z_{22})T_0.$$

By (4.2.8), we have

$$\left(\frac{T}{K}\right)^\alpha = \left(z_1 + \frac{\alpha K_1 T}{K}\right)\frac{N^\beta}{a_1 K_1}.$$

(4.2.12)

Substituting (4.2.12) into (4.2.11), we get

$$z - T = \left(\frac{\sigma_1}{\lambda_1} + \frac{\sigma_2}{\lambda_2\Lambda}\right)\left(z_1 + \frac{\alpha\Lambda T}{1 + \Lambda}\right)\frac{1}{\beta a_1}.$$

(4.2.13)

The two equations, (4.2.9) and (4.2.13), contain two variables, Λ and T. We now show that the two equations have a unique solution. Substituting (4.2.9) into (4.2.13) yields

$$\Lambda^2 + b_1\Lambda - b_2 = 0$$

(4.2.14)

where

$$b_1 \equiv \frac{(a_1 - a_2)\alpha z + a_1 z_2 - a_2 z_1 + \alpha\sigma_2 z_1 / \beta\lambda_2 - \alpha\sigma_1 z_1 / \beta\lambda_1}{(a_2 + \alpha\sigma_1 / \beta\lambda_1)z_2},$$

$$b_2 \equiv \frac{(a_2 + \alpha\sigma_2 / \beta\lambda_2)z_1}{(a_1 + \alpha\sigma_1 / \beta\lambda_1)z_2}.$$

(4.2.15)

The equation, (4.2.15), has two solutions. Since it is necessary to require Λ to be positive, we see that (4.2.15) has a unique positive solution as follows

$$\Lambda = -\frac{b_1}{2} + \left(\frac{b_1^2}{4} + b_2\right)^{1/2}. \tag{4.2.16}$$

From (4.2.9), we directly obtain T. We thus determine the equilibrium values of Λ and T.

It is now shown that all other variables can be uniquely expressed as functions of Λ and T^h. From (4.2.12), we get the two countries' capital stocks as follows:

$$K_1 = \left\{\left(z_1 + \frac{\alpha \Lambda T}{1 + \Lambda}\right)\frac{(1 + \Lambda)^\alpha}{a_1 T^\alpha \Lambda^\alpha}\right\}^{1/\beta} N, \quad K_2 = \frac{K_1}{\Lambda}. \tag{4.2.17}$$

By (4.2.6), we get r and w_{jm}. From (4.2.2) and (4.2.3), we directly get: C_j, S_j, Y_j, T_{jm} and T_{jm}^h ($= T_0 - T_{jm}$). By (4.1.1) and (4.1.2), N_{jm} and N_j are obtained. The trade gap E is given by (4.2.4). From (4.1.2) and (4.1.5), we have F_j. All variables are explicitly solved. Summarizing the above discussion, we have the following proposition.

Proposition 4.2.1.
The dynamic system has a unique equilibrium.

We will not provide stability conditions because the issue is too complicated.

4.3 Time Allocation and Trade Patterns

This section examines trade patterns and compares living conditions and time allocation of the two countries. Since it is generally difficult to explicitly interpret the analytical results, a few special cases are examined.

Case I $a_1 = a_2$

By the definitions of a_1 and a_2, we may rewrite the condition $a_1 = a_2$ as follows

$$\frac{\sigma_{11} + \sigma_{12} + \xi_1}{\lambda_1} = \frac{\sigma_{21} + \sigma_{22} + \xi_2}{\lambda_2}.$$

The term $\sigma_{j1} + \sigma_{j2} + \xi_j$ is the sum of the husband's and the wife's propensities to use leisure time, and the family's propensity to consume goods in country j. We may thus call the term as country j's propensity to enjoy. The requirement $a_1 = a_2$ means that the ratio of country 1's propensity to enjoy and country 1's propensity to hold wealth is equal to the ratio of country 2's. We may thus interpret the requirement as that the family preferences are 'identical' in the two countries.

From the discussion in the preceding section, in this case the ratio of capital stocks $\Lambda = K_1 / K_2$ between the two countries is given by

$$\Lambda = \frac{z_{11} + z_{12}}{z_{21} + z_{22}}. \tag{4.3.1}$$

The ratio Λ is equal to the ratio, $(z_{11} + z_{12})/(z_{21} + z_{22})$, of the sums of the husband's and the wife's human capital levels in the two countries. As the two countries have an identical family preference, this conclusion is acceptable.

By (4.2.2) and (4.2.3), we have

$$\frac{T_{11}^h}{T_{21}^h} = \left(\frac{1 + z_{12}/z_{11}}{1 + z_{22}/z_{21}}\right)\frac{\lambda_2\sigma_{11}}{\lambda_1\sigma_{21}}, \quad \frac{T_{12}^h}{T_{22}^h} = \left(\frac{1 + z_{11}/z_{12}}{1 + z_{21}/z_{22}}\right)\frac{\lambda_2\sigma_{12}}{\lambda_1\sigma_{22}},$$

$$\frac{C_1}{C_2} = \frac{\lambda_2\xi_1}{\lambda_1\xi_2}\Lambda, \quad \frac{Y_1}{Y_2} = \frac{\xi_1/\lambda_1 + \delta_k}{\xi_2/\lambda_2 + \delta_k}\Lambda. \tag{4.3.2}$$

We see that even in the case of $z_1 = z_2$ and $a_1 = a_2$ (which implies $\Lambda = 1$), the consumption levels and time allocation structures of the two countries may be varied due to differences in the wife's and the husband's human capital levels and the propensities to use leisure time.

From the definitions of T_j^h, $T_{jm}^h = T_0 - T_{jm}$, (4.2.4), (4.2.6) and (4.3.1), we get

$$E = \frac{\sigma_2/\lambda_2 - \sigma_1/\lambda_1}{\beta K^\alpha (TN)^\beta} K_1 K_2. \tag{4.3.4}$$

The trade direction is only dependent on the difference of the ratios of the propensities to use leisure time and to hold wealth between the two countries. The difference in the human capital levels between the two countries does not affect the direction of equilibrium trade patterns. If $\sigma_2/\lambda_2 > \sigma_1/\lambda_1$ (which means,

$\xi_2 / \lambda_2 < \xi_1 / \lambda_1$ because of $a_1 = a_2$), then $E > 0$. Country 1 utilizes some of country 2's capital stocks. The conclusions are intuitively acceptable.

Case II $a_1 > a_2$ and $z_1 = z_2$

The requirement, $a_1 > a_2$, means that the ratio of country 1's propensity to enjoy and country 1's propensity to hold wealth is equal to the ratio of country 2's. This simply means that country 1's propensity to consum is stronger than country 2. The condition, $z_1 = z_2$, implies that the sum of the husband's and wife's human capital levels in country 1 is equal to that in country 2.

We now show that $\Lambda < 1$ is held at the equilibrium. By (4.2.16), $\Lambda < 1$ is guaranteed if

$$\frac{b_1}{2} + 1 > \left(\frac{b_1^2}{4} + b_2 \right)^{1/2} \tag{4.3.5}$$

where $1 + b_1 / 2 > 0$. The inequality, (4.3.5), is satisfied if $b_2 < 1 + b_1$. By (4.2.15), it is easy to check that this inequality is satisfied. This conclusion is quite expectable because country 1 is 'less patient' in consuming than country 2. From (4.2.2) and (4.2.3), we have

$$\frac{T_{1m}^h}{T_{2m}^h} = \frac{\lambda_2 \sigma_{1m} z_{2m}}{\lambda_1 \sigma_{2m} z_{1m}} \Lambda, \quad \frac{C_1}{C_2} = \frac{\lambda_2 \xi_1}{\lambda_1 \xi_2} \Lambda, \quad \frac{Y_1}{Y_2} = \frac{\xi_1 / \lambda_1 + \delta_k}{\xi_2 / \lambda_2 + \delta_k} \Lambda. \tag{4.3.6}$$

If without further specifying the parameter values, it is not easy to explicitly judge the comparative results. If it is further required that the male labor force in the two countries have an equal level of human capital, i.e., $z_{11} = z_{21}$, then we have

$$\frac{T_{1m}^h}{T_{2m}^h} = \frac{\lambda_2 \sigma_{1m}}{\lambda_1 \sigma_{2m}} \Lambda, \quad m = 1, 2.$$

If $\lambda_2 \sigma_{1m} / \lambda_1 \sigma_{2m} < 1$, $T_{1m}^h / T_{2m}^h < 1$. In the case of $\lambda_2 \sigma_{1m} / \lambda_1 \sigma_{2m} > 1$, T_{1m}^h / T_{2m}^h may be either greater or less than unity. We may similarly discuss C_1 / C_2 and Y_1 / Y_2. By (4.2.4), we get

$$E = \left(\frac{T_1}{T_2} - \Lambda \right) \frac{T_2 K_2}{T}.$$

In the case of $T_1 / T_2 \geq 1$, $E > 0$. In the case of $T_1 / T_2 < 1$, E may be either positive or negative.

4.4 The Impact of the Wife's Human Capital

This section examines the effects of changes in the human capital level z_{12} of country 1's female labor force. Since the equilibrium problem is explicitly given, it is analytically easy to carry out the comparative analysis. Since it is quite difficult to explicitly interpret results, for illustration we require $a_1 = a_2$ and $\sigma_2 / \lambda_2 = \sigma_1 / \lambda_1$ to be held in this section.

By (4.3.4), $E = 0$ is held at the equilibrium. Taking derivatives of (4.4.1) with respect to z_{12} yields

$$\frac{d\Lambda}{dz_{12}} = \frac{\Lambda}{z_{11} + z_{12}} > 0. \tag{4.4.1}$$

We conclude that an improvement in the human capital level of country 1's female labor force increases the ratio of capital stocks between countries 1 and 2.

By (4.2.13) and $\sigma_2 / \lambda_2 = \sigma_1 / \lambda_1$, we get

$$T = \frac{\xi_1 + \delta_k \lambda_1 + \delta_k}{\sigma_1 + \beta \xi_1 + \delta_k \beta \lambda_1} \beta z. \tag{4.4.2}$$

By (4.4.2), we have

$$\frac{1}{T} \frac{dT}{dz_{12}} = \frac{T_0}{z} > 0. \tag{4.4.3}$$

From (4.2.17) and $K = K_2(1 + \Lambda)$, we obtain

$$\frac{1}{K} \frac{dK}{dz_{12}} = \frac{1}{K_1} \frac{dK_1}{dz_{12}} = \frac{1}{z_{11} + z_{12}} > 0, \quad \frac{dK_1}{dz_{12}} = 0. \tag{4.4.4}$$

Country 1's and the world's capital stocks, K_1 and K, are increased and country 2's capital stocks, K_2, is not affected.

By (4.1.8), (4.2.2), (4.2.3) and (4.2.6), we get

$$\frac{1}{C_j}\frac{dC_j}{dz_{12}} = \frac{1}{Y_j}\frac{dY_j}{dz_{12}} = \frac{1}{F_j}\frac{dF_j}{dz_{12}} = \frac{1}{K_j}\frac{dK_j}{dz_{12}}, \quad j = 1, 2,$$

$$\frac{1}{w_{12}}\frac{dw_{12}}{dz_{12}} = \frac{1}{z_{12}} > 0, \quad \frac{dw_{j1}}{dz_{12}} = \frac{dw_{22}}{dz_{12}} = \frac{dr}{dz_{12}} = 0,$$

$$\frac{1}{T_{12}^h}\frac{dT_{12}^h}{dz_{12}} = -\frac{z_{11}}{(z_{11} + z_{12})z_{12}} < 0, \quad \frac{1}{T_{11}^h}\frac{dT_{11}^h}{dz_{12}} = \frac{1}{K_1}\frac{dK_1}{dz_{12}}, \quad \frac{dT_{2m}^h}{dz_{12}} = 0.$$

$$(4.4.5)$$

Summarizing the results in this section, we have the following corollary.

Corollary 4.4.1.
Let $a_1 = a_2$ and $\sigma_2 / \lambda_2 = \sigma_1 / \lambda_1$. Then, an improvement in the human capital level, z_{12}, of country 1's female labor force has following impact on the world economy: the world capitals K and the world output, $F_1 + F_2$, are increased, the rate of interest r is not affected; country 1's capital stocks K_1, output F_1, consumption level C_1, and income level Y_1, male leisure time T_{11}^h, and female wage rate w_{12}, are increased, country 1's female leisure time, T_{12}^h, is decreased, and male wage rate w_{11} is not affected; and country 2's capital stocks K_2, output F_2, consumption level C_2, income level Y_2, time allocation T_{2m}^h, and wage rates w_{2m}, are not affected.

It should be remarked that the comparative analysis is conduced under the strict conditions, $a_1 = a_2$ and $\sigma_2 / \lambda_2 = \sigma_1 / \lambda_1$. In general, it is very difficult to explicitly determine effects of changes in any parameters on the equilibrium structure of the world economy.

4.5 Concluding Remarks

This chapter proposed a two-country trade model with endogenous savings, consumption, time allocation and sexual division of labor. We built the trade model to explain endogenous accumulation of capital and international distribution of capital in the world economy in which the domestic markets in each country are perfectly competitive, international product and capital markets are freely mobile and labor is internationally immobile. We showed how the national differences in human capital levels of two sexes and preferences for consumption, time allocation and wealth accumulation determine the trade patterns and national differences in living conditions. We argued that trade patterns are not only determined by international comparative advantages in technology, but also influenced by preferences for leisure time and propensity to hold wealth. We also analyzed the effects of changes in the human capital level of country 1's female labor force on the world economy under some strict conditions.

5 Growth and Trade Patterns with National Public Goods

The previous chapters are concerned with international trade patterns and world economic growth without government intervention. But governments may intervene economic growth in different ways (Auerbach and Feldetein, 1990, 1991). It is significant to examine how government's intervention may affect world trade. This chapter is concerned with a special form of government intervention. We propose a two-country growth model with public sector attributes. The model describes a dynamic interaction between government policy, capital accumulation, national and international distribution of capital and labor, division of labor and capital distribution within each country. We analyze how differences in public policy, human capital and preference structures between countries may affect the global economy.

5.1 The Trade Model with Public Goods

Like in the preceding chapters, we are concerned with an economic system consisting of two countries, indexed by 1 and 2, respectively. Each country has one (private) industrial and one public sector. The public good is supplied and consumed nationally. Capital stocks and labor force are employed to produce the commodities and supply public goods. It is assumed that the two countries' industrial product is qualitatively homogenous and is either consumed or invested. We assume that each country has a homogenous population. Anyone in the system is free to choose his profession and there is no international migration. We select industrial commodity to serve as numeraire, with all the other prices being measured relative to its price. We neglect transportation cost of commodities between and within countries. The national government provides domestic public goods. The governments exhaust the internally generated revenues on the provision of the public good. There are no benefit or cost spillovers in either consumption or production of the public good from one country to the other. We introduce

N_j — country j's fixed population, $j = 1, 2$;

$K_j(t)$ — the level of capital stocks owned by country j at time t;

$E(t) > (<) 0$ — country 2's (1's) capital stocks employed by country 1 (2);

i, p — subscript index denoting industrial and public sectors, respectively;

$\Pi \equiv \{(i,1), (p,1), (i,2), (p,2)\}$ — the classification set of the production sectors, for instance, $(i,1)$ denotes country 1's industrial sector;

$K_{qj}(t)$ and $N_{qj}(t)$ — the capital stocks and labor force employed by sector $(q,j) \in \Pi$;

$F_{qj}(t)$ — the output level of sector $(q,j) \in \Pi$;

$k_j(t)$ — the level of capital stocks owned by per person in country j;

$c_j(t)$ and $s_j(t)$ — the consumption and savings of per person in country j;

τ_j — the fixed tax rate on the industrial sector in country j; and

$w_j(t)$ and $r(t)$ — country j's wage and the rate of interest.

We now describe the model.

The two sectors
The production functions of the public sectors in the two countries are specified as follows

$$F_{pj}(t) = K_{pj}^{\alpha_{pj}} (z_{pj} N_{pj})^{\beta_{pj}}, \quad \alpha_{pj}, \beta_{pj} > 0, \quad j = 1, 2 \tag{5.1.1}$$

in which z_{pj} are country j's levels of human capital of the public sector. Production functions of the industrial sectors in the two countries are specified as follows

$$F_{ij}(t) = K_{ij}^{\alpha_{ij}} (z_{ij} N_{ij})^{\beta_{ij}}, \quad \alpha_{ij} + \beta_{ij} = 1, \quad \alpha_{ij}, \beta_{ij} > 0, \quad j = 1, 2 \tag{5.1.2}$$

in which z_{ij} are country j's levels of human capital in industrial production. It should be remarked that we omit possible effects of public goods on productivity of the industrial sector. In fact, it is conceptually not difficult to take account of the possible impact by assuming that F_{ij} are dependent on F_{pj}.

We assume that perfect competition dominates the industrial sectors in the two countries. The marginal conditions of the industrial sectors are thus given by

$$r = \frac{(1 - \tau_j)\alpha_{ij} F_{ij}}{K_{ij}}, \quad w_j = \frac{(1 - \tau_j)\beta_{ij} F_{ij}}{N_{ij}}, \quad j = 1, 2. \tag{5.1.3}$$

Behavior of households

The net income, y_j, per person in country j consists of the wage income w_j and interest payment rk_j, i.e.

$$y_j(t) = rk_j + w_j, \quad j = 1, 2. \tag{5.1.4}$$

It is assumed that person j's utility level $U_j(t)$ is dependent on the supply level F_{jp} / N_j per capita of the public good, the consumption level $c_j(t)$ of goods, and the level of the person's wealth, $k_j(t) + s_j(t) - \delta_k k_j(t)$, where δ_k is the fixed depreciation rate of capital. For simplicity, the utility functions are specified as follows

$$U_j(t) = A_j \left(\frac{F_{pj}}{N_j} \right) c_j^{\xi_j} (k_j + s_j - \delta_k k_j)^{\lambda_j}, \quad \xi_j \, \lambda_j > 0, \quad j = 1, 2 \tag{5.1.5}$$

in which ξ_j and λ_j are person j's propensities to consume commodity and to own wealth. In (5.1.5), A_j are continuous functions of the average level of public goods (and services).

Person j's budget constraint is given by

$$c_j + s_j = y_j, \quad j = 1, 2. \tag{5.1.6}$$

Person j maximizes the person's utility (5.1.5) subject to its budget constraint (5.1.6). The optimal problems have the following solutions

$$c_j = \xi_j \rho_j \Omega_j, \quad s_j = \lambda_j \rho_j \Omega_j - \delta k_j \tag{5.1.7}$$

where

$$\Omega_j \equiv y_j + (1 - \delta_k)k_j, \quad \rho_j \equiv \frac{1}{\xi_j + \lambda_j}, \quad \delta \equiv 1 - \delta_k.$$

According to the definitions of k_j and s_j, the capital accumulation of person j is given by

$$\frac{dk_j}{dt} = s_j - \delta_k k_j.$$

Substituting s_j in (5.1.7) into these equations yields

$$\frac{dk_j}{dt} = \lambda_j \rho_j \Omega_j - k_j, \quad j = 1, 2. \tag{5.1.8}$$

Full employment of the production factors and balance of demand and supply

The levels K_j of country j's capital stocks are given by

$$K_j = k_j N_j, \quad j = 1, 2. \tag{5.1.9}$$

By the definitions of K_{qj}, E and K_j, we have

$$K_{i1} + K_{p1} - E = K_1, \quad K_{i2} + K_{p2} + E = K_2. \tag{5.1.10}$$

The labor force is fully employed in each country, i.e.

$$N_{ij} + N_{pj} = N_j, \quad j = 1, 2. \tag{5.1.11}$$

As product is either consumed or invested, we have the following relation

$$\sum_j (c_j + s_j) N_j = F_{i1} + F_{i2}. \tag{5.1.12}$$

The government behavior

The revenue of country j's government at time t consists tax income on the industrial sector $\tau_j F_{ij}$. The government's budget is distributed between the wage payment $w_j N_{pj}$ for the workers and interest payment rK_{pj} for the capital stocks employed by the public sector, i.e.

$$w_j N_{pj} + rK_{pj} = \tau_j F_{ij}, \quad j = 1, 2. \tag{5.1.13}$$

We assume that the government will use its tax revenue in such a way that the output F_{pj} of the public sector is maximal. It should be remarked that the goal of the government may be more complicated. For instance, it is quite reasonable to suggest that country j's government may maximize some aggregated social welfare function subject to its revenue constraint.

Maximizing F_{qj} in (5.1.1) subject to (5.1.13) yields

$$rK_{pj} = \alpha_j F_{ij}, \quad w_j N_{pj} = \beta_j F_{ij}, \quad j = 1, 2 \tag{5.1.14}$$

where

$$\alpha_j \equiv \frac{\tau_j \alpha_{pj}}{\alpha_{pj} + \beta_{pj}}, \quad \beta_j \equiv \frac{\tau_j \beta_{pj}}{\alpha_{pj} + \beta_{pj}}, \quad j = 1, 2.$$

We have thus built the model. There are 26 endogenous variables, K_{qj}, N_{qj}, and F_{qj}, $(q, j) \in \Pi$, w_j, c_j, s_j, k_j, y_j, and U_j, $j = 1, 2$, E and r.

5.2 Equilibria of the Global Economy

This section examines conditions for existence of equilibria of the dynamic system. By (5.1.8), at equilibrium we have

$$\lambda_j \rho_j \Omega_j = k_j, \quad j = 1, 2. \tag{5.2.1}$$

Substituting (5.2.1) into (5.1.7) yields

$$c_j = \frac{\xi_j k_j}{\lambda_j}, \quad s_j = \delta_k k_j. \tag{5.2.2}$$

By (5.2.2) and (5.1.7), we get

$$y_j = \delta_j k_j, \quad j = 1, 2 \tag{5.2.3}$$

where $\delta_j \equiv \xi_j / \lambda_j + \delta_k$. By (5.2.3) and (5.1.4), we have

$$(\delta_j - r) k_j = w_j, \quad j = 1, 2. \tag{5.2.4}$$

Since it is necessary to require $k_j > 0$ and $w_j > 0$, we require

$$r < \delta_1 = \min\{\delta_j, j = 1, 2\}. \tag{5.2.5}$$

In (5.2.5), we require: $\delta_1 < \delta_2$, i.e., $\xi_1 / \lambda_1 < \xi_2 / \lambda_2$, which is interpreted as that country 1's consumers are more patient than country 2's (with regard to their own incomes). By (5.1.2) and (5.1.3), we have

$$w_j = \theta_j r^{-\alpha_{ij}/\beta_{ij}}$$

(5.2.6)

where

$$\theta_j \equiv (1 - \tau_j)^{1/\beta_{ij}} z_{ij} \beta_{ij} \alpha_{ij}^{\alpha_{ij}/\beta_{ij}}.$$

By (5.1.14), (5.1.3) and (5.1.4), we have

$$\frac{r}{w_j} = \frac{\alpha_{ij} N_{ij}}{\beta_{ij} K_{ij}} = \frac{\alpha_j N_{pj}}{\beta_j K_{pj}}, \quad j = 1, 2.$$

(5.2.7)

By (5.1.14) and (5.1.3), we have

$$\frac{N_{ij}}{N_{pj}} = \frac{(1 - \tau_j)\beta_{ij}}{\beta_j}, \quad j = 1, 2.$$

(5.2.8)

By (5.2.8) and (5.1.11), we solve the labor distribution as follows

$$N_{ij} = \frac{(1 - \tau_j)\beta_{ij} N_j}{\beta_j + (1 - \tau_j)\beta_{ij}}, \quad N_{pj} = \frac{\beta_j N_j}{\beta_j + (1 - \tau_j)\beta_{ij}}, \quad j = 1, 2.$$

(5.2.9)

By (5.2.7) and (5.2.8), we have

$$\frac{K_{ij}}{K_{pj}} = \frac{(1 - \tau_j)\alpha_{ij}}{\alpha_j}, \quad j = 1, 2.$$

(5.2.10)

By (5.2.10) and (5.1.12), we solve

$$K_{i1} = \tau_{i1}(K_1 + E), \quad K_{p1} = \tau_{p1}(K_1 + E), \quad K_{i2} = \tau_{i2}(K_2 - E),$$
$$K_{p2} = \tau_{p2}(K_2 - E)$$

(5.2.11)

where

$$\tau_{ij} \equiv \frac{(1-\tau_j)\alpha_{ij}}{\alpha_j + (1-\tau_j)\alpha_{ij}}, \quad \tau_{pj} \equiv \frac{\alpha_j}{\alpha_j + (1-\tau_j)\alpha_{ij}}, \quad j = 1, 2.$$

By (5.2.11), $rK_{ij} = (1-\tau_j)\alpha_{ij}F_{ij}$ in (5.1.3), and (5.1.2), we obtain

$$K_1 + E = \frac{z_1}{r^{1/\beta_{i1}}}, \quad K_2 - E = \frac{z_1}{r^{1/\beta_{i2}}} \tag{5.2.12}$$

where

$$z_j = \frac{z_{ij}N_{ij}}{\tau_{ij}}\left\{(1-\tau_j)\alpha_{ij}\right\}^{1/\beta_{ij}}, \quad j = 1, 2.$$

Using (5.1.10), (5.2.6), and (5.2.12), we obtain

$$k_j = \frac{\theta_j}{(\delta_j - r)r^{\alpha_{ij}/\beta_{ij}}}. \tag{5.2.13}$$

Substituting (5.2.2) into (5.1.12) yields

$$\sum_j \delta_j k_j N_j = \sum_j \frac{w_{ij}N_{ij}}{(1-\tau_j)\beta_{ij}} \tag{5.2.14}$$

where we use $w_j N_{ij} = (1-\tau_j)\beta_{ij}F_{ij}$ from (5.1.3). Substituting (5.2.6) and (5.2.13) into (5.2.14), we get

$$\Phi(r) \equiv \left(\frac{\delta_1 N_1}{\delta_1 - r} - \frac{N_{i1}}{(1-\tau_1)\beta_{i1}}\right)\theta r^\alpha + \frac{\delta_2 N_2}{\delta_2 - r} - \frac{N_{i2}}{(1-\tau_2)\beta_{i2}} = 0$$

$$\tag{5.2.15}$$

where $\theta \equiv \theta_1/\theta_2$ and $\alpha \equiv \alpha_{i2}/\beta_{i2} - \alpha_{i1}/\beta_{i1}$. It can be seen that the signs of

$$N_j - \frac{N_{ij}}{(1-\tau_j)\beta_{ij}} = N_j - \frac{N_j}{\beta_j + (1-\tau_j)\beta_{ij}}$$

are ambiguous. For convenience, we require: $\beta_j + (1-\tau_j)\beta_{ij} < 1$, i.e.

$$N_j < \frac{N_{ij}}{\beta_{ij}(1-\tau_j)}, \quad j=1, 2.$$

The requirements, $\beta_j + (1-\tau_j)\beta_{ij} < 1$, is guaranteed if country j's tax rate τ_j is not high. If $\beta_{ij} + \beta_{pj}/(\alpha_{pj} + \beta_{pj})$ hold, the above requirements are satisfied.

The function $\Phi(r)$ has the following properties

$$\Phi(0) < 0, \quad \Phi(\delta_1) > 0.$$

This implies that the equation $\Phi(r) = 0$ has at least one solution for $0 < r < \delta_1$. It is difficult to explicitly judge whether or not the equation has a unique meaningful solution. For simplicity, we require: $\alpha = 0$, i.e., $\alpha_{i1} = \alpha_{i2}$. The condition simply means that the industrial sectors in the two countries have an identical production function. Under this requirement, we obtain two solutions of (5.2.15) as follows

$$r = \upsilon \pm (\upsilon_1^2 + \upsilon_2)^{1/2} \tag{5.2.16}$$

where

$$\upsilon_1 \equiv \frac{\delta_1 + \delta_2 - n_1 - n_2}{2}, \quad \upsilon_2 \equiv \delta_1 n_2 + \delta_2 n_1 - \delta_1\delta_2,$$

$$n_j \equiv \upsilon_0\delta_j\theta N_j, \quad \upsilon_0 \equiv \left(\frac{\theta N_{i1}}{(1-\tau_1)\beta_{i1}} + \frac{N_{i2}}{(1-\tau_2)\beta_{i2}} \right)^{-1} > 0$$

Since

$$2\upsilon_1 = \left\{ \frac{\theta N_{i1}}{(1-\tau_1)\beta_{i1}} + \frac{N_{i2}}{(1-\tau_2)\beta_{i2}} - \frac{\theta N_1}{N_2} \right\}\upsilon_0\delta_1$$

$$+ \left\{ \frac{\theta N_{i1}}{(1-\tau_1)\beta_{i1}} + \frac{N_{i2}}{(1-\tau_2)\beta_{i2}} - \frac{N_1}{N_2} \right\}\upsilon_0\delta_2 > 0,$$

$$\upsilon_2 = \left\{ \theta N_1 - \frac{\theta N_{i1}}{(1-\tau_1)\beta_{i1}} + N_2 - \frac{N_{i2}}{(1-\tau_2)\beta_{i2}} \right\}\upsilon_0\delta_1\delta_2 < 0$$

where we use $\beta_j + (1 - \tau_j)\beta_{ij} < 1$, we see that the equation, (5.2.15), has two positive solutions in the case that the term

$$v_1^2 + v_2 = \frac{(\delta_1 - \delta_2 - n_1 - n_2)^2}{4} + \frac{n_2(\delta_1 - \delta_2)}{2}$$

is positive. It is direct to show that only one solution

$$r = v_1 - (v_1^2 + v_2)^{1/2}$$

satisfies $0 < r < \delta_1$. Summarizing the above discussion, we obtain the following result.

Proposition 5.2.1.
We require: $\delta_1 < \delta_2$ and $\alpha_{i1} = \alpha_{i2}$. The dynamic system has a unique equilibrium. The equilibrium values of all the variables are given by the following procedure: r by (5.2.16) $\rightarrow$ w_j, $j = 1, 2$, by (5.2.6) $\rightarrow$ N_{qj}, $(q, j) \in \Pi$, by (5.2.9) $\rightarrow$ $K_1 + E$ and $K_2 - E$ by (5.2.12) $\rightarrow$ K_{qj} by (5.2.11) $\rightarrow$ F_{qj} by (5.1.1) $\rightarrow$ F_{ij} by (5.1.2) $\rightarrow$ k_j by (5.2.13) $\rightarrow$ K_j by (5.1.9) $\rightarrow$ E by (5.2.12) $\rightarrow$ c_j and s_j by (5.2.2) $\rightarrow$ y_j by (5.2.3) $\rightarrow$ U_j by (5.1.5).

We have thus solved the equilibrium problems. We now examine the impact of changes in some parameters on the equilibrium structure of the dynamic system.

5.3 The Impact of Changes in the Tax Rate

This section is concerned with the impact of changes in country 1's tax rate, τ_1, on the equilibrium structure of the world economy. Taking derivatives of $r = v_1 - (v_1^2 + v_2)^{1/2}$ with respect to τ_1 yields

$$2(v_1 - r)\frac{dr}{d\tau_1} = -2r\frac{dv_1}{d\tau_1} - \frac{dv_2}{d\tau_1} \tag{5.3.1}$$

in which $(v_1^2 + v_2)^{1/2} = v_1 - r > 0$ and

$$2\frac{d\upsilon_1}{d\tau_1} = \frac{n_1}{(1-\tau_1)\beta_{i1}} - n_1\tau^* - n_2\tau^*,$$

$$\frac{d\upsilon_2}{d\tau_1} = \delta_2 n_1\tau^* + \delta_1 n_2\tau^* - \frac{\delta_2 n_1}{(1-\tau_1)\beta_{i1}}$$

where

$$\tau^* \equiv \frac{\alpha_{i1}\theta N_{i1}}{\upsilon_0 \beta_{i1}^2 (1-\tau_1)^2}.$$

We see that the rate of interest r may be either increased or reduced.

By (5.2.6), we have

$$\frac{\beta_{i1}}{w_1}\frac{dw_1}{d\tau_1} = -\frac{1}{1-\tau_1} - \frac{\alpha_{i1}}{r}\frac{dr}{d\tau_1} < 0, \quad \frac{\beta_{i2}}{w_2}\frac{dw_2}{d\tau_1} = -\frac{\alpha_{i2}}{r}\frac{dr}{d\tau_1} < 0. \qquad (5.3.2)$$

In the case of $dr / d\tau_1 > (<) 0$, the wage rates in two countries are reduced (increased) as country 1's tax rate is increased. Taking derivatives of (5.2.9) with respect to τ_1 yields

$$\frac{dN_{p1}}{d\tau_1} = -\frac{dN_{p1}}{d\tau_1} = \frac{\beta_{i1} - \beta_{p1}/(\alpha_{p1} + \beta_{p1})}{\beta_1 + (1-\tau_1)\beta_{i1}} N_{p1},$$

$$\frac{dN_{p2}}{d\tau_1} = \frac{dN_{p2}}{d\tau_1} = 0. \qquad (5.3.3)$$

The labor force employed by country 1's public sector is increased and the labor force by country 1's industrial sector is reduced. Country 2's labor distribution is not affected.

By (5.1.9) and (5.2.13), we have

$$\frac{1}{K_1}\frac{dK_1}{d\tau_1} = \frac{1}{k_1}\frac{dk_1}{d\tau_1} = \frac{r - \alpha_{i1}\delta_1}{(\delta_1 - r)r\beta_{i1}}\frac{dr}{d\tau_1} - \frac{1}{(1-\tau_1)\beta_{i1}},$$

$$\frac{1}{K_2}\frac{dK_2}{d\tau_1} = \frac{1}{k_2}\frac{dk_2}{d\tau_1} = \frac{r - \alpha_{i1}\delta_2}{(\delta_2 - r)r\beta_{i1}}\frac{dr}{d\tau_1}. \qquad (5.3.4)$$

The signs of $dk_j / d\tau_1$ are ambiguous. By (5.2.2) and (5.2.3), we have

$$\frac{1}{c_j}\frac{dc_j}{d\tau_1} = \frac{1}{y_j}\frac{dy_j}{d\tau_1} = \frac{1}{k_j}\frac{dk_j}{d\tau_1}, \quad j = 1, 2. \tag{5.3.5}$$

By (5.2.12), we obtain

$$\frac{dE}{d\tau_1} = N_2 \frac{dk_2}{d\tau_1} - \frac{K_2 - E}{r\beta_{i1}}\frac{dr}{d\tau_1}. \tag{5.3.6}$$

By (5.2.11), (5.1.1) and (5.1.2), we obtain

$$\frac{1}{K_{q1}}\frac{dK_{q1}}{d\tau_1} = \frac{1}{N_{i1}}\frac{dN_{i1}}{d\tau_1} - \frac{1}{(1-\tau_1)\beta_{i1}} - \frac{1}{r\beta_{i1}}\frac{dr}{d\tau_1},$$

$$\frac{1}{K_{q2}}\frac{dK_{q2}}{d\tau_1} = -\frac{1}{r\beta_{i1}}\frac{dr}{d\tau_1}, \quad \frac{1}{F_{q1}}\frac{dF_{q1}}{d\tau_1} = \frac{\beta_{q1}}{N_{i1}}\frac{dN_{i1}}{d\tau_1} + \frac{\alpha_{q1}}{K_{i1}}\frac{dK_{i1}}{d\tau_1},$$

$$\frac{1}{F_{q2}}\frac{dF_{q2}}{d\tau_1} = \frac{\alpha_{q2}}{K_{q2}}\frac{dK_{q2}}{d\tau_1}, \quad q = i, p. \tag{5.3.7}$$

5.4 The Impact of Changes in the Population

This section is concerned with the impact of changes in country 1's population, N_1, on the equilibrium structure of the world economy. Taking derivatives of $r = \upsilon_1 - (\upsilon_1^2 + \upsilon_2)^{1/2}$ with respect to N_1 yields

$$2(\upsilon_1 - r)\frac{dr}{dN_1}$$

$$= \left\{ \frac{1 - r/\delta_1}{\beta_1 + (1-\tau_1)\beta_{i1}} - \frac{1 - r/\delta_2}{\beta_2 + (1-\tau_2)\beta_{i2}} \right\} \upsilon_0^2 \delta_1 \delta_2 N_2 \tag{5.4.1}$$

where

$$(\upsilon_1^2 + \upsilon_2)^{1/2} = \upsilon_1 - r > 0.$$

The sign of dr / dN_1 is the same as that of the term

$$\frac{1 - r / \delta_1}{\beta_1 + (1 - \tau_1)\beta_{i1}} - \frac{1 - r / \delta_2}{\beta_2 + (1 - \tau_2)\beta_{i2}}.$$

Since $1 - r / \delta_2 > 1 - r / \delta_1 > 0$, the sign of dr / dN_1 is negative (ambiguous) in the case of

$$\beta_1 + (1 - \tau_1)\beta_{i1} > (<) \beta_2 + (1 - \tau_2)\beta_{i2}.$$

We require: $\beta_1 + (1 - \tau_1)\beta_{i1} > \beta_2 + (1 - \tau_2)\beta_{i2}$, i.e.

$$\left(\frac{\beta_{p1}}{\alpha_{p1} + \beta_{p1}} - \beta_{i1} \right)\tau_1 > \left(\frac{\beta_{p2}}{\alpha_{p2} + \beta_{p2}} - \beta_{i2} \right)\tau_2. \qquad (5.4.2)$$

This is guaranteed, for instance, if

$$\frac{\beta_{p1}}{\alpha_{p1} + \beta_{p1}} - \beta_{i1} \geq \frac{\beta_{p2}}{\alpha_{p2} + \beta_{p2}} - \beta_{i2} > (<) 0$$

and $\tau_1 > \tau_2$. Under (5.4.2), the rate of interest is reduced as country 1's population is increased.

By (5.2.6), we have

$$\frac{\beta_{i1}}{w_j} \frac{dw_j}{dN_1} = -\frac{\alpha_{i1}}{r} \frac{dr}{dN_1} > 0, \quad j = 1, 2. \qquad (5.4.3)$$

The wage rates in two countries are increased. Taking derivatives of (5.2.9) with respect to N_1 yields

$$\frac{1}{N_{p1}} \frac{dN_{p1}}{dN_1} = \frac{1}{N_{i1}} \frac{dN_{i1}}{dN_1} = \frac{1}{N_1} > 0, \quad \frac{dN_{p2}}{dN_1} = \frac{dN_{i2}}{dN_1} = 0, \quad j = 1, 2.$$

$$(5.4.4)$$

The numbers of labor employed by country 1's two sectors are increased. Country 2's labor distribution is not affected.

By (5.1.9) and (5.2.13), we obtain

$$\frac{1}{K_1}\frac{dK_1}{dN_1} = \frac{1}{k_1}\frac{dk_1}{dN_1} + \frac{1}{N_1}, \quad \frac{1}{K_2}\frac{dK_2}{dN_1} = \frac{1}{k_2}\frac{dk_2}{dN_1}. \tag{5.4.5}$$

Country j's capital stocks per capita is increased (reduced) in the case of $r > (<) \alpha_{i1}\delta_j$. By (5.2.2) and (5.2.3)

$$\frac{1}{c_j}\frac{dc_j}{dN_1} = \frac{1}{y_j}\frac{dy_j}{dN_1} = \frac{1}{k_j}\frac{dk_j}{dN_1}, \quad j = 1, 2 \tag{5.4.6}$$

hold. The signs of dc_j / dN_1 and dy_j / dN_1 are ambiguous. By (5.2.12), we obtain

$$\frac{dE}{dN_1} = N_2 \frac{dk_2}{dN_1} - \frac{K_2 - E}{r\beta_{i1}}\frac{dr}{dN_1}. \tag{5.4.7}$$

By (5.2.11), (5.1.1) and (5.1.2), we obtain

$$\frac{1}{K_{q1}}\frac{dK_{q1}}{dN_1} = \frac{1}{N_1} - \frac{1}{r\beta_{i1}}\frac{dr}{dN_1} > 0, \quad \frac{1}{K_{q2}}\frac{dK_{q2}}{dN_1} = -\frac{1}{r\beta_{i1}}\frac{dr}{dN_1} > 0,$$

$$\frac{1}{F_{q1}}\frac{dF_{q1}}{dN_1} = \frac{\alpha_{q1}}{K_{q1}}\frac{dK_{q1}}{dN_1} + \frac{\beta_{i1}}{N_1} > 0, \quad \frac{1}{F_{q2}}\frac{dF_{q2}}{dN_1} = \frac{\alpha_{q2}}{K_{q2}}\frac{dK_{q2}}{dN_1} > 0,$$

$$q = i, p. \tag{5.4.8}$$

As country 1's population is increased, the output levels of the two countries' two sectors are reduced.

6 Growth, Trade, and International Migration

So far we assumed that capital and goods are freely mobile among nations but people are internationally immobile. This requirement is strict for modern economies. Although there are some dynamic models in the literature of trade theory with growth as mentioned in Chapter 2, issues about interactions between growth, trade and migration are not well addressed within a compact analytical framework. It is apparently not only economic factors that determine international migration patterns. Factors such as differences in social status, accessibility to friendship, climates and social environment in the home country and the foreign country are significant in affecting people's movement. It is necessary to examine migration issues within a framework that takes account of behavior of all the participants in the global economy.

Various theoretical models are proposed to deal with issues related to international migration (e.g., Bhagwati and Hamada, 1974, Rodriguez, 1975, Bhagwati, 1976, Bhagwati and Srinivasan, 1983, Djajic and Milbourne, 1988, Zhang, 1990b, Rauch, 1991a). It may be argued that only a few theoretical models with migration treat the world economy as a dynamic whole. Since the world has become more and more connected due to widely spread free trades and free movement of people, issues related to dynamic interdependence of economic development in different countries and international migration are becoming increasingly significant. The purpose of this chapter is to address the issue of dynamic interdependence between economic growth and international migration within a compact framework. We develop a dynamic model with endogenous capital accumulation and international migration to gain insights into possible relationships between international migrants and economic growth of the world economy. As far as production and capital accumulation are concerned, the model in this chapter is developed within the same framework as represented in the preceding chapters.

It is not an easy matter to develop a theoretical model which takes account of both capital accumulation and international migration within a compact framework. In modern economies, labor and capital are quickly mobile between nations. It may be reasonable to assume that capital movement equalizes rate of interest between nations. But there are different principles for analyzing temporary equilibrium conditions for labor movement in a dynamic international framework. For example, in the theoretical literature on international economics two principles have been proposed to analyze labor movement. One is that labor movement, if costs associated with professional or locational changes are neglected, equalizes wage rates between nations. This assumption is limited if nations provide different levels of amenity (such as national cultures, freedom, climates and pollution) and have different technologies. The other one is that free movement of people equalizes utility levels which they may obtain in different countries. Although this assumption is quite acceptable for analyzing issues related to movement of people, it is not easy to apply the principle within a compact dynamic framework with international differences in life styles and wage rates. One of the reasons is that it is difficult to examine issues related to ownership of capital in a dynamic world economy. If wage rates and life styles (including saving behavior) are internationally different and people may freely move within the world economy, how to calculate each individual's capital and his income in a dynamic world economy is not an easy matter. In this chapter, we solve this issue by utilizing a utility function proposed by Chapter 2.

This chapter is organized as follows. Section 6.1 defines the model. Section 6.2 provides the conditions for the existence of unique equilibrium. Section 6.3 examines the impact of improvement in the amenity levels that people of the migrating country obtain in the home and foreign countries on the world economic structure. Section 6.4 examines the impact of improvement in the level of human capital of people in the migrating country on the world economic structure. Section 6.5 concludes the chapter.

6.1 The Growth Model with Trade and Migration

We are concerned with an economic system of two countries, indexed by $j = 1, 2$, respectively. We assume that country 1's population has no incentives to migrate to country 2 and country 2's population has incentive and freedom to migrate to country 1. From theoretical points of view, we may have various possible combinations of migration pattern. For instance, it is quite reasonable to assume the existence of bilateral migration. People with low level of human capital in a developed economy may go to work in a less developed economy in order to utilize some advantages he may obtain from his native country, and vice versa. From the discussion below, it can be seen that it is conceptually not difficult to introduce this case into our framework. For simplicity, we are concerned with unilateral international migration. We omit any possible economic cost associated with migration.

To describe the model, we introduce the following indexes

N_j — the fixed population of country j, $j = 1, 2$;

$N_h(t)$ and $N_m(t)$ — the number of country 2's people who remain in country 2 and who migrate to country 1 at time t, respectively;

$\Pi \equiv \{1, h, m\}$ — the classification set of the world population; 1 denotes country 1's native people, h denotes country 2's people remaining in the home country and m denotes country 2's people migrating to country 1;

$k_q(t)$ — the capital stocks owned by per person $q \in \Pi$;

$K_j(t)$ — the level of capital stocks owned by country j;

$E(t) > (<)$ — country 2's (1's) capital stocks employed by country 1 (2);

$F_j(t)$ — country j's output;

$c_q(t)$ and $s_q(t)$ — the consumption and savings of per person q, $q \in \Pi$; and

$r(t)$ and $w_q(t)$ — the rate of interest and the wage rate of person q, $q \in \Pi$.

It is assumed that labor and capital are always fully employed. The world capital stocks $K(t)$ and country j's qualified labor force $N_j^*(t)$ are given by

$$K_1 = k_1 N_1 + k_m N_m, \quad K_2 = k_h N_h, \quad K = K_1 + K_2,$$
$$N_1^* = z_1 N_1 + z_m N_m, \quad N_2 = z_h N_h \tag{6.1.1}$$

where z_q is the level of person q's human capital, $q \in \Pi$. The parameters z_q measure productivity of person q. Country 2's people may have different levels of productivity when they work in the two countries. One of common conditions for migration is that people may more effectively use their talents in foreign countries. As shown late, differences in the amenities that the two countries provide for country 2's people and in the levels of human capital that country 2's people exhibit in the two countries play a significant role in determining migration.

The production functions of the two countries are specified as follows

$$F_1 = (K_1 + E)^{\alpha_1} N_1^{*\beta_1}, \quad F_2 = (K_2 - E)^{\alpha_2} N_2^{*\beta_2},$$
$$\alpha_j + \beta_j = 1, \quad \alpha_j, \beta_j > 0, \quad j = 1, 2 \tag{6.1.2}$$

where $K_1 + E$ and $K_2 - E$ are the capital stocks employed by countries 1 and 2, respectively. We assume that labor markets are perfectly competitive and migrants are not discriminated in country 1. The marginal conditions are given by

$$r = \frac{\alpha_1 F_1}{K_1 + E} = \frac{\alpha_2 F_2}{K_2 - E}, \quad w_1 = \frac{\beta_1 z_1 F_1}{N_1^*}, \quad w_m = \frac{\beta_1 z_m F_1}{N_1^*},$$

$$w_h = \frac{\beta_2 z_h F_2}{N_2^*}.$$ (6.1.3)

By (6.1.3), we have

$$\frac{w_1}{w_m} = \frac{z_1}{z_m}, \quad \frac{w_h}{w_m} = \frac{\beta_2 z_h F_2 N_1^*}{\beta_1 z_m F_1 N_2^*}.$$

The wage ratio w_1 / w_m between person 1 and person m is only related to the ratio of their levels of human capital. Although person m and person h have the same nationality and have homogenous human capital, the ratio of their wage rates w_h / w_m is dependent not only on the ratio of levels of human capital which they exhibit in different countries, but also on differences in the production functions. If the two countries' production function is identical, i.e., $\alpha_1 = \alpha_2$, it can be shown

$$\frac{w_h}{w_m} = \frac{z_h}{z_m}.$$

The wage ratio w_h / w_m is only dependent on the ratio of their levels of human capital in the two countries. If we interpret z_q as working time of person q, the conclusions are intuitively obvious.

It is assumed that the utility level $U_q(t)$ of person q is dependent on his temporary consumption level $c_q(t)$ and his wealth, $k_q(t) + s_q(t) - \delta_k k_q(t)$, where δ_k is the fixed depreciation rate of capital. The utility functions $U_q(t)$ are specified as follows

$$U_q(t) = A_q c_q^{\xi_q} (k_q + s_q - \delta_k k_q)^{\lambda_q},$$
$$\xi_q, \lambda_q > 0, \ \xi_q + \lambda_q = 1, \ q \in \Pi.$$ (6.1.4)

Here, we call ξ_q and λ_q person q's propensities to consume and to hold wealth, respectively. Like in Chapter 2, the temporal utility function takes account of the future by the preference structure parameters, ξ_q and λ_q. If λ_q becomes larger, we interpret that person q becomes more patient. The parameter A_q is the level of amenity that person q obtains. Countries 1 and 2 may offer different levels of amenity for country 2's people. This implies that A_h and A_m may be different. If country 2's people get no amenity in the foreign country (i.e., $A_m = 0$), there should be no migration. We have analyzed the trade model without migration. On the other hand, if country 2 offers no amenity to its people, then all the people from country 2 will migrate to country 1 (if country 1 allows). In this case, the trade model becomes a two-group growth model as developed in Zhang (1999a). We will not examine these two extreme cases. This chapter is concerned with the case that country 2's people exist in the two countries. It should be noted that it is quite reasonable to assume that A_h and A_m are endogenous variables. For instance, A_m may be positively (e.g., because of forming a large community of migrants from the same cultural background) or negatively (e.g., because of strengthened discrimination against migrants) dependent on N_m.

Since country 2's people are internationally freely mobile, the utility levels that country 2's people obtain in the two countries should be the same, i.e.

$$U_h(t) = U_m(t), \; if \; 0 < N_m, \; N_h < N_2. \tag{6.1.5}$$

It should be noted that the dynamic behavior of the system are examined in Chapter 2 when $N_m = 0$ (i.e., in the case of no international migration).

The net income y_q of person q is given by

$$y_q(t) = rk_q + w_q, \; q \in \Pi. \tag{6.1.6}$$

Households in each country have two decision variables, c_q and s_q. The budget constraints are given by

$$c_q + s_q = y_q, \; q \in \Pi. \tag{6.1.7}$$

Person q maximizes $U_q(t)$ in (6.1.4) subject to the above budget constrain. The optimal problem has the following unique solution

$$c_q = \xi_q y_q + (1 - \delta_k)\xi_q k_q, \; s_q = \lambda_q y_q - (1 - \delta_k)\xi_q k_q, \; q \in \Pi. \tag{6.1.8}$$

We see that the consumption level of each person is positively related to his net income and his capital stocks; and each person's savings is positively related to his net income but negatively on related to his capital stocks.

The capital accumulation of person q is given by

$$\frac{dk_q}{dt} = s_q - \delta_k k_q, \quad q \in \Pi. \tag{6.1.9}$$

Substituting s_q in (6.1.8) into these equations yields

$$\frac{dk_q}{dt} = \lambda_q y_q - (\xi_q + \delta_k \lambda_q)k_q, \quad q \in \Pi. \tag{6.1.10}$$

As product is either consumed or invested, we have

$$\sum_{q \in \Pi}(c_q + s_q)N_q = F_1 + F_2. \tag{6.1.11}$$

Country 2's people either maintain at the home country or migrate to the foreign country, i.e.

$$N_h(t) + N_m(t) = N_2. \tag{6.1.12}$$

We have thus built the model. The system consists of 26 endogenous variables, k_q, c_q, s_q, y_q, w_q, U_q, $q \in \Pi$, N_h, N_m, K_j, F_j, $j = 1, 2$, E, and r. It also contains the same number of independent equations. We now examine the behavior of the system.

6.2 Equilibrium of the Global Economy

This section examines conditions that the system has equilibria. By (6.1.10), at equilibrium we have

$$y_q = \delta_q k_q, \quad q \in \Pi \tag{6.2.1}$$

where $\delta_q \equiv \xi_q / \lambda_q + \delta_k$. By (6.1.6) and (6.2.1), we have

$$(\delta_q - r) = w_q, \quad q \in \Pi. \tag{6.2.2}$$

Since it is necessary to require: $k_q > 0$ and $w_q > 0$, we have to require

$$\min \left\{ \delta_q, \ q \in \Pi \right\} > r.$$

For simplicity, we assume that migrants have the highest propensity to hold wealth, i.e.

$$\lambda_m > \max \left\{ \lambda_1, \lambda_h \right\}.$$

It can be seen that we may similarly discuss the cases that some other group has the highest propensity to hold wealth. Since $\delta_q = 1 / \lambda_q - 1 + \delta_k$, we see that

$$\min \left\{ \delta_q, q \in \Pi \right\} = \delta_m.$$

Hence the condition, $\min \left\{ \delta_q, q \in \Pi \right\} > r$ becomes

$$\delta_m > r. \tag{6.2.3}$$

Using $w_1 / w_m = z_1 / z_m$ and (6.2.2), we obtain

$$\frac{k_1}{k_m} = \left(\frac{\delta_m - r}{\delta_1 - r} \right) \frac{z_1}{z_m}. \tag{6.2.4}$$

Substituting (6.2.1) into (6.1.8) yields

$$c_q = \frac{\xi_q k_q}{\lambda_q}, \ s_q = \delta_k k_q, \ q \in \Pi. \tag{6.2.5}$$

Substituting (6.2.2) into (6.1.4) and then using (6.1.5), we get

$$\frac{k_h}{k_m} = A, \ A \equiv \left(\frac{\lambda_h}{\xi_h} \right)^{\xi_h} \left(\frac{\xi_m}{\lambda_m} \right)^{\xi_m} \frac{A_m}{A_h}. \tag{6.2.6}$$

The ratio k_h / k_m of levels of capital stocks owned by country 2's people who maintain at the home country and migrate to country 1 is dependent on the ratio of amenity levels that country 2's people obtain in the two countries and difference in the life styles that they experience in the two countries. If country 2's people have the same level of propensities to hold wealth, i.e., $\lambda_m = \lambda_h$ in the two countries, then $k_h / k_m = A_m / A_h$ holds. If country 2's people socially suffer in country 1 in comparison to their home country, i.e., $A_m < A_h$, then at equilibrium migrants own more capital stocks than their countrymen. Otherwise, equilibrium cannot be maintained under the free migration institution.

By

$$r = \frac{\alpha_1 F_1}{K_1 + E} = \frac{\alpha_2 F_2}{K_2 - E}$$

in (6.1.3) and (6.1.2), we directly obtain

$$\frac{N_1^*}{K_1 + E} = \left(\frac{r}{\alpha_1}\right)^{1/\beta_1}, \quad \frac{N_2^*}{K_2 - E} = \left(\frac{r}{\alpha_2}\right)^{1/\beta_2}. \tag{6.2.7}$$

From (6.1.2), (6.2.7) and w_q, $q \in \Pi$ in (6.1.3), we get

$$w_1 = \left(\frac{\alpha_1}{r}\right)^{a_1} \beta_1 z_1, \quad w_m = \left(\frac{\alpha_1}{r}\right)^{a_1} \beta_1 z_m, \quad w_h = \left(\frac{\alpha_2}{r}\right)^{a_2} \beta_2 z_h \tag{6.2.8}$$

where $a_j \equiv \alpha_j / \beta_j$. Substituting w_m and w_h in (6.2.8) into (6.2.2), we get

$$(\delta_m - r)k_m = \left(\frac{\alpha_1}{r}\right)^{a_1} \beta_1 z_m, \quad (\delta_h - r)k_h = \left(\frac{\alpha_2}{r}\right)^{a_2} \beta_2 z_h.$$

By the above two equations and $k_h / k_m = A$ in (6.2.6), we get

$$\Phi(r) \equiv \frac{\delta_h - r}{\delta_m - r} - a_0 r^{a_1 - a_2} = 0, \quad a_0 \equiv \frac{\beta_2 z_h \alpha_2^{a_2}}{\beta_1 z_m \alpha_1^{a_1} A}. \tag{6.2.9}$$

In the case of $a_1 > a_2$ (i.e., $\alpha_1 > \alpha_2$), we have

$$\Phi(0) > 0, \quad \Phi(\delta_m) > 0,$$

$$\Phi' = \frac{\delta_h - \delta_m}{(\delta_m - r)^2} - (a_1 - a_2)a_0 r^{a_1 - a_2 - 1}, \quad \delta_m > r > 0.$$

The equation $\Phi(r) = 0$ may have none or multiple solutions for $\delta_m > r > 0$.

In the case of $a_1 < a_2$, we have

$$\Phi(0) < 0, \quad \Phi(\delta_m) > 0, \quad \Phi' > 0, \quad for \ \delta_m > r > 0.$$

The equation $\Phi(r) = 0$ has a unique solution for $\delta_m > r > 0$.

In the case of $a_1 = a_2$, by (6.2.9) we solve

$$r = \frac{\delta_m z / A - \delta_h}{z / A - 1} \tag{6.2.10}$$

where $z \equiv z_h / z_m$. By (6.2.10) and $\delta_h > \delta_m$, we see that (6.2.3) is guaranteed if $z / A > \delta_h / \delta_m > 1$. This condition is guaranteed if country 2's people obtain a very low amenity level in the foreign country. It can be seen that whether or not the problem has a meaningful solution (with the existence of country 2's people in the two countries) is dependent on comparative conditions of how people use their talents, of what kinds of life styles they choose to live and of how they are treated in the two countries. For convenience of interpretation, we are only concerned with the case of $a_1 = a_2$.

Assumption 6.2.1.
In the remainder of this chapter, we require: $a_1 = a_2$ and $z / A > \delta_h / \delta_m$.

Under Assumption 6.2.1 $\Phi(r) = 0$ has a unique solution for $\delta_m > r > 0$. By (6.2.6), we solve w_q, $q \in \Pi$. We solve k_q by (6.2.2), y_q by (6.2.1), and c_q and s_q by (6.2.5), respectively. By (6.1.7), (6.1.11), and (6.1.3), we get

$$\sum_q \beta_1 y_q N_q = \frac{w_m N_1^*}{z_m} + \frac{w_h N_2^*}{z_h} \tag{6.2.11}$$

where y_q and w_q are known. By (6.2.11), (6.1.12) and the definitions of N_j^* in (6.1.1), we solve

$$N_m = \frac{w_1 N_1 + w_h N_2 - \beta_1 y_1 N_1 - \beta_1 y_h N_2}{w_h - w_m + \beta_1 y_m - \beta_1 y_h}, \quad N_h = N_2 - N_m.$$

$$\tag{6.2.12}$$

It is necessary to require: $0 < N_m < N_2$. Since it is not easy to interpret the conditions that the inequalities, $0 < N_m < N_2$, are guaranteed, we omit further examining them. By (6.2.12) and (6.1.12), we directly obtain K_j and N_j^*, $j = 1, 2$. By (6.2.7), we have

$$\frac{N_1^*}{K_1 + E} = \frac{N_2^*}{K_2 - E}.$$

From this equation we obtain

$$E = \frac{K_2 N_1^* - K_1 N_2^*}{N_1^* + N_2^*}. \tag{6.2.13}$$

If country 2's level of capital stocks owned by per qualified capita is higher (lower) than country 1's level of capital stocks owned by per qualified capita, i.e., $K_2 / N_2^* > (<) K_1 / N_1^*$, then country 2's (1's) capital stocks are employed by country 1 (2), i.e., $E > (<) 0$. Summarizing the above discussion, we get the following proposition.

Proposition 6.2.1.
Assume: $\lambda_m > \max\{\lambda_h, \lambda_1\}$, $a_1 = a_2$ and $z / A > \delta_h / \delta_m$. If N_m given by (6.2.12) satisfies $0 < N_m < N_2$, then the trade model has a unique equilibrium. The equilibrium values of all the variables are given by the following procedure: r by (6.2.10) $\rightarrow w_q$, $q \in \Pi$, by (6.2.8) $\rightarrow k_q$ by (6.2.2) $\rightarrow y_q$ by (6.2.1) $\rightarrow c_q$ and s_q by (6.2.5) $\rightarrow U_q$ by (6.1.4) $\rightarrow N_m$ by (6.2.12) $\rightarrow N_h = N_2 - N_m \rightarrow K_j$ and N_j^*, $j = 1, 2$, by (6.1.1) $\rightarrow E$ by (6.2.13) $\rightarrow F_j$ by (6.1.2).

Since it is difficult to explicitly interpret the conditions, for illustration we calculate a special case. We take on the following parameter values:

$$\delta_k = 0, \; z_1 = z_m = 1, \; z_h = 0.8, \; A_m = 1, \; N_2 = 2N_1, \; \alpha_1 = 1/2,$$
$$\lambda_1 = \frac{1}{8}, \; \lambda_m = \frac{1}{6}, \; \lambda_h = \frac{1}{7}, \; A_h = \frac{25}{16}. \tag{6.2.14}$$

The requirement $\delta_k = 0$ neglects capital depreciation. The condition $A_m = 1$ is required only for convenience of representation. The requirement $N_2 = 2N_1$

means that country 2's population is twice as many as country 1's population. This requirement is significant since it can be shown that if N_1 is much smaller than N_2 (for instance, $N_2 = 5N_1$), N_m has no meaningful solutions in our example. We assume that migrants work as effectively as country 1's native labor force, i.e., $z_1 = z_m = 1$. The requirement $z_h = 0.8$ implies that country 2's people work less effectively in the home country than in the foreign country. We assume that the people who maintain at the home country are assumed to obtain a higher amenity level, to maintain a lower propensity to hold wealth and to exhibit a lower level of talent utilization efficiency than their countrymen in the foreign country.

By Proposition 6.2.1 and (6.2.14), we directly calculate the unique equilibrium values of the variables as follows

$$r = 3.07, \ w_1 = w_m = 0.081, \ w_h = 0.065, \ k_1 = 0.021, \ k_m = 0.042,$$

$$k_h = 0.021, \ y_1 = c_1 = 0.145, \ y_m = c_m = 0.211, \ y_h = c_h = 0.133,$$

$$N_m = 0.127, \ K_1 = 0.015, \ F_1 = 0.09, \ F_2 = 0.122,$$

$$K_2 = 0.019, \ N_1^* = 0.627, \ N_2^* = 0.698, \ E = -0.002. \tag{6.2.15}$$

It should be noted that the immigrant has a higher consumption level and owns more capital stocks than the native resident in the long term because of, for instance, 'depressed' social environment or 'show-off' psychology (which results in high propensity to save).

6.3 The Impact of Amenity on Trade and Migration

This section examines the effects of changes in the amenity levels that country 2's people obtain in the home and foreign countries in the equilibrium structure. By the definition of A, a change in A may be caused by shifts in A_m, A_h, ξ_h, ξ_m or λ_h. In this section, a change in A is assumed to be caused by changes in A_m or A_h. For convenience, we specify some parameters as in (6.2.14). We also use the calculated results in (6.2.15).

By (6.2.10), we have

$$\frac{dr}{dA} = -\frac{\delta_h}{z-A} + \frac{r}{z-A} = -10.722 < 0. \tag{6.3.1}$$

As A_m (A_h) is increased (decreased), the rate of interest r is reduced. Since an improvement in A_m means that the home country becomes less attractive, more people tend to migrate to the foreign country. As country 2's people work harder and has a high propensity to hold wealth in the foreign country, it is intuitively acceptable that the rate of interest is reduced (due to the re-distribution of labor force and other forces).

Taking derivatives of (6.2.8) with respect to A yields

$$\frac{dw_1}{dA} = \frac{dw_m}{dA} = -\frac{a_1 w_1}{r}\frac{dr}{dA} = 0.284 > 0,$$

$$\frac{dw_h}{dA} = -\frac{a_2 w_h}{r}\frac{dr}{dA} = 0.227 > 0. \tag{6.3.2}$$

An increase in A increases the wage rates of all the groups in the world economy.

By (6.2.2), we obtain

$$\frac{dk_1}{dA} = \frac{dw_1/dA + k_1 dr/dA}{\delta_1 - r} = 0.016 > 0,$$

$$\frac{dk_m}{dA} = \frac{dw_m/dA + k_m dr/dA}{\delta_m - r} = -0.087 < 0,$$

$$\frac{dk_h}{dA} = \frac{dw_h/dA + k_h dr/dA}{\delta_h - r} = -0.004 < 0. \tag{6.3.3}$$

As A is increased, the level of capital stocks owned by per capita of country 1's native people is increased but the levels of capital stocks of per capita born in country 2 are reduced, irrespective of whether they maintain in or leave away from the home country.

By (6.2.1) and (6.2.5), we directly obtain

$$\frac{dy_1}{dA} = \frac{dc_1}{dA} = \delta_1 \frac{dk_1}{dA} = 0.111 > 0,$$

$$\frac{dy_m}{dA} = \frac{dc_m}{dA} = \delta_m \frac{dk_m}{dA} = -0.436 < 0,$$

$$\frac{dy_h}{dA} = \frac{dc_h}{dA} = \delta_h \frac{dk_h}{dA} = -0.022 < 0. \tag{6.3.4}$$

Taking derivatives of (6.2.12) with respect to A yields

$$\frac{dN_m}{dA} =$$

$$\frac{N_1 dw_1/dA + N_2 dw_h/dA - \beta_1 N_1 dy_1/dA - \beta_1 N_2 dy_h/dA}{w_1 N_1 + w_h N_2 - \beta_1 y_1 N_1 - \beta_1 y_h N_2} N_m -$$

$$\frac{dw_h/dA - dw_m/dA + \beta_1 dy_m/dA - \beta_1 dy_h/dA}{w_h - w_m + \beta_1 y_m - \beta_1 y_h} N_m = 16.412 > 0,$$

$$\frac{dN_h}{dA} = -\frac{dN_m}{dA} = -16.412 < 0. \tag{6.3.5}$$

As the home country's life amenity becomes more deteriorated, more people will migrate to the foreign country.

By (6.1.1) and (6.1.3), we get

$$\frac{dK_1}{dA} = N_1 \frac{dk_1}{dA} + N_m \frac{dk_m}{dA} + k_m \frac{dN_m}{dA} = 0.686 > 0,$$

$$\frac{dK_2}{dA} = N_h \frac{dk_h}{dA} + k_h \frac{dN_h}{dA} = -0.368 < 0,$$

$$\frac{dN_1^*}{dA} = z_m \frac{dN_m}{dA} = 16.412 > 0, \quad \frac{dN_2^*}{dA} = z_h \frac{dN_h}{dA} = -13.13 < 0,$$

$$\frac{dF_1}{dA} = \frac{w_m dN_1^*/dA + N_1^* dw_m/dA}{\beta_1 z_m} = 3.028 > 0,$$

$$\frac{dF_2}{dA} = \frac{w_h dN_2^*/dA + N_2^* dw_h/dA}{\beta_2 z_h} = -0.696 < 0. \tag{6.3.6}$$

The levels of country 1's (2's) qualified labor input, total capital stocks and output are increased (reduced).

By $r = \alpha_1 F_1/(K_1 + E)$ in (6.1.3), we obtain

$$\frac{dE}{dA} = \frac{\alpha_1}{r}\frac{dF_1}{dA} - \frac{\alpha_1 F_1}{r^2}\frac{dr}{dA} - \frac{dK_1}{dA} = 0.912 > 0. \tag{6.3.7}$$

The value of E is increased. Since E is negative, the trade gap is reduced. Summarizing the above analysis we obtain the following proposition.

Corollary 6.3.1.

Let (6.2.14) be held. The unique equilibrium of the dynamic system is given as in (6.2.15). An increase (decrease) in the amenity level A_m (A_h) that country 2's people obtain in the foreign (home) country has the following impact on the equilibrium structure of the world economy: (i) the levels $K_1 + E$ and N_1^* ($K_2 - E$ and N_2^*) of capital stocks and qualified labor force employed by country 1 (2) are increased (reduced); (ii) the output level F_1 (F_2) of country 1 (2) is increased (reduced); (iii) the number N_m of people who migrate from country 2 to country 1 is increased, and the value of the trade gap E is increased; (iv) the levels, k_1, y_1 and c_1, of capital stocks, net income and consumption of country 1's native people are increased, the levels, k_m, y_m and c_m, of capital stocks, net income and consumption of country 2's people who migrate to country 1 and the levels, k_h, y_h and c_h, of capital stocks, net income and consumption of country 2's people who maintain in country 2 are reduced; and (v) the rate of interest r is reduced, the wage rates, w_1, w_m and w_h, of the three groups are increased.

It should be remarked that the proposition is obtained under the strict requirements. If we specify the parameters differently, effects on some variables may be in the opposite directions.

6.4 The Impact of Human Capital on Trade and Migration

This section examines effects of changes in the level z_h of human capital that country 2's people exhibit in the home country on the equilibrium structure. We specify the parameters as in (6.2.14).

Taking derivatives of (6.2.10) with respect to z_h yields

$$\frac{dr}{dz_h} = \frac{\delta_m - r}{(z - A)z_m} = 7.063 > 0. \tag{6.4.1}$$

As the working efficiency of the labor force in country 2 is improved, the rate of interest is increased.

By (6.2.8), we obtain

$$\frac{dw_1}{dz_h} = \frac{dw_m}{dz_h} = -\frac{a_1 w_1}{r}\frac{dr}{dz_h} = -0.187 < 0,$$

$$\frac{dw_h}{dz_h} = \frac{w_h}{z_h} - \frac{a_2 w_h}{r}\frac{dr}{dz_h} = -0.068 < 0. \tag{6.4.2}$$

As the level of human capital is improved, the wage rates w_q of all the groups are reduced. Taking derivatives of (6.2.12) with respect to z_h yields

$$\frac{dk_1}{dz_h} = \frac{dw_1/dz_h + k_1 dr/dz_h}{\delta_1 - r} = -0.01 < 0,$$

$$\frac{dk_m}{dz_h} = \frac{dw_m/dz_h + k_m dr/dz_h}{\delta_m - r} = 0.058 > 0,$$

$$\frac{dk_h}{dz_h} = \frac{dw_h/dz_h + k_h dr/dz_h}{\delta_h - r} = 0.03 > 0. \tag{6.4.3}$$

Due to the improved human capital in country 2's labor force who stays at the home country, the level of capital stocks owned by per capita of country 1's native people is reduced but the levels of capital stocks of per capita born in country 2 are increased, irrespective of whether they maintain in or leave away from the home country.

By (6.2.1) and (6.2.5), we obtain

$$\frac{dy_1}{dz_h} = \frac{dc_1}{dz_h} = \delta_1 \frac{dk_1}{dz_h} = -0.073 < 0,$$

$$\frac{dy_m}{dz_h} = \frac{dc_m}{dz_h} = \delta_m \frac{dk_m}{dz_h} = 0.286 > 0,$$

$$\frac{dy_h}{dz_h} = \frac{dc_h}{dz_h} = \delta_h \frac{dk_h}{dz_h} = 0.182 > 0. \tag{6.4.4}$$

Taking derivatives of (6.2.2) with respect to z_h yields

$$\frac{dN_m}{dz_h} =$$

$$\frac{N_1 dw_1/dz_h + N_2 dw_h/dz_h - \beta_1 N_1 dy_1/dz_h - \beta_1 N_2 dy_h/dz_h}{w_1 N_1 + w_h N_2 - \beta_1 y_1 N_1 - \beta_1 y_h N_2} N_m -$$

$$\frac{dw_h / dz_h - dw_m / dz_h + \beta_1 dy_m / dz_h - \beta_1 dy_h / dz_h}{w_h - w_m + \beta_1 y_m - \beta_1 y_h} N_m = -10.886 < 0,$$

$$\frac{dN_h}{dz_h} = -\frac{dN_m}{dz_h} = 10.886 > 0. \tag{6.4.5}$$

If country 2's people utilize their talents more effectively in the home country, then some of the people who migrated to the foreign country will return to the home country.

Taking derivatives of (6.1.1) and (6.1.3) with respect to z_h yields

$$\frac{dK_1}{dz_h} = N_1 \frac{dk_1}{dz_h} + N_m \frac{dk_m}{dz_h} + k_m \frac{dN_m}{dz_h} = -0.463 < 0,$$

$$\frac{dK_2}{dz_h} = N_h \frac{dk_h}{dz_h} + k_h \frac{dN_h}{dz_h} = 0.268 > 0,$$

$$\frac{dN_1^*}{dz_h} = z_m \frac{dN_m}{dz_h} = -10.886, \quad \frac{dN_2^*}{dz_h} = z_h \frac{dN_h}{dz_h} + N_h = 9.582,$$

$$\frac{dF_1}{dz_h} = \frac{w_m dN_1^* / dz_h + N_1^* dw_m / dz_h}{\beta_1 z_m} = -2.007 < 0,$$

$$\frac{dF_2}{dz_h} = \frac{w_h dN_2^* / dz_h + N_2^* dw_h / dz_h}{\beta_2 z_h} - \frac{F_2}{z_h} = 1.288 > 0. \tag{6.4.6}$$

The levels of country 1's (2's) qualified labor input, total capital stocks and output are reduced (increased).

By $r = \alpha_1 F_1 / (K_1 + E)$ in (6.1.3), we obtain

$$\frac{dE}{dz_h} = \frac{\alpha_1}{r} \frac{dF_1}{dz_h} - \frac{\alpha_1 F_1}{r^2} \frac{dr}{dz_h} - \frac{dK_1}{dz_h} = 0.102 > 0. \tag{6.4.7}$$

The value of E is increased. Since E is negative, the trade gap is reduced. Summarizing the above analysis we obtain the following proposition.

Corollary 6.4.1.

Let (6.2.14) be held. An increase in the level z_h of human capital of country 2's people who maintain at the home country has the following impact on the equilibrium structure of the world economy: (i) the levels $K_1 + E$ and N_1^* ($K_2 - E$ and N_2^*) of capital stocks and qualified labor force employed by country 1 (2) are decreased (increased); (ii) the output level F_1 (F_2) of country 1 (2) is reduced (increased); (iii) the number N_m of people who migrate from country 2 to country 1 is reduced, and the value of the trade gap E is increased; (iv) the levels, k_1, y_1 and c_1, of capital stocks, net income and consumption of country 1's native people are reduced, the levels, k_m, y_m and c_m, of capital stocks, net income and consumption of country 2's people who migrate to country 1 and the levels, k_h, y_h and c_h, of capital stocks, net income and consumption of country 2's people who maintain in country 2 are increased; and (v) the rate of interest r is increased, the wage rates, w_1, w_m and w_h, of the three groups are reduced.

6.5 Concluding Remarks

This chapter analyzed the dynamic interdependence between world economic growth, trade patterns and migration. The world economy consists of two countries and three groups of people. We showed how differences in social and economic conditions of the two countries and preferences and human capital structure of the world population affect trade and migration patterns and the global economic structure. We discussed the conditions for existence of economic equilibria and examined the effects of changes in amenity and human capital on the equilibrium structure.

This model may be extended in multiple ways. As shown later, we may extend the framework to include multiple sectors and introduce endogenous human capital. It is important to take account of tariffs, transportation costs and possible costs of migration. We may relax the assumption of homogenous population of each country. It is also important to take account of national resources such as land. Utilization of public goods may cause congestion problems and migration may worsen environment. Too many migrants may cause the natives to strengthen discrimination which reduces wage rate and social amenity that migrants obtain in the foreign country. It is quite obvious that the government may add migration restriction when too many migrants come in.

7 Trade with Endogenous Capital and Knowledge

The previous chapters examined various aspects of international trades. We showed how trade patterns are related to capital accumulation, preferences and sexual division of labor. But in all these models we assumed that human capital is endogenously given. This chapter suggests a dynamic one-commodity and multiple-country trade model to examine interactions between savings rates, trade, knowledge utilization and creativity. Although our model is similar to the dynamic one-commodity and two-country trade model with endogenous human capital (e.g., Wang, 1990), we treat knowledge differently. We consider knowledge as an international public good in the sense that all countries access to knowledge and the utilization of knowledge by one country does not affect that by others. Due to cultural differences, educational systems and policies, knowledge utilization efficiency and creativity differ between countries.

Knowledge creation and utilization is the driving force of modern economic development. A main issue in economics is concerned with dynamic interactions between economic growth, knowledge creation and utilization. The literature on economic development has recently been centered on identifying different aspects of dynamic interactions between growth and knowledge accumulation. One of the first seminal attempts to render technical progress endogenous in growth models was initiated by Arrow (1962) emphasizing one aspect of knowledge accumulation - learning by doing. Uzawa (1965) introduced a sector specifying in creating knowledge into growth theory. The knowledge sector utilizes labor and the existing stock of knowledge to produce new knowledge which enhances productivity of the production sector. Another approach was taken by, for instance, Kennedy (1964), Weisäcker (1966), Drandakis and Phelps (1966), and Samuelson (1965), who took account of the assumption of "inducement through the factor prices". Schultz (1981) emphasized the incentive effects of policy on investment in human capital. There are many other studies on endogenous technical progresses (e.g., Sato and Tsutsui, 1984, Nelson and Winter, 1982, Dosi, Pavitt and Soete, 1990). In Romer (1986), knowledge is taken as an input in the production function and competitive equilibrium is rendered consistent with increasing aggregate returns owing to externalities. It is assumed that knowledge displays increasing marginal productivity but new knowledge is produced by investment in research which exhibits diminishing returns. Various other issues related to innovation, diffusion of technology and behavior of economic agents under various institutions have been discussed in the literature. There are also many other models emphasizing different aspects, such as education, trade, R&D policies, entrepreneurship, division of labor, learning through trading, brain drain, economic geography, of dynamic interactions among economic structure, development and knowledge (e.g., Dollar, 1986, Krugman, 1991, Rauch, 1991b, Stokey, 1991, Barro and Sal-i-Martin, 1995). It may be argued that there is a theoretical limitation in those works. Capital and knowledge have not been integrated into a compact theoretical framework with economic structures and free markets. For instance, in the works by Grossman and Helpman (1991) physical capital is almost totally neglected. In this chapter, we develop a trade model with endogenous knowledge as well as capital accumulation.

7.1 The Model with Capital and Knowledge

The economic production is similar to that in the previous chapters. The system consists of multiple nations, indexed by $j = 1, ..., J$. Only one good is produced in the system. The good is assumed to be composed of homogeneous qualities, and to be produced by employing three factors of production - labor, capital and knowledge. Market conditions are similar to those in the trade models in Chapters 2-4. Each country has a fixed labor force, N_j, ($j = 1, ..., J$). Let prices be measured in terms of the commodity and the price of the commodity be unity. We denote by $w_j(t)$ and $r_j(t)$ respectively the wage and interest rate in the j th country. In the free trade system, the interest rate is identical in all countries

$$r(t) = r_j(t) \ (j = 1, ..., J).$$

Production and capital accumulation
We specify the production functions as follows

$$F_j(t) = Z^{m_j} (K_j + E_j)^\alpha N_j^\beta, \ \alpha + \beta = 1, \ \alpha, \beta > 0,$$
$$m_j \geq 0, \quad j = 1, ..., J \qquad (7.1.1)$$

in which $Z \ (> 0)$ is the world knowledge stock at time t, $K_j(t)$ are the capital stocks owned by country j, and $E_j(t) > (<) 0$ are foreign capital stocks (home capital stocks located abroad). Here, we call m_j country j's knowledge utilization efficiency parameter. If we interpret $Z^{m_j/\beta} N_j$ as country j's human capital or qualified labor force, we see that the production function is a neoclassical one and homogeneous of degree one with the inputs.

As cultures, political systems and educational and training systems vary between countries, m_j will be varied. Equation (7.1.1) implies that if the labor force and capital stocks employed by two countries are identical, then the difference in output between the two countries is only determined by the difference between their knowledge utilization efficiency.

According to the definitions of E_j, we have

$$\sum_{j=1}^{J} E_j = 0. \tag{7.1.2}$$

The marginal conditions are given by

$$r_j = \frac{\alpha F_j}{K_j + E_j}, \quad w_j = \frac{\beta F_j}{N_j}. \tag{7.1.3}$$

For simplicity, we assume that the savings rates s_j, $j = 1, ..., J$, are constant. The capital accumulation of country j is given by

$$\frac{dK_j}{dt} = s_j F_j - \delta_k K_j \tag{7.1.4}$$

where δ_k is the depreciation rate of capital.

Knowledge accumulation
Similarly to Zhang (1999), we propose the following possible dynamics of knowledge

$$\frac{dZ}{dt} = \sum_{j=1}^{J} \frac{\tau_j F_j}{Z^{\varepsilon_j}} - \delta_z Z \tag{7.1.5}$$

in which τ_j (≥ 0) and ε_j ($j = 1, ..., J$), and δ_z (≥ 0) are parameters. We interpret $\tau_j F_j / Z^{\varepsilon_j}$ as contribution to knowledge accumulation by country j through learning by doing. In order to explain this equation, we consider a simple case in which the world consists of a single country and knowledge is a function of the total industrial output during a certain historical period

$$Z(t) = a_1 \{ \int_0^t F(\theta) d\theta \}^{a_2} + a_3$$

in which a_1, a_2 and a_3 are positive parameters. The above equation implies that the effects of economic activities upon knowledge accumulation have properties of decreasing return to scale effects in the case of $(0 \leq a_2 \leq 1)$. It is not difficult to see that a_1 and a_3 can be interpreted as measurements of the efficiency of 'learning by doing' by the production sector. Taking the derivatives of the equation yields

$$\frac{dZ}{dt} = \frac{\tau_i F}{Z^\varepsilon} - \delta_z Z$$

in which $\tau_i \equiv a_1 a_2$ and $\varepsilon \equiv 1 - a_2$.

We are mainly interested in how different combinations of knowledge utilization efficiency parameters m_j, savings rates s_j, scale effects in knowledge accumulation ε_j, and knowledge accumulation efficiencies τ_j may affect the world economic development.

We have thus built the model which explains the endogenous accumulation of capital and knowledge and the international distribution of capital under the assumptions of perfect competition and international immobility of the labor force. We now examine the properties of the system.

7.2 The Dynamics of the Trade System

We now show that the dynamics of the trade system can be represented by two different equations of the world capital and knowledge. From (7.1.2), we have

$$\frac{(K_1 + E_1)N_j}{(K_j + E_j)N_1} = Z^{-q_j}, \quad j = 2, ..., J \tag{7.2.1}$$

where $q_j \equiv (m_j - m_1) / \beta$.

Substituting (7.2.1) into (7.1.1) yields

$$F_j = n_j Z^{q_j} F_1, \quad j = 2, ..., J \tag{7.2.2}$$

in which $n_j \equiv N_j / N_1$. From (7.2.1), we directly obtain the following lemma.

Lemma 7.2.1.
At any point of time, the ratio of the capital stocks employed per capita and that of the incomes between any two countries in the trade system are only determined by the difference in the knowledge utilization efficiency parameters between the two countries.

Define the world capital stock by $K = \sum_j K$. Utilizing $\sum_j E_j = 0$ and (7.2.1), we have

$$K_1 + E_1 = K - \sum_{j \neq 1}(K_j + E_j) = K - (K_1 + E_1)(\frac{H_0}{N_1} - 1)$$

$$(7.2.5)$$

where

$$H_0 \equiv \sum_{j \neq 1} N_j Z^{q_j}.$$

$$(7.2.6)$$

From (7.1.1), (7.2.1) and (7.2.5), we have

$$K_1 + E_1 = \frac{N_1 K}{H_0}, \quad F_1 = N_1 Z^{m_1}\left(\frac{K}{H_0}\right)^{\alpha}.$$

$$(7.2.7)$$

From (7.2.1), (7.2.2) and (7.2.7), we can explicitly express $K_j + E_j$ and F_j as functions of K and Z. Hence, we can rewrite the dynamics (7.1.4) and (7.1.5) in terms of K and Z as follows

$$\frac{dK}{dt} = H_k(Z)K^{\alpha} - \delta_k K, \quad \frac{dZ}{dt} = H_z(Z)K^{\alpha} - \delta_z Z$$

$$(7.2.8)$$

where

$$H_k(Z) \equiv \frac{\sum_j s_j N_j Z^{q_j}}{H_0^{\alpha}} Z^{m_1}, \quad H_z(Z) \equiv \frac{\sum_j H_j(Z)}{H_0^{\alpha}},$$

$$H_j \equiv \tau_j N_j Z^{q_j + m_1 - \varepsilon_j}, \quad j = 1, ..., J.$$

$$(7.2.9)$$

Equilibrium of the system is determined by

$$K = \left(\frac{H_k}{\delta_k}\right)^{1/\beta}, \quad H_z(Z)K^{\alpha} = \delta_z Z. \tag{7.2.10}$$

Substituting K in (7.2.10) into the right-hand side equation in (7.2.10), we see that the equilibrium problem is to find a positive Z such that

$$\Phi(Z) \equiv \left(\frac{H_k}{\delta_k}\right)^{\alpha/\beta} \frac{H_z}{Z} - \delta_z = \Phi_0(Z)\sum_j \Phi_j(Z) - \delta_z = 0 \tag{7.2.11}$$

in which

$$\Phi_0(Z) \equiv \left(\frac{\sum_j s_j \phi_j(Z)}{\sum_j \phi_j(Z)}\right)^{\alpha/\beta}, \quad \phi_j(Z) \equiv N_j Z^{m_j/\beta},$$

$$\Phi_j(Z) \equiv \left(\frac{1}{\delta}\right)^{\alpha/\beta} \tau_j N_j Z^{x_j}, \quad x_j \equiv \frac{m_j}{\beta} - \varepsilon_j - 1, \quad j = 1, ..., J.$$

$$\tag{7.2.12}$$

As m_j is country j's knowledge utilization efficiency and ε_j is country j's return to scale effects of knowledge in knowledge accumulation, we may interpret x_j as measurement of return to scale effects of knowledge in the whole system. We may thus make the following interpretations of the parameters. We say that country j's knowledge utilization and creation exhibits increasing (decreasing) return to scale effects in the dynamic system when $x_j > (<) 0$.

When $x_j = 0$ for all j, we have $\Phi_0(Z) = \delta_z$, i.e.

$$\sum_j (s_j - \delta_z^{\beta/\alpha})\phi_j(Z) = 0. \tag{7.2.13}$$

As $\phi_j > 0$, $\Phi(Z) = 0$ has infinite positive solutions in the case of $s_j = \delta_z^{\beta/\alpha}$ for all j. If $s_j > \delta_z^{\beta/\alpha}$ for all j or $s_j < \delta_z^{\beta/\alpha}$ for all j, it has no solution. If $s_j < \delta_z^{\beta/\alpha}$ for some of j and $s_j > \delta_z^{\beta/\alpha}$ for the others, then it may have solutions. In the remainder of this chapter, we omit the case of $x_j = 0$ for all j.

We can check directly that when $x_j > (<) \, 0$ for all j, $\Phi(Z) = 0$ has at least one solution. To check the uniqueness, we take derivatives of (7.2.11) with respect to Z

$$\frac{Z}{\Phi_0}\Phi' = \sum_j x_j \Phi_j + \alpha_0(Z) \sum_{j=1}^{J-1} \sum_{k>j}^{J} M_{jk} \phi_k(Z) \phi_j(Z) \qquad (7.2.14)$$

where Φ' is the derivative of Φ with respect to Z and

$$\alpha_0(Z) \equiv \left(\frac{\sum_j \Phi_j(Z)}{\sum_j s_j \phi_j(Z) \sum_j \phi_j(Z)} \right) \frac{\alpha}{\beta^2} > 0,$$

$$M_{jk} \equiv (m_k - m_j)(s_j - s_k). \qquad (7.2.15)$$

From (7.2.14), we see that when $x_j < (>) \, 0$ and $M_{jk} < (>) \, 0$ for all j and k ($j = 1, ..., J - 1$, $k = j + 1, ..., J$), then $\Phi'(Z) < (>) \, 0$ for all positive $Z > 0$. Accordingly, we conclude that when $x_j < (>) \, 0$ and $M_{jk} < (>) \, 0$ for all j and k, there is a unique equilibrium. If $M_{jk} < 0$ for some of j and k and $M_{jk} > 0$ for the other j and k, then Φ' may be either positive or negative, i.e., $\Phi(Z) = 0$ may have multiple solutions.

When $x_j < 0$ for some j and $x_j > 0$ for the other j, $\Phi(Z) > 0$ and $\Phi(\infty) > 0$. Accordingly, a necessary and sufficient condition for the existence of equilibria is that there exists a positive number Z_0 such that $\Phi(Z_0) \leq 0$. Moreover, if $\Phi(Z_0) < 0$, the system must have multiple equilibria.

When the trade system has multiple equilibria, we cannot compare the trade system with the autarky system. Hence, the remainder of this study limits our discussion to those cases in which the system has a unique equilibrium.

Proposition 7.2.1.
In the free trade system, we have: (i) when $x_j < 0$ for all j and $M_{jk} \leq 0$ for all j ($= 1, ..., J - 1$) and all k ($j < k \leq J$), the system has a unique stable equilibrium; and (ii) when $x_j > 0$ for all j and $M_{jk} \geq 0$ for all j ($= 1, ..., J - 1$) and all k ($j < k \leq J$), the system has a unique unstable equilibrium.

We may check the stability conditions by directly calculating the eigenvalues. We have just interpreted the conditions $x_j > 0$ or $x_j < 0$. The conditions $(m_k - m_j)(s_j - s_k) < (>) 0$ simply mean that when country j's savings rate is higher than that in country k, country j's knowledge utilization efficiency is higher (lower) than that of country k. Hence, the above proposition can be interpreted as follows: i) if the countries' knowledge utilization efficiency is low, all the countries exhibit decreasing returns, and the difference in the savings rates between any two countries has the same sign as that in the knowledge utilization efficiency parameters between the two countries; then the system has a unique stable equilibrium; ii) if the countries' knowledge utilization efficiency is high, all the countries exhibit increasing returns, and the difference in the savings rates between any two countries has the opposite sign to that in the knowledge utilization efficiency parameters between the two countries; then the system has a unique unstable equilibrium.

It is should be mentioned that the requirements in Proposition 7.2.1 are very strict. If we relax any of them, then the system may have multiple equilibria. As we are mainly interested in examining the impact of free trade upon the system, we will not analyze the behavior of the system when it has multiple equilibria.

7.3 The Global Economy in the Autarky System

In order to explain the impact of free trade, we examine an international system in which people have freedom in exchange of ideas, but there is neither trade nor migration among countries. That is, $E_j = 0$ for all j and r_j are not globally identical.

The (n + 1)-dimensional dynamics are defined by (7.1.4) and (7.1.5). Equilibrium is defined by

$$
K_j^* = \left(\frac{s_j}{\delta_k}\right)^{1/\beta} N_j Z^{*m_j/\beta} = \frac{s_j^{\alpha/\beta}\phi_j(Z^*)}{\delta_k^{1/\beta}},
$$
$$
\Phi^*(Z^*) \equiv \sum_j s_j^{\alpha/\beta}\Phi_j(Z^*) - \delta_z = 0 \qquad (7.3.1)
$$

in which Φ_j and x_j are defined in (7.2.12). In the remainder of this chapter, superscript $*$ stands for values of variables or functions in the autarky system.

Our task is to find whether $\Phi^* = 0$ has a positive solution. We may directly check that if $x_j \geq 0$ for all j (i.e., $\Phi^*(0) < 0$, $\Phi^*(\infty) > 0$, and $\Phi^{*\prime}(Z^*) > 0$ for $Z^* > 0$) or $x_j \leq 0$ for all j (i.e., $\Phi^*(0) > 0$, $\Phi^*(\infty) < 0$, and $\Phi^{*\prime}(Z^*) < 0$ for $Z^* > 0$), the system has a unique positive equilibrium. For any of the remaining $2^J - 2$ combinations of $x_j > 0$ or $x_j < 0$ for all j, the system has either two equilibria or none. We proved the case of $x_1 > 0$ and $x_j < 0$, $j = 2, ..., J$. The other cases can be checked in the same way. Since $x_1 > 0$, $x_j < 0$, $\Phi^*(0) > 0$ and $\Phi^*(\infty) > 0$. This means that $\Phi^* = 0$ has either no solution or multiple solutions. As $Z^* \Phi^{*\prime} = \sum_j x_j \Phi_j$, $\Phi^{*\prime}$ may be either positive or negative, depending upon the parameter values. If $\Phi^* = 0$ has more than two solutions, there are at least two values of Z^* such that $\Phi^* = 0$. Since $d(Z^* \Phi^{*\prime})/dZ^* > 0$ strictly holds for $Z^* > 0$, it is impossible for $\Phi^* = 0$ to have more than two solutions. A necessary and sufficient condition for the existence of two equilibria is that there exists a value of Z_0^* such that $\Phi^*(Z_0^*) < 0$.

Proposition 7.3.1.
We omit the case of $x_j = 0$ for all j.

If $x_j \leq 0$ for all j, then there is a unique equilibrium.

If $x_j \geq 0$ for all j, then there is a unique equilibrium.

For any of the remaining $(2^J - 2)$ combinations of $x_j > 0$ or $x_j < 0$ for all j, the system has either two equilibria or none.

It is important to note that if the conditions for the existence of a unique equilibrium for the trade system are satisfied, then the autarky system has a unique equilibrium, too. Hence, we can compare the equilibria in the two systems.

We do not determine the stability conditions for the general case, though we can prove the case of $J = 2$. It can be easily checked that in the case of $J = 2$, (i) if $x_j < 0$, $j = 1, 2$, the unique equilibrium is stable; (ii) if $x_j > 0$, $j = 1, 2$, the unique equilibrium is unstable; and (iii) if $x_1 < 0$ and $x_2 > 0$ ($x_1 > 0$ and $x_2 < 0$), the equilibrium with higher values of K and Z is unstable, and the other one is stable.

7.4 A Comparison of the Autarky and Trade Systems

This section examines the following two cases (a) when $x_j < 0$ and $M_{jk} \leq 0$ and (b) $x_j > 0$ and $M_{jk} \geq 0$ for all $j \, (= 1, ..., I - 1)$ and all $k \, (j < k \leq J)$, in which the two economic systems have unique equilibria.

From (7.2.11) and (7.3.1), we have

$$\left(\frac{\sum_j s_j \phi_j(Z)}{\sum_j \phi_j(Z)} \right)^{\alpha/\beta} \sum_j \Phi_j(Z) = \sum_j s_j^{\alpha/\beta} \Phi_j(Z^*) \tag{7.4.1}$$

in which Z^* and Z are the equilibrium values of the autarky and trade systems, respectively and ϕ_j are positive functions of Z. From (7.4.1), we see that it is not easy to generally determine whether $Z > Z^*$ or $Z < Z^*$. But we may consider a special case in which τ_1 is large and $\tau_j \, (j = 2, ..., J)$ are small (e.g., $\tau_j = 0$). This implies that only country 1 makes important contribution to world knowledge growth. The other countries may effectively utilize knowledge, but not make important contribution to the knowledge growth. Under this requirement, (7.4.1) may be approximately written as

$$\left(\frac{\sum_j s_j \phi_j(Z)}{\sum_j \phi_j(Z)} \right)^{\alpha/\beta} \Phi_1(Z) = s_1^{\alpha/\beta} \Phi_1(Z^*). \tag{7.4.2}$$

We have

$$\Phi_1(Z) < \Phi_1(Z^*), \quad if \ s_1 = s_m ,$$
$$\Phi_1(Z) > \Phi_1(Z^*), \quad if \ s_1 = s_M \tag{7.4.3}$$

where

$$s_m \equiv \min\{s_j, \ j = 1, ..., J\}, \ s_M \equiv \max\{s_j, \ j = 1, ..., J\}.$$

By the definition of Φ_1, (7.4.3) can be rewritten as follows

$$Z^{x_1} < Z^{*x_1}, \quad if \ s_1 = s_m; \ Z^{x_1} > Z^{*x_1}, \quad if \ s_1 = s_M . \tag{7.4.4}$$

We have the following conclusions

(i) if $x_1 > 0$ and $s_1 = s_m$, then $Z < Z^*$;

(ii) if $x_1 > 0$ and $s_1 = s_M$, then $Z > Z^*$;

(iii) if $x_1 < 0$ and $s_1 = s_m$, then $Z > Z^*$; and

(iv) if $x_1 < 0$ and $s_1 = s_M$, then $Z < Z^*$. $\qquad$ (7.4.5)

We see that even in the extreme case that only one country makes an important contribution to knowledge growth, the trade may either reduce or increase world knowledge in the long term, depending on the combinations of the savings rates and the knowledge utilization efficiency parameters.

By (7.2.10) and (7.3.1), we have

$$
\frac{K}{K^*} = \frac{\left(\sum_j \phi_j\right)^{1/\beta}}{\left(\sum_j N_j Z^{*m_j/\beta}\right)^{\alpha/\beta} \sum_j s_j^{\alpha/\beta} \phi_j^*} < \frac{\sum_j \phi_j}{\sum_j s_j^{\alpha/\beta} \phi_j^*} \qquad (7.4.6)
$$

in which ϕ_j^* is the value of $\phi_j(Z)$ evaluated at Z^* and $K^* (= \sum_j K_j^*)$ is the world capital stock in the autarky system. Hence, if

$$
\frac{Z}{Z^*} = s_j^{\alpha/m_j} < 1, \quad \text{for all } j \qquad (7.4.7)
$$

then $K / K^* < 1$. That is, when trade greatly reduces the knowledge stock, then the world capital stock is reduced in the long term. It can be seen that (7.4.7) may be valid only in cases (i) and (ii) when $Z < Z^*$. In cases (ii) and (iii), it is much too difficult to explicitly judge the impact of trade upon capital accumulation.

From (7.2.2), (7.2.10) and (7.3.1), the impact upon the income of the j th country is given by

$$
\frac{F_j}{F_j^*} = \left(\frac{Z}{Z^*}\right)^{m_j/\beta} \frac{\left(\sum_k s_k^{\alpha/\beta} \phi_k / s_j\right)^{\alpha/\beta}}{\sum_k \phi_k}. \qquad (7.4.8)
$$

We see that F_j / F_j^* is determined by combinations of the savings rates and the knowledge utilization efficiency parameters. In particular, when $x_1 < 0$ and

$$s_1 = s_M,$$

$$F_1 < F_1^*$$

where we use

$$\frac{Z}{Z^*} < 1, \quad \left(\sum_k \frac{s_k^{\alpha/\beta} \phi_k}{s_1} \right)^{\alpha/\beta} < \sum_k \phi_k.$$

It is difficult to make general judgments about the impact of trade upon the income distribution between the countries.

We will not interpret the above conclusions in detail as the conditions are clearly given by different combinations of the savings rates s_j and the knowledge utilization efficiency parameters m_j.

7.5 Concluding Remarks

This chapter constructed a model to show that the traditional belief that free trade is beneficial is valid only under certain circumstances (see Baldwin, 1992). Our simple model illustrates how difficult it is to make explicit conclusions about the impact of trade upon economic growth.

We analyzed the two extreme cases - complete autarky and trade without any trade barriers. It is important to examine the impact of trade upon the world economies with different trade barriers.

8 Global Economic Growth with Trade and Research

The preceding chapter introduced endogenous knowledge into the neoclassical trade model. The model was built on the assumption that knowledge accumulates through 'learning by doing' without any resources utilization. This assumption is strict in the sense that knowledge creation requires resources. A fundamental character of modern industrial economies is the deliberate large-scale quest for knowledge. The number of workers who generate and manipulate knowledge and information has increasingly become a larger share of the working population. A common important economic question faced with modern economies is how to distribute national resources among knowledge creation, knowledge utilization, education and economic development. It may be argued that national economic comparative advantage among developed economies is mainly due to its advantage in science and technology. Although it is often argued that governments should play a significant role in shaping development of science and technology, the question regarding the appropriate role for governments in encouraging economic growth by supporting scientific research remains vexed. Issues related to whether or not an increased budget for science will improve living conditions both in domestic and international terms are well raised but seldom examined for different conditions.

The purpose of this chapter is to introduce research into the framework proposed in Chapter 7. This chapter is concerned with interdependence of capital and knowledge accumulation under government's intervention in research. Although economists have recently developed a number of models to investigate similar issues (Grossman and Helpman, 1991, Aghion and Howitt, 1998 Jensen and Wong, 1998), this chapter treats problems related to interdependence between trade and research in a way different from the contemporary literature. Like in the preceding chapter, we still accept the assumption of perfect competition in international capital markets and domestic labor markets.

This chapter is organized as follows. Section 8.1 presents the basic model. Section 8.2 expresses the dynamics of the trade system in the term of knowledge and capital. Section 8.3 provides the conditions for existence of equilibria and stability in the model. Section 8.4 examines the impact of trade on knowledge accumulation and economic growth. Section 8.5 studies the impact of changes in the knowledge accumulation efficiency on the free trade system Section 8.6 concludes the chapter.

The appendix provides the conditions for existence of equilibria and stability of the autarky system.

8.1 The Model with Trade and Research

We consider a two-country and two-sector system. The two countries are indexed by j ($j = 1, 2$), respectively. Each country has one industry and one university, indexed by subscripts i and r, respectively. Country j has a fixed labor force N_j. Let prices be measured in terms of the commodity and the price of the commodity be unity. We denote $w_j(t)$ and $r_j(t)$ country j's wage rate and rate of interest. In a free trade system, $r(t) = r_1(t) = r_2(t)$. Rates of interest may not be equal in an autarky system. We introduce

$Z(t)$ — the knowledge stock of the world at time t;

$K_j(t)$ — the capital stocks owned by country j, $j = 1, 2$;

$E(t) > (<) \, 0$ — country 1's (2's) capital stocks employed by country 2 (1);

$K(t) = K_1(t) + K_2(t)$ — the capital stock of the world;

$N_{qj}(t)$ and $K_{qj}(t)$ — the labor force and capital stocks employed in country j's

sector q ($q = i, r$); and

τ_j ($0 \le \tau_j < 1$) — country j's tax rate on the production sector.

The behavior of the production sectors
We assume that the industrial production is carried out by combining knowledge, capital, and labor force. We specify the production functions, $F_j(t)$, $j = 1, 2$, as follows

$$F_j(t) = Z^{m_j} K_{ij}^{\alpha} N_{ij}^{\beta}, \quad \alpha + \beta = 1, \quad \alpha, \beta > 0, \quad m_j \ge 0, \quad j = 1, 2$$

$$(8.1.1)$$

in which m_j is country j's knowledge utilization efficiency parameter. If we interpret $Z^{m_j / \beta} N_{ij}$ as country j's human capital or qualified labor force, we see that the production function is a neoclassical one and homogeneous of degree one with the inputs. As cultures, political systems and educational and training systems vary between countries, m_j will be varied. Equation (8.1.1) implies that if the labor force and capital employed by the two countries are identical, then the difference in output between the two countries is only determined by their difference in knowledge utilization.

The marginal conditions are given by

$$r_j = \frac{(1 - \tau_j)\alpha F_j}{K_{ij}}, \quad w_j = \frac{(1 - \tau_j)\beta F_j}{N_{ij}}.$$
(8.1.2)

Capital and knowledge accumulation
Country j's national income Y_j is given by

$$Y_j(t) = r_j K_j + w_j N_j, \quad j = 1, 2.$$
(8.1.3)

Denote by s_j ($j = 1, 2$) country j's savings rate out of Y_j. For simplicity, we assume that the savings rates, s_j, are constant. The capital accumulation of country j is given by

$$\frac{dK_j}{dt} = s_j F_j - \delta_k K_j$$
(8.1.4)

where δ_k is the depreciation rate of capital.

Similarly to Zhang (1999a), we propose the following possible dynamics of knowledge

$$\frac{dZ}{dt} = \sum_{j=1}^{2} \left(\frac{\tau_{ij} F_j}{Z^{\varepsilon_{ij}}} + \tau_{rj} Z^{\varepsilon_{rj}} K_{rj}^{\alpha_{rj}} N_{rj}^{\beta_{rj}} \right) - \delta_z Z$$
(8.1.5)

in which τ_{qj} (≥ 0), $\alpha_{rj} \geq 0$), β_{rj} (≥ 0), ε_{qj} ($j = 1, 2, q = i, r$), and δ_z (≥ 0) are parameters. In this chapter we omit possible contribution to knowledge growth through research by private companies. We interpret $\tau_{ij} F_j / Z^{\varepsilon_{ij}}$ as contribution to knowledge accumulation by country j through 'learning by doing' as in Chapter 7. We call the term, $\tau_{rj} Z^{\varepsilon_{rj}} K_{rj}^{\alpha_{rj}} N_{rj}^{\beta_{rj}}$, the contribution to knowledge growth by country j's university. This term is interpreted as that country j's knowledge production is positively related to the capital stocks K_{rj} and the number of scientists N_{rj} employed by the university. To interpret the parameters ε_{rj} we note that on the one hand, as the knowledge stock is increased, the universities may more effectively utilize the traditional knowledge to discover new theorems; on the other hand, a large stock of knowledge may make discovery of new knowledge difficult. This implies that the parameters ε_{rj} may be either positive or negative, depending on the characteristics of knowledge creation that occurs in the university.

As N_{rj} and K_{rj} are paid by the government's tax income, we have

$$\tau_j F_j = r_j K_{rj} + w_j N_{rj}, \quad j = 1, 2. \tag{8.1.6}$$

We now determine N_{rj} and K_{rj}. For simplicity, we assume that the government decides the number of scientists and the capital stock of the university in the following way

$$N_{rj} = n_j N_j, \quad K_{r1} = g_1(K_1 - E), \quad K_{r2} = g_2(K_2 + E), \quad 0 < n_j, g_j < 1 \tag{8.1.7}$$

where n_j and g_j are the policy variables fixed by the government. We assume that n_j and g_j are exogenously given. It should be remarked that this assumption may be relaxed by assuming that the governments optimize research outputs, subjecting to the research budgets (Zhang, 1999a). We can interpret (8.1.7) as that the number of scientists and the total capital stocks employed by the university are linearly proportional to the population and the total capital stock of the country, respectively. Our concern is to examine the impact of the policy parameters n_j and g_j on the trade pattern.

Full employment of labor and capital
We assume that labor and capital are fully employed. This assumption is expressed as follows

$$N_{ij} = (1 - n_j)N_j, \quad K_{i1} + (1 - g_1)E = (1 - g_1)K_1,$$
$$K_{i2} - (1 - g_2)E = (1 - g_2)K_2, \quad j = 1, 2. \tag{8.1.8}$$

From (8.1.2), (8.1.6) and (8.1.8), we determine the tax rates as follows

$$\tau_j = 1 - \frac{(1 - g_j)(1 - n_j)}{1 - \beta g_j - \alpha n_j}, \quad j = 1, 2. \tag{8.1.9}$$

Each country's tax rate is determined by the country's research policy. It is straightforward to show $1 > \tau_j > 0$. From (8.1.2), (8.1.3) and (8.1.6), we obtain

$$Y_j = F_j, \quad j = 1, 2. \tag{8.1.10}$$

We have completed building the model of international trade with endogenous knowledge. As there are 18 time-dependent endogenous variables, K_{ij}, K_{rj}, K_j, N_{ij}, N_{rj}, F_j, Y_j, w_j ($j = 1, 2$), r, Z and 18 independent equations, the system may have solutions. The important parameters are the knowledge utilization parameters m_j, the savings rates s_j, the government research policy parameters n_j and g_j. We now show how these different forces affect dynamic patterns of international trade.

8.2 The Dynamics of the Free Trade System

In order to examine dynamic properties of the free trade system, it is necessary to write the dynamics in a form that can be investigated. First, we show that the dynamics can be actually described by two differential equations with $K(t)$ and $Z(t)$ as variables. Moreover, the rest variables in the system are explicitly given as functions of $K(t)$ and $Z(t)$ at any point of time.

First, from (8.1.2) we get

$$r = \frac{(1 - \tau_1)\alpha F_1}{K_{i1}} = \frac{(1 - \tau_2)\alpha F_2}{K_{i2}}.$$

From this equation and (8.1.1), we solve

$$\frac{K_1 - E}{K_2 + E} = nZ^m \tag{8.2.1}$$

where

$$m \equiv \frac{m_1 - m_2}{\beta}, \quad n \equiv \left(\frac{1 - \tau_1}{1 - \tau_2}\right)^{1/\beta} \left(\frac{1 - g_2}{1 - g_1}\right) \frac{N_{i1}}{N_{i2}}.$$

From (8.2.1), we get

$$E = \frac{K_1 - nZ^m K_2}{1 + nZ^m}.$$

Substituting this relation into (8.1.1) yields

$$F_1 = \alpha_1 Z^m f(K,Z), \quad F_2 = \alpha_2 f(K,Z) \tag{8.2.2}$$

in which

$$f \equiv Z^{m_2} K^\alpha f_1^\alpha(Z), \quad f_1(Z) \equiv \frac{1}{1 + nZ^m}, \quad \alpha_1 \equiv \left(\frac{1 - g_2}{N_{i2}}\right)^\alpha N_{i1},$$

$$\alpha_2 \equiv (1 - g_2)^\alpha N_{i2}^\beta.$$

From (8.2.2) and (8.2.3), we have the following lemma.

Lemma 8.2.1.
In the free trade system, the ratios of income per capita and wage rates between the two countries are given by

$$\frac{y_1}{y_2} = \frac{1 - n_1}{1 - n_2} Z^m, \quad \frac{w_1}{w_2} = \left(\frac{1 - \tau_1}{1 - \tau_2}\right) \frac{y_1}{y_2} \tag{8.2.4}$$

where $y_j \equiv Y_j / N_j$.

Lemma 8.2.1 implies that for given research policy the ratios of incomes per capita and wage rates between the two countries are determined by their difference in knowledge utilization efficiency. A country's income per capita and wage rate tend to be low if it devotes more capital and labor force to the university. In particular, when the two countries have the same knowledge utilization efficiency, i.e., $m_1 = m_2$, the ratios y_1 / y_2 and w_1 / w_2 are only related to the research parameters n_j and g_j, $j = 1, 2$. The country with heavier investment in research tends to be poorer than the other one.

Adding the two equations in (8.1.4) yields

$$\frac{dK}{dt} = s_1 F_1 + s_2 F_2 - \delta_k K . \tag{8.2.5}$$

Substituting (8.2.2) into (8.2.5) and (8.1.7) and substituting (8.2.1) and (8.2.2) into (8.1.5), we get

$$\frac{dK}{dt} = f_0(Z)f(K,Z) - \delta_k K, \quad \frac{dZ}{dt} = \sum_{j=1}^{2} \left(\phi_{ij} + \phi_{rj} \right) - \delta_z Z \tag{8.2.6}$$

where

$$f_0(Z) \equiv \alpha_1 s_1 Z^m + \alpha_2 s_2, \quad \phi_{i1} \equiv \alpha_1 \tau_{i1} Z^{m-\varepsilon_{i1}} f(K,Z),$$
$$\phi_{i2} \equiv \alpha_2 \tau_{i2} Z^{-\varepsilon_{i2}} f(K,Z), \quad \phi_{r1} \equiv \tau_{r1} (n_1 N_1)^{\beta_{r1}} (g_1 n)^{\alpha_{r1}} Z^{\alpha_{r1} m + \varepsilon_{r1}} (Kf)^{\alpha_{r1}},$$
$$\phi_{r2} \equiv \tau_{r2} (n_2 N_2)^{\beta_{r2}} g_2^{\alpha_{r2}} Z^{\varepsilon_{r2}} (Kf_1)^{\alpha_{r2}}.$$

The next section examines behavior of the dynamic system.

8.3 Equilibria and Stability Conditions

Before guaranteeing existence of equilibria, we determine the equilibrium trade pattern. As shown in Section 8.2, the trade pattern is determined by

$$E = \left(K_1 - nZ^m K_2 \right) f_1.$$

On the other hand, from (8.1.4) we have $K_j = s_j F_j / \delta_k$ at equilibrium. Utilizing these two relations, (8.2.2), and (8.2.3), we obtain the following relation

$$E = \frac{(1-g_1)s_1 - (1-g_2)s_2}{(1-g_1)\delta_k} \alpha_1 f f_1 Z^m . \tag{8.3.1}$$

We call $(1-g_j)s_j$ country j's net savings rate out of its income.

Lemma 8.3.1.
The equilibrium trade pattern is determined by the difference of the net savings rates between the two countries. That is, if $(1-g_1)s_1 > (1-g_2)s_2$, country 1's capital

is employed by country 2, and vice versa. If $(1 - g_1)s_1 = (1 - g_2)s_2$, there is no trade.

In the remainder of this chapter, we assume

$$q \equiv \frac{(1 - g_1)s_1}{(1 - g_2)s_2} > 1. \tag{8.3.2}$$

This requirement is satisfied when country 1 has either a higher savings rate or a lower ratio of the research capital than country 2. In particular, when country 1 has both a higher savings rate and a lower ratio of the research capital than country 2, (8.3.2) holds.

The following equations determine equilibria of (8.2.6)

$$f_0(Z)f(K,Z) = \delta_k K, \quad \sum_{j=1}^{2}\left(\phi_{ij} + \phi_{rj}\right) = \delta_z Z. \tag{8.3.3}$$

From the first equation in (8.3.3), we have

$$K = f_2(Z) \equiv \left(\frac{f_0 f_1^{\alpha} Z^{m_2}}{\delta_k}\right)^{1/\beta}. \tag{8.3.4}$$

Substituting (8.3.4) into the second equation in (8.3.3) yields

$$\Phi(Z) \equiv \sum_{j=1}^{2}\left\{\Phi_{ij}(Z) + \Phi_{rj}(Z)\right\} - \delta_z = 0 \tag{8.3.5}$$

in which

$$\Phi_{i1} \equiv \frac{\alpha_1 \tau_{i1} \delta_k Z^{m - \varepsilon_{i1} - 1} f_2}{f_0}, \quad \Phi_{i2} \equiv \frac{\alpha_2 \tau_{i2} \delta_k Z^{-\varepsilon_{i2} - 1} f_2}{f_0},$$

$$\Phi_{r1} \equiv \tau_{r1}(n_1 N_1)^{\beta_{r1}} (g_1 n)^{\alpha_{r1}} Z^{\alpha_{r1} m + \varepsilon_{r1} - 1}(f\!f_2)^{\alpha_{r1}},$$

$$\Phi_{r2} \equiv \tau_{r2}(n_2 N_2)^{\beta_{r2}} g_2^{\alpha_{r2}} Z^{\varepsilon_{r2} - 1}(f_1 f_2)^{\alpha_{r2}}. \tag{8.3.6}$$

We introduce the following four parameters

$$x_{ij} \equiv \frac{m_j}{\beta} - \varepsilon_{ij} - 1, \quad x_{rj} \equiv \frac{\alpha_{rj} m_j}{\beta} + \varepsilon_{rj} - 1. \tag{8.3.7}$$

From the definitions of the parameters, m_j, ε_{ij}, α_{rj}, and ε_{rj}, it can be seen that x_{ij} and x_{rj} may be either positive or negative. We can show that any of 16 combinations of $x_{ij} \geq 0$ or $x_{ij} < 0$ and $x_{rj} \geq 0$ or $x_{rj} < 0$ is economically meaningful. We say that the contribution to knowledge accumulation by country j's industrial sector exhibits increasing (decreasing) returns to scale in the system if $x_{ij} > 0$ ($x_{ij} < 0$). Similarly, we say that the contribution to knowledge accumulation by country j's university exhibits increasing (decreasing) returns to scale in the system if $x_{rj} > 0$ ($x_{rj} < 0$).

In the two cases of $x_{ij} < 0$, $x_{rj} < 0$, $j = 1, 2$ ($x_{ij} > 0$, $x_{rj} > 0$, $j = 1, 2$), we directly have

$$\Phi(0) > (<) \, 0 \text{ and } \Phi(+\infty) < (>) \, 0.$$

Accordingly, the equation, $\Phi(Z) = 0$, has positive solutions. By (8.3.5), we have

$$Z\Phi' = \sum_{j=1}^{2} \left\{ (x_{ij} + \alpha m \delta_0)\Phi_{ij} + (x_{rj} + \alpha_{rj} m \delta_0)\Phi_{rj} \right\} \tag{8.3.8}$$

where

$$\delta_0 \equiv \left(1 - \frac{1}{q}\right) \alpha_1 s_1 \beta f_0 f_1 Z^m > 0.$$

We see that when $x_{ij} < 0$, $x_{rj} < 0$, and $m < 0$, $j = 1, 2$, we have $\Phi'(Z) < 0$ for any positive Z. When $x_{ij} > 0$, $x_{rj} > 0$, and $m > 0$, $j = 1, 2$, we have $\Phi'(Z) > 0$ for any positive Z. This means that in the two cases there is a unique equilibrium. It is straightforward to check that in the case of $x_{ij} < 0$, $x_{rj} < 0$, and $m < 0$, $j = 1, 2$, the unique equilibrium is stable. In the case of $x_{ij} > 0$, $x_{rj} > 0$, and $m > 0$, $j = 1, 2$, the unique equilibrium is unstable. Summarizing the above discussion, we have the following proposition.

Proposition 8.3.1.

(i) If $x_{ij} < 0$, $x_{rj} < 0$, and $m < 0$, $j = 1, 2$, the trade system has a unique stable equilibrium;

(ii) If $x_{ij} > 0$, $x_{rj} > 0$, and $m > 0$, $j = 1, 2$, the trade system has a unique unstable equilibrium.

From the above interpretations of x_{ij} and x_{rj}, we may interpret the proposition as follows. If the two countries' industrial sectors and universities exhibit increasing (decreasing) returns in knowledge accumulation, the global economy is unstable (stable).

As shown in the appendix, if the conditions in (i) or (ii) of the above proposition are satisfied, similar conclusions hold for the autarky system. The uniqueness of equilibrium in the two systems is important for examining the impact of international trade on the world economy.

It should be remarked that the trade system may have multiple equilibria under other possible combinations of the parameters. As we are mainly concerned with the impact of free trade on the world economy and changes in some parameters, we limit our discussion to the above two cases.

8.4 Does Free Trade Benefit the World Economy?

This section examines the impact of trade on the two economies. With the parameters fixed, we compare the equilibria in the autarky and trade systems. The existence of equilibria and stability conditions of the autarky system are discussed in Appendix A. 8.1.

This section is only concerned with the following two cases: (i) $x_{ij} < 0$, $x_{rj} < 0$, and $m < 0$, $j = 1, 2$; (ii) $x_{ij} > 0$, $x_{rj} > 0$, and $m > 0$, $j = 1, 2$. From Proposition 8.3.1 and Proposition 8.A.1.1 in Appendix A.8.1, we know that the two systems have unique equilibria in the two cases. We now compare them.

The equilibrium values of knowledge in the two systems are respectively given by (8.3.5) and (8.A.1.3). From the two equations, we have the following relation

$$\sum_{j=1}^{2} \left\{ \Phi_{ij}(Z) + \Phi_{rj}(Z) \right\} = \sum_{j=1}^{2} \left\{ \Phi_{ij}^{*}(Z^{*}) + \Phi_{rj}^{*}(Z^{*}) \right\}$$

where Z and Z^* are the equilibrium values of knowledge in the autarky and free trade systems, respectively. In the remainder of this section, subscript * always refers to the functions and equilibrium values of variables in the autarky system. We rewrite the above equation as follows

$$\sum_{j=1}^{2}\left\{\Phi_{ij}(Z) - \Phi_{ij}^*(Z^*) + \Phi_{rj}(Z) - \Phi_{rj}^*(Z^*)\right\} = 0. \tag{8.4.1}$$

In order to judge the sign of $Z - Z^*$, we simplify (8.4.1). For convenience of discussion, we require that τ_{i1}, τ_{i2} and τ_{r1} are so small that we can omit the terms associated with them in (8.4.1). In particular, we require

$$\tau_{i1} = \tau_{i2} = \tau_{r1} = 0.$$

This requirement means that possible contribution to knowledge accumulation through learning by doing by the two countries' industrial sectors and through research by country 1's university is negligible. From the definitions of Φ_{ij}, Φ_{ij}^*, Φ_{rj}, and Φ_{rj}^* and the above requirement, (8.4.1) becomes

$$\Phi_{r2}(Z) - \Phi_{r2}^*(Z^*) = 0.$$

By the definitions of $\Phi_{r2}(Z)$ and $\Phi_{r2}^*(Z^*)$, we get the following relation between Z and Z^* from the above equation

$$\tau_{r2}(n_2 N_2)^{\beta_{r2}} g_2^{\alpha_{r2}} Z^{\varepsilon_{r2}-1}(f_1 f_2)^{\alpha_{r2}} = \tau_{r2}(s_2^* g_2)^{\alpha_{r2}} N_{r2}^{\beta_{r2}} Z^{*x_{r2}}. \tag{8.4.2}$$

Substituting f_1 in (8.2.3) and f_2 in (8.3.4) into (8.4.2) yields

$$\left(\frac{Z^*}{Z}\right)^x = \frac{q N_1 Z^m + q_0}{N_1 Z^m + q_0} > 1 \tag{8.4.3}$$

where

$$x \equiv \frac{\beta x_{r2}}{\alpha_{r2}}, \quad q_0 \equiv \left(\frac{1-g_1}{1-g_2}\right)\frac{1-n_2}{1-n_1} > 0.$$

In (8.4.3) we use $q > 1$ to guarantee $\left(Z^*/Z\right)^x > 1$. It can be seen that the sign of x is the same as that of x_{r2}. We conclude that if $x_{r2} > (<)\,0$, we have $Z^* > (<)\,Z$. This implies that if the contribution to knowledge accumulation by country 2's university exhibits decreasing (increasing) returns to scale in the system, the equilibrium level of knowledge is higher (lower) in the autarky system than in the free trade system. This implies that free trade may not expand knowledge in the long term.

By (8.2.4) and (8.A.1.2), we have

$$\frac{K^*}{K} = \frac{s_1^* Z^{*m_1/\beta} + s_2^* Z^{*m_2/\beta}}{f_0 f_1^\alpha Z^{m_2}/\delta_k^{1/\beta}} =$$

$$(q^{1/\beta} Z^{*m} + q_0 N_0) \frac{\left(Z^m + q_0 N_0\right)^{\alpha/\beta}}{\left(qZ^m + q_0 N_0\right)^{1/\beta}} \left(\frac{Z^*}{Z}\right)^{m_2/\beta}$$

$$> \frac{q^{1/\beta} Z^{*m} + q_0 N_0}{qZ^m + q_0 N_0} \left(\frac{Z^*}{Z}\right)^{m_2/\beta} \tag{8.4.4}$$

where $N_0 \equiv N_2/N_1$. If $Z^*/Z > q^{\alpha/\beta m} > 1$, then $K^*/K > 1$. If $Z^*/Z < q^{\alpha/\beta m}$, K^*/K may be either greater or less than unity.

We can examine the impact of free trade on the other variables in the system. As the results are obtained with a complicated combination of the parameters, we will not represent them.

Lemma 8.4.1.
The equilibrium level of knowledge in the autarky system is higher than in the free trade system, i.e., $Z^* > Z$, if the following four conditions are satisfied: (1) $(1 - g_1)s_1 > (1 - g_2)s_2$; (2) $x_{ij}, x_{rj} > 0$, $j = 1, 2$; (3) $m_1 > m_2$; and (4) $\tau_{r1} > 0$ and $\tau_{i1} = \tau_{i2} = \tau_{r1} = 0$. Moreover, if $Z^*/Z > q^{\alpha/\beta m}$, then $K^* > K$.

The above lemma may be interpreted as follows. If (1) country 1's net savings rate is higher than country 2's; (2) the two countries' industrial sectors and universities exhibit increasing returns to scale in knowledge accumulation; (3) country 1 applies knowledge more effectively than country 2 in economic production; and (4) the two countries' industrial sectors and country 1's university make little contribution to knowledge creation and country 2's knowledge creation efficiency is high, we can conclude that free trade would reduce knowledge in the long term.

Moreover, if the reduction in knowledge is significant, the world capital stock is also reduced. The above lemma thus shows the possibility that free trade does not benefit the world economy.

The trade model in this chapter illustrates complex of international trade among economies with different characteristics. We demonstrated that it is possible that free trade may benefit no economy in the world. It should be remarked that it is also possible to identify some cases that free trade may benefit all economies in the global system. Our model shows how difficult to explicitly judge the impact of trade on the global economy

8.5 The Impact of Knowledge Accumulation Efficiency

This section examines the impact of changes in the knowledge accumulation efficiency parameters τ_{ij} and τ_{rj} $(j = 1, 2)$ on the free trade system. As we can similarly examine effects in the autarky system, we limit our investigation to the free trade system. For illustration, we are concerned only with changes in τ_{r2}. In this section we are concerned with the following two cases

(i) $x_{ij} < 0$, $x_{rj} < 0$, and $m < 0$, $j = 1, 2$;

(ii) $x_{ij} > 0$, $x_{rj} > 0$, and $m > 0$, $j = 1, 2$.   (8.5.1)

We know that in these cases there is a unique equilibrium in the trade system.

Taking derivatives of (8.2.4) and (8.3.5) with respect to τ_{r2} yields

$$\beta \frac{dK}{d\tau_{r2}} = \left(m_2 + \frac{\alpha_1 s_1 m Z^m}{f_0} - \alpha n m f_1 Z^m \right) \frac{dZ}{d\tau_{r2}},$$

$$-\Phi' \frac{dZ}{d\tau_{r2}} = \frac{\Phi_{r2}}{\tau_{r2}} > 0.$$ (8.5.1)

In case (i) ((ii)), we have $\Phi' < (>) 0$. We see that in case (i) ((ii)), the equilibrium level of knowledge is increased (reduced) as the knowledge accumulation efficiency is improved. It is straightforward to see that in case (i), the world capital stock is increased.

In case (i), by (8.2.2) and (8.1.2) we get

$$\frac{dF_{ij}}{d\tau_{r2}} > 0, \quad j = 1, 2,$$

$$\frac{d(w_1/w_2)}{d\tau_{r2}} = \frac{d(F_{i1}/F_{i2})}{d\tau_{r2}} = \frac{\alpha_1 m Z^{m-1}}{\alpha_2} \frac{dZ}{d\tau_{r2}} < 0. \tag{8.5.3}$$

Summarizing the above discussion, we have the following corollary.

Corollary 8.5.1.

Assume that $x_{ij} < 0$, $x_{rj} < 0$, and $m < 0$, $j = 1, 2$ in the free trade system. An increase in τ_{ij} or τ_{rj} ($j = 1, 2$) has the following impact on the world economy: (1) the equilibrium levels of knowledge and world capital stocks are increased; (2) the wage rates and production output in all the national economies are increased; and (3) country 2 economically benefits more than country 1.

It is important to note that if $x_{ij} > 0$, $x_{rj} > 0$, and $m > 0$, $j = 1, 2$, the effects of changes in τ_{ij} or τ_{rj} ($j = 1, 2$) are the opposite to these given by Corollary 8.5.1.

8.6 Research, Knowledge, and Trade

This chapter suggested a one-sector trade model with endogenous knowledge. We examined the impact of trade on the global economy. We proved that the traditional belief that free trade is desirable may be invalid under certain conditions. Although economists demonstrated invalidity of the traditional belief when perfect competition is not assumed, we discussed the issue under the traditional assumption of perfect competition. This chapter investigated some special cases of the general model. It is possible to get more insights into complexity of international trade by examining other possible combinations of the parameters.

Appendix

A.8.1 Equilibria and Stability of the Autarky System

In the autarky system, we have $E = 0$. Moreover, r_1 may not equal r_2. The dynamics are given by

$$\frac{dK_j}{dt} = s_j F_j - \delta_k K_j,$$

$$\frac{dZ}{dt} = \sum_{j=1}^{2} \left(\frac{\tau_{ij} F_j}{Z^{\varepsilon_{ij}}} + \tau_{rj} Z^{\varepsilon_{rj}} K_{rj}^{\alpha_{rj}} N_{rj}^{\beta_{rj}} \right) - \delta_z Z. \qquad (8.A.1.1)$$

Equilibria are given by

$$K_j = s_j^* Z^{*m_j/\beta}, \quad \Phi^*(Z^*) \equiv \sum_{j=1}^{2} \left\{ \Phi_{ij}^*(Z^*) + \Phi_{rj}^*(Z^*) \right\} - \delta_z = 0 \quad (8.A.1.2)$$

in which

$$\Phi_{ij}^* \equiv (1 - g_j)^{\alpha} \tau_{ij} s_j^{*\alpha} N_{ij}^{\beta} Z^{*x_{ij}}, \quad \Phi_{rj}^* \equiv \tau_{rj} N_{rj}^{\beta_{rj}} (s_j^* g_j)^{\alpha_{rj}} Z^{*x_{rj}},$$

$$s_j^* \equiv \left(\frac{s_j}{\delta_k} \right)^{1/\beta} (1 - g_j)^{\alpha/\beta} N_{ij}. \qquad (8.A.1.3)$$

It is straigtforward to prove the following proposition.

Proposition 8.A.1.1.
(i) If $x_{ij} < 0$, and $x_{rj} < 0$, $j = 1, 2$, the autarky system has a unique stable equilibrium;
(ii) If $x_{ij} > 0$, and $x_{rj} > 0$, $j = 1, 2$, the autarky system has a unique unstable equilibrium;
(iii) For any of the remaining 14 possible combinations of $x_{ij} > (\leq) 0$, $x_{rj} > (\leq) 0$, $j = 1, 2$, the autarky system has two equilibria. When the system has two equilibria, the one with lower values of Z is stable and the other one is unstable.

9 Trade Patterns in a Multi-Group and Multi-Sector Global Economy

There are a few formal theoretical models that explicitly deal with issues related to international trade patterns with multiple groups and economic structures. The previous chapters analyzed trade patterns with capital, knowledge and multiple groups. But these frameworks are limited to the case that the world economy produces a single (highly aggregated) good which can be used as either for consumption or investment. In the remainder of this book, we are concerned with world economies with multiple products.

It may be said that structural interdependence among ownership structures of production and consumption resources (such as land and capital), production and consumption structures, and markets is one of the most important topics in economics. It is desirable to develop an economic system which takes account of complexity of this structural interdependence in a consistent way. Since the pioneering works of Leontief (e.g., Leontief, 1949, 1966), numerous theoretical studies on economic structures have been published (e.g., Sraffa, 1960, Brody, 1970, Pasinetti, 1981, 1983). The Leontief multi-sector model has been applied to different economic systems of multiple regions and countries (Isard, 1953, Duchin, 1989). Although the input-output system has proved to be effective for analyzing economic structures with complicated linkages among various production sectors in multi-regional or multi-national systems, it is analytically difficult to introduce endogenous behavior of households. This chapter constructs an equilibrium multi-sector model with endogenous household behavior to show how demand and supply with a specified ownership structure are structurally interdependent in a simplified agricultural world. Although the construction of our model is strongly influenced by the Leontief input-output system, we try to emphasize the impact of consumption behavior and human capital structures of different groups of the population in different countries on the world economy.

This chapter is organized as follows. Section 9.1 defines the international trade model with multiple groups of the population and multiple kinds of products. Section 9.2 examines conditions for the trade system to have equilibria. Section 9.3 analyzes effects of changes in resources (of labor and land) on the world economic structure. Section 9.4 examines impact of changes in the landlords' preference on the economic system. Section 9.5 concludes the chapter. The appendix proves the results in Section 9.3.

9.1 The Multi-Group and Multi-Sector Model

We are concerned with a world economic system which consists of two countries, indexed by $j = 1, 2$, respectively. Each country has two fixed resources, labor and land. It is assumed that the quality of land is homogenous within each country. This assumption may be relaxed according the analytical way proposed by Morishima (1989). The population within each country is classified into two groups, workers and landlords. It is assumed that the people from the same group are identical in preference and human capital, but people of different groups may have different preferences and human capital. It is assumed that landlords do not work in field and live on the land revenue. Workers work in fields and are paid in wages which are their only income resource. Although it is conceptually not difficult to relax this classification by allowing the existence of another group who owns (some of) the land and work in fields, we limit our discussion to the two groups.

It is assumed that land quality and climates may vary between the two countries. Here, land quality and climates may be considered as given technologies to countries. National differences in land quality and climates thus imply that two countries have different advantages or disadvantages in producing certain kinds of goods. In this chapter, we classify economic production into country-specified and agricultural sectors. The country-specified sector produces goods which can be produced only by the country. We omit any possibility that the country-specified goods are produced by the other country (due to technology, climate, land quality or any other reasons). Country-specified goods (simply called country j's goods) are consumed by the two countries. The agricultural sectors in the two countries produce the same kind of agricultural goods. The agricultural commodity is selected to serve as numeraire. Perfect competition is assumed to prevail in markets both within each country and between the two countries. Commodities are traded without any barriers such as transport costs or tariffs. Any possibility of international migration is omitted. We also omit possibility of selling and buying land in international land markets. We introduce

i, a — subscript indexes for country-specified and agricultural sectors, respectively;

L_j — country j's fixed land, $j = 1, 2$;

N_{j1} and N_{j2} — country j's fixed number of landlords and workers;

N_{qj} — the number of workers employed by country j's sector q, $j = 1, 2$, $q = i, a$;

L_{qj} — the land employed by country j's sector q;

C_{aj1} and C_{aj2} — the consumption levels of agricultural goods by country j's landlords and workers, respectively;

C_{k1j1} and C_{kj2} — the consumption levels of country k's goods by country j's landlords and workers, k, $j = 1, 2$;

F_{qj} — the output levels of country j's sector q; and

w_j, p_j and R_j — country j's wage rate, the price of country j's goods and country j's land rent.

The production functions of the world economy are specified as follows:

$$F_{qj} = (q_{qk}L_{qj})^{\alpha_{qj}}(z_{qj}N_{qj})^{\beta_{qj}},$$
$$\alpha_{qj} + \beta_{qj} = 1, \quad \alpha_{qj}, \beta_{qj} > 0, \quad q = i, a, \quad j = 1, 2$$

where q_{qk} and z_{qk} are respectively indicators of land quality and workers' human capital for country j's sector q. For simplicity of analysis, we require $\alpha_{a1} = \alpha_{a2}$ which simply implies that the two countries have the same agricultural production function. We rewrite the above production functions as follows

$$F_{qj} = \theta_{qk}L_{qj}^{\alpha_{qj}}N_{qj}^{\beta_{qj}}, \quad \theta_{qj} \equiv q_{qj}^{\alpha_{qj}}z_{qj}^{\beta_{qj}}. \tag{9.1.1}$$

The marginal conditions are given by

$$R_j = \frac{\alpha_{aj}F_{aj}}{L_{aj}} = \frac{\alpha_{ij}p_jF_{ij}}{L_{ij}}, \quad w_j = \frac{\beta_{aj}F_{aj}}{N_{aj}} = \frac{\beta_{ij}p_jF_{ij}}{N_{ij}}. \tag{9.1.2}$$

The net incomes Y_{kj} of the two groups in the two countries are given by

$$Y_{j1} = R_jL_j, \quad Y_{j2} = w_jN_j. \tag{9.1.3}$$

It is assumed that there is an aggregated utility function for each group in each country. It is further assumed that a typical household's utility level is dependent on its consumption levels of two countries' goods and agricultural goods. The utility functions are specified as follows

$$U_{jk} = C_{ajk}^{\mu_{jk}}C_{1jk}^{\xi_{jk}}C_{2jk}^{\eta_{jk}}, \quad \mu_{jk}, \xi_{jk}, \eta_{jk} > 0, \quad j, k = 1, 2 \tag{9.1.4}$$

where U_{j1} and U_{j2} represent respectively the utility levels of country j's landlords and workers. It should be remarked that some group may not consume some goods. For instance, country 1's workers may not consume country 2's goods. This case may be taken into account by letting $\eta_{12} = 0$.

The financial budget constraints are given by

$$C_{ajk} + p_1 C_{1jk} + p_2 C_{2jk} = Y_{jk}, \quad j, k = 1, 2. \tag{9.1.5}$$

Each group maximizes its utility subject to its budget constrains. The optimal problems have the following unique solutions

$$C_{ajk} = \mu_{jk} \rho_{jk} Y_{jk}, \quad p_1 C_{1jk} = \xi_{jk} \rho_{jk} Y_{jk}, \quad p_2 C_{2jk} = \eta_{jk} \rho_{jk} Y_{jk} \tag{9.1.6}$$

where

$$\rho_{jk} \equiv \frac{1}{\mu_{jk} + \xi_{jk} + \eta_{jk}}.$$

The balances of demand for and supply of agricultural goods are given by

$$\sum_{j,k} C_{ajk} = F_{a1} + F_{a2}. \tag{9.1.7}$$

According to the definition of country-specified goods, we have the following demand-supply conditions

$$\sum_{m,k=1}^{2} C_{jmk} = F_{ij}, \quad j = 1, 2. \tag{9.1.8}$$

The trade balance conditions are given by

$$\begin{aligned}
F_{a1} - C_{a11} - C_{a12} + p_1 C_{121} + p_1 C_{122} &= p_2 C_{211} + p_2 C_{212}, \\
F_{a2} - C_{a21} - C_{a22} + p_2 C_{211} + p_2 C_{212} &= p_1 C_{121} + p_1 C_{122}.
\end{aligned} \tag{9.1.9}$$

The left-hand sides of the above equations are country j's net exports and the right-hand sides are its net imports.

It is assumed that the land and labor force are fully employed in the two countries, i.e.

$$L_{aj} + L_{ij} = L_j, \quad N_{aj} + N_{ij} = N_{j2}, \quad j = 1, 2. \tag{9.1.10}$$

It is straightforward to show that with (9.1.6), (9.1.5) are not independent of the other equations in the system. Adding the two equations in (9.1.9) yields (9.1.7). We now show that (9.1.8) are not independent of the other equations in the system. First, by (9.1.2) and (9.1.3), we have

$$F_{ij} = Y_{j1} + Y_{j2} - F_{aj}.$$

Substituting F_{aj} in (9.1.9) and Y_{j1} and Y_{j2} in (9.1.5) into the above equations, we get (9.1.8). We may thus omit (9.1.6), (9.1.7) and (9.1.8) in the remainder of this chapter. We have thus built the model. The system has 38 independent variables, L_{aj}, L_{ij}, N_{aj}, N_{ij}, F_{aj}, F_{ij}, C_{ajk}, C_{1jk}, C_{2jk}, Y_{jk}, U_{jk}, p_j, w_j, and R_j ($j, k = 1, 2$). It also contains the same number of independent equations. We now solve the equilibrium problem.

9.2 The Existence of Equilibrium

This section examines under what conditions the economic system has equilibria. First, by (9.1.2) we have

$$\frac{L_{ij}}{L_{aj}} = \frac{\alpha_{ij}\beta_{aj}}{\alpha_{aj}\beta_{ij}} \frac{N_{ij}}{N_{aj}}. \tag{9.2.1}$$

Using (9.1.10) and (9.2.1), we obtain

$$\frac{L_j}{L_{aj}} = \frac{\alpha_j + \alpha_{ij}\beta_{aj}N_j / N_{aj}}{\alpha_{aj}\beta_{ij}} \tag{9.2.2}$$

where $\alpha_j = \alpha_{aj} - \alpha_{ij}$. Substituting C_{ajk}, C_{1jk}, and C_{2jk} in (9.1.6) into (9.1.9) yields

$$
\begin{aligned}
F_{a1} + \xi_{21}p_{21}Y_{21} + \xi_{22}p_{22}Y_{22} = \\
(\mu_{11} + \eta_{11})p_{11}Y_{11} + (\eta_{12} + \mu_{12})p_{12}Y_{12}, \\
F_{a2} + \eta_{11}p_{11}Y_{11} + \eta_{12}p_{12}Y_{12} = \\
(\mu_{21} + \xi_{21})p_{21}Y_{21} + (\mu_{22} + \xi_{22})p_{22}Y_{22}.
\end{aligned} \tag{9.2.3}
$$

By (9.1.3) and (9.1.2), we have

$$Y_{j1} = \frac{\alpha_{aj} L_j F_{aj}}{L_{aj}}, \quad Y_{j2} = \frac{\beta_{aj} N_j F_{aj}}{N_{aj}}.$$

Substituting these equations into (9.2.3), we have

$$\left(\frac{\alpha_{a2} \xi_{21} \rho_{21} L_2}{L_{a2}} + \frac{\xi_{22} \rho_{22} \beta_{a2} N_2}{N_{a2}} \right) F_{a2} =$$

$$\left\{ (\mu_{11} + \eta_{11}) \frac{\alpha_{a1} \rho_{11} L_1}{L_{a1}} + (\eta_{12} + \mu_{12}) \frac{\beta_{a1} \rho_{12} N_1}{N_{a1}} - 1 \right\} F_{a1},$$

$$\left(\eta_{11} \rho_{11} \frac{\alpha_{a1} L_1}{L_{a1}} + \eta_{12} \rho_{12} \frac{\beta_{a1} N_1}{N_{a1}} \right) F_{a1}$$

$$= \left\{ (\mu_{21} + \xi_{21}) \rho_{21} \frac{\alpha_{a2} L_2}{L_{a2}} + (\mu_{22} + \xi_{22}) \rho_{22} \frac{\beta_{a2} N_2}{N_{a2}} - 1 \right\} F_{a2}.$$

$$(9.2.4)$$

As F_{aj} are functions of L_{aj} and N_{aj}, we see that the four independent equations (9.2.2) and (9.2.4) contain four variables, L_{aj} and N_{aj}, $j = 1, 2$. We now solve the equations.

Substituting (9.2.2) into (9.2.4) yields

$$\left(\frac{a_{11}}{N_{a1}} - b_{11} \right) F_{a1} = \left(\frac{a_{12}}{N_{a2}} + b_{12} \right) F_{a2},$$

$$\left(\frac{a_{21}}{N_{a1}} + b_{21} \right) F_{a1} = \left(\frac{a_{22}}{N_{a2}} - b_{22} \right) F_{a2} \qquad (9.2.5)$$

where

$$a_{11} \equiv \left\{ \frac{\eta_{11} + \mu_{11}}{\beta_{i1}} \alpha_{i1} \rho_{11} + (\eta_{12} + \mu_{12}) \rho_{12} \right\} \beta_{a1} N_1 > 0,$$

$$a_{12} \equiv \left(\frac{\alpha_{i2} \xi_{21} \rho_{21}}{\beta_{i2}} + \xi_{22} \rho_{22} \right) \beta_{a2} N_2 > 0,$$

$$a_{21} \equiv \left(\frac{\alpha_{i1}\eta_{11}\rho_{11}}{\beta_{i1}} + \eta_{12}\rho_{12} \right)\beta_{a1}N_1 > 0,$$

$$a_{22} \equiv \left\{ \frac{\eta_{21} + \mu_{21}}{\beta_{i2}}\alpha_{i2}\rho_{21} + (\eta_{22} + \mu_{22})\rho_{22} \right\}\beta_{a2}N_2 > 0,$$

$$b_{jj} \equiv 1 - \left(1 - \frac{\beta_{aj}}{\beta_{ij}} \right)(\eta_{j1} + \mu_{j1})\rho_{j1} > 0, \quad b_{12} \equiv \frac{\alpha_2\xi_{21}\rho_{21}}{\beta_{i1}},$$

$$b_{21} \equiv \frac{\alpha_1\xi_{11}\rho_{11}}{\beta_{i2}} \qquad\qquad (9.2.6)$$

in which $(\eta_{j1} + \mu_{j1})\rho_{j1} < 1$ are used. It is necessary to require

$$\frac{a_{jj}}{N_{a1}} \geq b_{jj}. \qquad\qquad (9.2.7)$$

If $N_{aj} = 0$, country j does not produces agricultural goods. If $a_{jj}/b_{jj} = N_{aj}$, it implies that agricultural production is produced only in country j. We are only concerned with the case that both countries produce agricultural product, i.e., $a_{jj}/b_{jj} > N_{aj}$, $j = 1, 2$. We omit the possibility that agricultural goods are produced only in one country.

Dividing the first equation in (9.2.5) by the second one, we get

$$\left(\frac{a_{11}}{N_{a1}} - b_{11} \right)\left(\frac{a_{22}}{N_{a2}} - b_{22} \right) = \left(\frac{a_{12}}{N_{a2}} + b_{12} \right)\left(\frac{a_{21}}{N_{a1}} + b_{21} \right). \qquad (9.2.8)$$

In the case of $\alpha_{i1} = \alpha_{i2} = \alpha_{a1}$ (i.e., $b_{jj} = 1$, $\alpha_j = b_{12} = b_{21} = 0$), we directly have

$$N_{a1} = a_{11} - \frac{a_{12}a_{21}}{a_{22} - N_{a2}}.$$

In the other cases, we have

$$N_{a1} = \frac{A_{11} - A_{12}N_{a2}}{A_{21} + A_{22}N_{a2}} \qquad\qquad (9.2.9)$$

where

$$A_{11} \equiv a_{11}a_{22} - a_{21}a_{12}, \quad A_{12} \equiv a_{21}b_{12} + a_{11}b_{22},$$
$$A_{21} \equiv a_{12}b_{21} + a_{22}b_{11}, \quad A_{22} \equiv b_{12}b_{21} - b_{11}b_{22}. \tag{9.2.10}$$

By (9.2.2), we have

$$\frac{L_{a1}}{L_{a2}} = \left(\frac{\alpha_2 + \alpha_{i2}\beta_{a2}N_2 / N_{a2}}{\alpha_1 + \alpha_{i1}\beta_{a1}N_1 / N_{a1}} \right) \frac{\beta_{i1}L_2}{\beta_{i2}L_2}. \tag{9.2.11}$$

Substituting F_{aj} in (9.1.1) into the first equation in (9.2.5) and then using (9.2.11), we have the following equation to determine N_{a2}

$$\Phi(N_{a2}) = \left(\frac{\alpha_2 N_{a2} + \alpha_{i2}\beta_{a2}N_2}{\alpha_1 N_{a1} + \alpha_{i1}\beta_{a1}N_1} \right) \frac{\beta_{i1}L_1}{\beta_{i2}L_2} - \left(\frac{a_{12} + b_{12}N_{a2}}{a_{11} - b_{11}N_{a1}} \frac{\theta_{a2}}{\theta_{a1}} \right)^{1/\alpha_{a1}}$$
$$= 0 \tag{9.2.12}$$

in which N_{a1} is a function of N_{a2} explicitly defined in (9.2.9).

It is easy to check that for any solution N_{a2} of (9.2.12), all other variables are uniquely determined by the following procedure: N_{aj}, $j = 1, 2$, by (9.2.12) $\rightarrow$ $N_{ij} = N_j - N_{aj} \rightarrow L_{aj}$ by (9.2.2) $\rightarrow L_{ij} = L_j - L_{aj} \rightarrow F_{aj}$ and F_{ij} by (9.1.1) $\rightarrow R_j$ and w_j by (9.1.2) $\rightarrow Y_{j1}$ and $Y_{j2} \rightarrow p_j = w_j N_{ij} / \beta_{ij}F_{ij}$ by (9.1.2) $\rightarrow C_{aj1}, C_{aj2}, C_{qj1}, C_{qj2}, q, j = 1, 2$ by (9.1.6) $\rightarrow U_{j1}$ and U_{j2} by (9.1.4).

Hence, our only task in examining the existence of equilibria is to investigate under what conditions $\Phi(N_{a2}) = 0$ has solutions. It is analytically not difficult to provide conditions for the existence of solutions of the equation

$$\Phi(N_{a2}) = 0, \quad N_2 > N_{a2} > 0.$$

If $\Phi(0)$ and $\Phi(N_2)$ have the opposite signs, the equation has at least one solution for $N_2 > N_{a2} > 0$. If the sign of $d\Phi / dN_{a2}$ is changed for $N_2 > N_{a2} > 0$, the equation has a unique solution. If $\Phi(0)$ and $\Phi(N_2)$ have the same sign, then the problem has either multiple solutions or no solution. Unfortunately, it is not easy to explicitly interpret the analytical conclusions. Here, for simplicity of discussion we are concerned with a special case.

Let us consider the case of $\alpha_{i1} = \alpha_{i2} = \alpha_{a1}$. Under this requirement, we have

$$N_{a1} = a_{11} - a_{12}\theta, \quad N_{a1} = a_{22} - \frac{a_{21}}{\theta}$$

(9.2.13)

where

$$\theta \equiv \left(\frac{L_2 N_1}{L_1 N_2}\right)^{\alpha_{a1}} \frac{\theta_{a2}}{\theta_{a1}}.$$

We require $N_j > N_{aj} > 0$. By (9.2.13), we directly have that $N_{a2} > 0$ if

$$\frac{a_{11}}{a_{12}} > \theta > \frac{a_{21}}{a_{22}}.$$

(9.2.14)

Using

$$(\mu_{j1} + \eta_{j1})\alpha_{i2}\rho_{j1} + (\eta_{j2} + \mu_{j2})\beta_{i1}\rho_{j2} < 1$$

where

$$(\mu_{j1} + \eta_{j1})\rho_{j1} < 1, \quad (\eta_{j2} + \mu_{j2})\rho_{j2} < 1, \quad \alpha_{i1} + \beta_{i1} = 1$$

we obtain

$$N_j > N_{aj} > 0$$

for any N_{aj} given by (9.2.13). Accordingly, if inequalities (9.2.14) are satisfied, we uniquely solve $N_{a2} > 0$ as a function of the parameters. By the definitions of a_{qj} and θ, (9.2.14) may be rewritten as follows

$$\frac{(\mu_{11} + \eta_{11})\alpha_{i1}\rho_{11} + (\eta_{12} + \mu_{12})\beta_{i1}\rho_{12}}{\beta_{i2}\xi_{22}\rho_{22} + \alpha_{21}\xi_{21}\rho_{21}} > \frac{F_{a2}(L_2, N_2)}{F_{a1}(L_1, N_1)}$$

$$> \frac{\beta_{i1}\eta_{12}\rho_{12} + \alpha_{i1}\eta_{11}\rho_{11}}{(\mu_{21} + \xi_{21})\alpha_{i2}\rho_{21} + (\xi_{22} + \mu_{22})\beta_{i2}\rho_{22}} \tag{9.2.15}$$

where $F_{aj}(L_j, N_j)$ are the output level of country j's agricultural sector when the total land and labor are employed by the agricultural sector. In the case that the two countries have identical resources and productivity, i.e.

$$F_{a1}(L_1, N_1) = F_{a2}(L_2, N_2)$$

the above inequality is held if

$$(\mu_{11} + \eta_{11})\alpha_{i1}\rho_{11} + (\eta_{12} + \mu_{12})\beta_{i1}\rho_{12} > \beta_{i1}\eta_{12}\rho_{12} + \alpha_{i1}\eta_{11}\rho_{11},$$
$$(\mu_{21} + \xi_{21})\alpha_{i2}\rho_{21} + (\xi_{22} + \mu_{22})\beta_{i2}\rho_{22} > \beta_{i2}\xi_{22}\rho_{22} + \alpha_{21}\xi_{21}\rho_{21}.$$
$$\tag{9.2.16}$$

Here, we interpret the two terms, $(\mu_{11} + \eta_{11})\alpha_{i1}\rho_{11} + (\eta_{12} + \mu_{12})\beta_{i1}\rho_{12}$ and $\beta_{i2}\xi_{22}\rho_{22} + \alpha_{21}\xi_{21}\rho_{21}$, in the first inequality in (9.2.15) as the 'weighted' sum of country 1's propensities to consume agricultural goods and country 2's country-specified goods and the 'weighted' sum of country 2's propensities to consume country 1's goods, respectively. The first inequality simply says that the weighted sum of country 1's propensities to consume agricultural goods and country 2's country-specified goods is higher than the weighted sum of country 2's propensities to consume country 1's goods. If this inequality is not held, the agricultural production is concentrated in country 2. Similarly, we may interpret the second inequality.

Proposition 9.2.1.
In the remainder of this chapter, we assume that $\alpha_{i1} = \alpha_{i2} = \alpha_{a1}$ and (9.2.14) are satisfied. The world economy has a unique equilibrium.

We examined the equilibrium problem. The remainder of this chapter examines effects of changes in some parameters on the world economy.

9.3 The Impact of Labor Force and Land

This section examines the impact of resources on the world economic structure. First, we are concerned with changes in country 1's labor force. Taking derivatives of (9.2.13) and $N_{ij} = N_j - N_{aj}$ with respect to N_1 yields

$$\frac{1}{N_{a1}}\frac{dN_{a1}}{dN_1} = \frac{N_{a1} + \beta_{a1}a_{12}\theta}{N_{a1}N_1} > 0,$$

$$\frac{1}{N_{i1}}\frac{dN_{i1}}{dN_1} = \frac{N_1 - a_{11} + \alpha_{a1}a_{12}\theta}{N_{i1}N_1} > 0, \quad \frac{1}{N_{a2}}\frac{dN_{a2}}{dN_1} = -\frac{\beta_{a1}a_{a1}\theta,}{\theta N_1} < 0,$$

$$\frac{1}{N_{i2}}\frac{dN_{i2}}{dN_1} = -\frac{1}{N_{i2}}\frac{N_{a2}}{dN_1} > 0 \tag{9.3.1}$$

where $N_1 - a_{11} > 0$ is used in determining the sign of dN_{a1} / dN_1. As the number N_1 of country 1's workers is increased, the laborers, N_{a1} and N_{i1}, employed country 1's two sectors are increased, and the number, N_{a1} (N_{i1}), employed by country 2's agricultural (country-specified) sector is reduced (increased). We will not explain the results in detail. It can be seen that to examine how a change in N_1 affects any variable, it is necessary to examine how all the equations in the system are affected.

Taking derivatives of (9.2.1) and (9.2.2) with respect to N_1 yields

$$\frac{dL_{a1}}{dN_1} = -\frac{dL_{i1}}{dN_1} = \frac{\beta_{a1}a_{12}\theta L_{a1}}{N_{a1}N_1} > 0, \quad \frac{1}{L_{q2}}\frac{dL_{q2}}{dN_1} = \frac{1}{N_{q2}}\frac{dN_{q2}}{dN_1},$$

$$q = i, a. \tag{9.3.2}$$

Country 1's agricultural (country-specified) sector employs more (less) land, and Country 2's agricultural (country-specified) sector employs less (more) land.

By (9.1.1), (9.3.1) and (9.3.2), we obtain

$$\frac{1}{F_{a1}}\frac{dF_{a1}}{dN_1} = \frac{\alpha_{a1}}{L_{a1}}\frac{dL_{a1}}{dN_1} + \frac{\beta_{a1}}{N_{a1}}\frac{dN_{a1}}{dN_1} > 0,$$

$$\frac{1}{F_{i1}}\frac{dF_{i1}}{dN_1} = \frac{N_1 - a_{11}}{N_{i1}N_1}\beta_{i1} > 0, \quad \frac{1}{F_{a2}}\frac{dF_{a2}}{dN_1} = -\frac{a_{21}\beta_{a1}}{\theta N_1} < 0,$$

$$\frac{1}{F_{i2}}\frac{dF_{i2}}{dN_1} = -\frac{1}{N_{i2}}\frac{dN_{a2}}{dN_1} > 0. \tag{9.3.3}$$

The output levels, F_{a1} and F_{i1}, of country 1's two sectors are increased, and the output level, F_{a2} (F_{i2}), of country 2's agricultural (country-specified) sector is reduced (increased). Taking derivatives of (9.1.2) with respect to N_1, we get the impact on the price structure as follows

$$\frac{1}{\alpha_{a1} w_1} \frac{dw_1}{dN_1} = -\frac{1}{\beta_{a1} R_1} \frac{dR_1}{dN_1} = -\frac{1}{N_1} < 0,$$

$$\frac{dw_2}{dN_1} = \frac{dR_2}{dN_1} = \frac{dp_1}{dN_1} = \frac{dp_2}{dN_1} = 0. \tag{9.3.4}$$

Country 1's wage rate (land rent) is reduced (increased). The prices p_j of the two country-specified goods, and country 2's wage rate and land rent are not affected. By (9.1.3), we get

$$\frac{1}{Y_{11}} \frac{dY_{11}}{dN_1} = \frac{1}{R_1} \frac{dR_1}{dN_1}, \quad \frac{1}{Y_{12}} \frac{dY_{12}}{dN_1} = \frac{\beta_{a1}}{N_1} > 0, \quad \frac{dY_{21}}{dN_1} = \frac{dY_{22}}{dN_1} = 0. \tag{9.3.5}$$

The income, Y_{11} (Y_{12}), of country 1's landlords (workers) reduced (increased), and the incomes, Y_{21} and Y_{22}, of country 2's two groups are not affected.

Taking derivatives of (9.1.6) with respect to N_1, we get the impact on the consumption components as follows

$$\frac{1}{C_{a11}} \frac{dC_{a11}}{dN_1} = \frac{1}{C_{111}} \frac{dC_{111}}{dN_1} = \frac{1}{C_{212}} \frac{dC_{212}}{dN_1} = \frac{1}{Y_{11}} \frac{dY_{11}}{dN_1} > 0,$$

$$\frac{1}{C_{a12}} \frac{dC_{a12}}{dN_1} = \frac{1}{C_{112}} \frac{dC_{112}}{dN_1} = \frac{1}{C_{212}} \frac{dC_{212}}{dN_1} = \frac{1}{Y_{12}} \frac{dY_{12}}{dN_1} > 0,$$

$$\frac{dC_{a21}}{dN_1} = \frac{dC_{121}}{dN_1} = \frac{dC_{221}}{dN_1} = \frac{dC_{a22}}{dN_1} = \frac{dC_{122}}{dN_1} = \frac{dC_{222}}{dN_1} = 0. \tag{9.3.6}$$

We have thus obtained the effects of changes in N_1 on the trade system. Summarizing the above analysis, we have the following lemma.

Lemma 9.3.1.
An increase in the number N_1 of country 1's workers has the following impact on the world economy: (1) on country 1's labor and land distribution and output: the levels, N_{a1} and N_{i1}, of labor inputs of the two sectors, and the levels of F_{a1} and F_{i1}, of the two sectors' output are increased; the agricultural (country-specified)

sector's land input, L_{a1} (L_{i1}), is increased (reduced); (2) on country 2 's labor and land distribution and output: the levels, N_{a2}, L_{a2}, and F_{a2} (N_{i2}, L_{i2}, and F_{i2}), of the agricultural (country-specified) sector's labor input, land input and output are reduced (increased); (3) on country 1 's price structure: the wage rate, w_1, is decreased, the land rent, R_1, is increased, and the price, p_1, of the country-specified goods is not affected; (4) on country 2 's price structure: the wage rate, w_2, the land rent, R_2, and the country-specified goods price, p_2, are not affected; (5) on country 1 's net income and consumption structure: the two groups' net incomes, Y_{11} and Y_{21}, consumption levels, C_{a11}, C_{111}, C_{211}, C_{a12}, C_{112}, and C_{a12}, of the three goods by country 1 's two groups are increased;   (6) on country 2 's net income and consumption structure: the two groups' net incomes, Y_{21} and Y_{22}, consumption levels, C_{a12}, C_{a21}, C_{121} C_{221}, C_{a22}, C_{122}, and C_{222}, of the three goods by country 1 's two groups are increased.

Similarly, we get effects of changes in country 1 's land L_1 on the world economic system as follows.

Lemma 9.3.2.
An increase in country 1 's land L_1 has the following impact on the world economy: (1) on country 1 's labor and land distribution and output: L_{a1}, L_{i1}, F_{a1} and F_{i1} are increased; N_{a1} (N_{i1}) is increased (reduced); (2) on country 2 's labor and land distribution and output: N_{a2}, L_{a2}, and F_{a2} (N_{i2}, L_{i2}, and F_{i2}) are reduced (increased); (3) on country 1 's price structure: w_1, is increased, R_1 is deceased, and p_1 is not affected; (4) on country 2 's price structure: w_2, R_2, and p_2, are not affected; (5) on country 1 's net income and consumption structure: Y_{11}, Y_{21}, C_{a11}, C_{111}, C_{221} C_{a12}, C_{211}, C_{212}, and C_{a12}, are increased; (6) on country 2 's net income and consumption structure: Y_{21}, Y_{22}, C_{222}, C_{a21}, C_{121} C_{112}, C_{122}, and C_{a22}, are increased.

The lemma is proved in Appendix A 9.1.

9.4 The Impact of Landlords' Propensity to Consume Foreign Goods

This section examines the effects of changes in the propensity μ_{11} of country 1's landlords to consume country 2's country-specified goods on the world economic structure. Taking derivatives of (9.2.13) and $N_{ij} = N_j - N_{aj}$ with respect to μ_{11}, we obtain

$$\frac{dN_{a1}}{d\mu_{11}} = -\frac{dN_{i1}}{d\mu_{11}} = \xi_{11}\alpha_{i1}\rho_{11}^2 N_1 > 0,$$

$$\frac{dN_{a2}}{d\mu_{11}} = -\frac{dN_{i2}}{d\mu_{11}} = -\frac{\xi_{11} + \mu_{11}}{\theta} a_{21}\alpha_{i1}\rho_{11}^2 N_1. \tag{9.4.1}$$

As country 1's landlords propensity to consume country 2's country-specified goods, some of the labor employed by country 1's country-specified sector are shifted to country 1's agricultural sector, and some of the labor employed by country 2's agricultural sector are shifted to country 2's country-specified sector.

By (9.2.1), (9.2.2) and (9.1.1), we directly obtain

$$\frac{1}{L_{qj}}\frac{dL_{qj}}{d\mu_{11}} = \frac{1}{F_{qj}}\frac{dF_{qj}}{d\mu_{11}} = \frac{1}{N_{qj}}\frac{dN_{qj}}{d\mu_{11}}, \quad q = i, a, \quad j = 1, 2. \tag{9.4.2}$$

We see that the sign of $dL_{qj}/d\mu_{11}$ and $dF_{qj}/d\mu_{11}$ is the same as that of $dN_{qj}/d\mu_{11}$. Taking derivatives of (9.1.2) and (9.1.3) with respect to μ_{11}, we obtain

$$\frac{dw_j}{d\mu_{11}} = \frac{dR_j}{d\mu_{11}} = \frac{dp_j}{d\mu_{11}} = \frac{dY_{1j}}{d\mu_{11}} = \frac{dY_{2j}}{d\mu_{11}} = 0. \tag{9.4.3}$$

The prices structure of the world economy and income levels are not affected. It should be remarked that the above conclusion is due to the strict assumption of $\alpha_{i1} = \alpha_{i2} = \alpha_{a1}$. For instance, in the case of $\alpha_{ij} > \alpha_{a1}$, (9.4.2) are not held.

Taking derivatives of (9.1.6) with respect to μ_{11}, we get the effects on the consumption structure as follows

$$\frac{1}{C_{a11}}\frac{dC_{a11}}{d\mu_{11}} = \frac{1}{C_{111}}\frac{dC_{111}}{d\mu_{11}} = -\rho_{11}, \quad \frac{1}{C_{211}}\frac{dC_{211}}{d\mu_{11}} = (\xi_{11} + \mu_{11})\rho_{11},$$

$$\frac{dC_{a12}}{d\mu_{11}} = \frac{dC_{112}}{d\mu_{11}} = \frac{dC_{212}}{d\mu_{11}} = \frac{dC_{a2j}}{d\mu_{11}} = \frac{dC_{12j}}{d\mu_{11}} = \frac{dC_{22j}}{d\mu_{11}} = 0. \qquad (9.4.4)$$

Country 1's landlords' consumption levels, C_{a11} and C_{111}, of agricultural goods and country 1's country-specified goods are reduced, and consumption level, C_{111}, of country 2's country-specified goods is increased, and the other groups' consumption levels are not affected.

Similarly, it is direct to analyze effects of changes in any group's preference parameters on the world economic structure.

9.5 Concluding Remarks

This chapter proposed a two-country trade equilibrium model. The population of each country is classified into workers and landlords. The workers live on the wage income and landlords on the land rent revenue. Each country produces country-specified and agricultural goods; each group consumes two country-specified and agricultural goods. Production has two factor inputs, land and labor. Agricultural and two country-specified goods are domestically and internationally freely mobile. We showed how the trade equilibrium can be determined and explicitly solved the model in a special case. We also examined the effects of changes in some parameters on the equilibrium structure of the world economy.

The model may be extended in different ways. For instance, there may be multiple kinds of ownership structures. It may be more suitable to classify the population into three groups. The added group may work as wage earners and get income from land ownership. This chapter may be considered to be appropriate only for agricultural economies.

Appendix

A.9.1 Checking Lemma 9.3.2

The proof is to take derivatives of the variables with respect to L_1. Similarly to the process of proving Lemma 9.3.1, we directly get the following results

$$\frac{dN_{a1}}{dL_1} = -\frac{dN_{i1}}{dL_1} = \frac{\alpha_{a1}a_{12}\theta,}{L_1} > 0,$$

$$\frac{dN_{a2}}{dL_1} = -\frac{dN_{i2}}{dL_1} = -\frac{\alpha_{a1}a_{21}}{\theta L_1} < 0,$$ (9.A.1.1)

$$\frac{1}{L_{a1}}\frac{dL_{a1}}{dL_1} = \frac{a_{11} - \beta_{a1}a_{12}\theta}{N_{a1}L_1} > 0,$$

$$\frac{1}{L_{i1}}\frac{dL_{i1}}{dN_1} = \frac{N_1 - a_{11} + \beta_{a1}a_{12}\theta}{N_{i1}L_1} > 0,$$

$$\frac{1}{L_{q2}}\frac{dL_{q2}}{dL_1} = \frac{1}{N_{q2}}\frac{dN_{q2}}{dL_1}, \quad q = i, a$$ (9.A.1.2)

$$\frac{1}{F_{a1}}\frac{dF_{a1}}{dL_1} = \frac{\alpha_{a1}}{L_{a1}}\frac{dL_{a1}}{dL_1} + \frac{\beta_{a1}}{N_{a1}}\frac{dN_{a1}}{dL_1} > 0,$$

$$\frac{1}{F_{i1}}\frac{dF_{i1}}{dL_1} = \frac{N_1 - a_{11}}{N_{i1}L_1}\alpha_{i1} > 0,$$

$$\frac{1}{F_{a2}}\frac{dF_{a2}}{dL_1} = -\frac{a_{21}\alpha_{a1}}{\theta L_1 N_{a2}} < 0, \quad \frac{1}{F_{i2}}\frac{dF_{i2}}{dL_1} = -\frac{1}{N_{i2}}\frac{dN_{a2}}{dL_1} > 0. \quad (9.A.1.3)$$

$$\frac{1}{\alpha_{a1}w_1}\frac{dw_1}{dL_1} = -\frac{1}{\beta_{a1}R_1}\frac{dR_1}{dL_1} = \frac{1}{L_1}, \quad \frac{dw_2}{dL_1} = \frac{dR_2}{dL_1} = \frac{dp_1}{dL_1} = \frac{dp_2}{dL_1} = 0,$$ (9.A.1.4)

$$\frac{1}{Y_{11}}\frac{dY_{11}}{dL_1} = \frac{\alpha_{a1}}{L_1}, \quad \frac{1}{Y_{12}}\frac{dY_{12}}{dN_1} = \frac{1}{w_1}\frac{dw_1}{dL_1} > 0, \quad \frac{dY_{21}}{dL_1} = \frac{dY_{22}}{dL_1} = 0,$$ (9.A.1.5)

$$\frac{1}{C_{a11}}\frac{dC_{a11}}{dL_1} = \frac{1}{C_{111}}\frac{dC_{111}}{dL_1} = \frac{1}{C_{211}}\frac{dC_{211}}{dL_1} = \frac{1}{Y_{11}}\frac{dY_{11}}{dL_1} > 0,$$

$$\frac{1}{C_{a12}}\frac{dC_{a12}}{dL_1} = \frac{1}{C_{112}}\frac{dC_{112}}{dL_1} = \frac{1}{C_{212}}\frac{dC_{212}}{dL_1} = \frac{1}{Y_{12}}\frac{dY_{12}}{dL_1} > 0,$$

$$\frac{dC_{a2j}}{dL_1} = \frac{dC_{12j}}{dL_1} = \frac{dC_{22j}}{dL_1} = 0$$ (9.A.1.6)

in which equation (9.A.1.*) corresponds to equation (9.4.*) in Section 9.4.

10 Global Growth, Trade, and Economic Structures

This chapter is concerned with dynamic relations between growth, economic structure and trade patterns in a two-country world economy. The model is similar to the two-country, two-good, two factor neoclassical trade. This chapter classifies national product into commodities and services. It is assumed that each country supplies and consumes both commodities and services. We hold that it is significant to classify national product into domestic services and international goods. The issues, for instance, about possible impact of changes of one country's preferences for its services on the long-run world economic structure cannot be analyzed within the one-commodity framework.

It may be argued that although economists have proposed different trade models with capital accumulation, relations between preferences and global growth with economic structures are not yet well examined. This chapter proposes a compact framework to analyze issues related to how preference structures of different economies determine international trade patterns, global growth, and economic structures. It is obvious that the world trade pattern is determined not only by differences in technology and resources, but also by preference structures of different countries.

When time and space are explicitly considered, services have their typical characteristics. In most cases, they are produced and consumed at the same time and at the same place. This means that services can be consumed only in the country in which they are supplied. In this chapter, it is assumed that services, such as hotels, restaurants, hospitals, education, transportation and communication systems, supplied by one country cannot be consumed by the other country. Any possible consumption by tourists is neglected in this chapter.

As shown in this chapter, our dynamic multi-sector model is much more difficult to analyze and exhibits some complicated behavior which make it difficult to provide explicit conclusions under general conditions. It should be remarked that the model developed in this chapter is similar to the trade model, for instance, by Eaton (1987) in many aspects. A main difference of our model from the Eaton model (in which only one country is explicitly considered) is that our trade model is not partial in the sense that our framework takes account of behavior of all consumers and producers in the world economy. In fact, it may be claimed that not only the Eaton model, most of dynamic trade models in the literature are partial in the sense that not all trade participants are taken into account in modeling. For instance, trade economists have been much concerned with economic behavior of small and open countries. By the assumption that an economy is small and open, it is reasonable to assume some of its economic variables like exchange rates and prices of some goods to be exogenous. From the perspective of general economic theory, such a partial approach is only for analytical convenience. When one analyzes trade issues, it may be quite misleading to only analyze behavior of one country and treat other countries' economic behavior as parameters.

It is worthwhile to mention that formal trade theory has not succeeded in handling with issues related to growth and economic structures. The one-sector trade model is not sufficient to provide insights into dynamic processes of division of labor and interdependence between division of labor, knowledge and efficiency. It is necessary to extend the one-sector economy into multiple ones. It may be argued that the main task of economics is to explain how economic structures are determined over time and space (Rostow, 1960, Kuznets, 1963, 1966, Lewis, 1955). Since the pioneering works of Leontief (e.g., Leontief, 1941, 1949, 1966), numerous theoretical studies on economic structure have been published (e.g., Sraffa, 1960, Nikaido, 1968, Morishima, 1964, 1969, Brody, 1970, Pasinetti, 1981, 1993, Arthur, Landesmann and Scazzieri, 1991). But it may be argued that formal trade theory has not yet succeeded in providing satisfactory frameworks for analyzing international trades with capital and knowledge accumulation. In this and next chapters we point out another possible directions in examining trade issues.

The outline of this chapter is as follows. Sector 10.1 represents the basic model. Section 10.2 provides conditions for existence of equilibria and stability. Section 10.3 examines effects of changes in country 1's savings rate on the world economy. Section 10.4 concludes the study. In the appendix, we prove the results in Section 10.2.

10.1 The Growth Model with Trade and Structures

We consider a two-country and two-sector system. The two countries are indexed by 1 and 2, respectively. Each country has two, industrial and service, sectors. The industrial and service sectors are indexed by i and s, respectively. It is assumed that only one commodity is produced in the system. The good is assumed to be composed of homogeneous qualities, and to be produced by employing two factors, labor and capital. Perfect competition is assumed to prevail in markets both within each country and between the countries, and commodities are traded without any barriers such as transport costs or tariffs. Any possibility of migration between the two countries is omitted. Domestic labor markets are assumed to be perfectly competitive. Each country has a fixed labor force. The single commodity is selected to serve as the numeraire. We introduce the following variables to describe the trade system

N_j — the fixed labor force of country j, $j = 1, 2$;

$K_j(t)$ — the level of capital stocks owned by country j at time t, $j = 1, 2$;

$E(t) > (<)$ — country 2's (1's) capital stocks employed by country 1 (2);

$K(t)$ — the level of the world capital stocks;

$N_{ij}(t)$ and $K_{ij}(t)$ — the labor force and capital stocks employed by country j's industrial sector;

$N_{sj}(t)$ and $K_{sj}(t)$ — the labor force and capital stocks employed by country j's service sector;

$F_{ij}(t)$ and $F_{sj}(t)$ — the output levels of country j's industrial and service sectors;

$C_{ij}(t)$ and $C_{sj}(t)$ — the consumption levels of the commodity and services by country j;

$p_j(t)$ and $w_j(t)$ — the prices of services and wage rates in country j ($j = 1, 2$); and

$r(t)$ — the rate of interest.

We now construct the model.

Production and capital and labor markets
It is assumed that the industrial production is carried out by combination of capital and labor force in the form of

$$F_{i1}(t) = K_{i1}^{\alpha}(zN_{i1})^{\beta}, \quad F_{i2}(t) = K_{i2}^{\alpha}N_{i2}^{\beta}, \quad \alpha + \beta = 1, \quad \alpha, \beta > 0$$

$$(10.1.1)$$

where α and β are parameters. From the discussion below, it can be seen that we can similarly carry out the analysis when the parameter α is varied between the two countries. The parameter z is interpreted as a measurement of per laborer's working time difference between the two countries. If $z > 1$, we say that country 1's workers work longer hours than country 2's workers. The above specified functional forms imply that the two countries have an identical production technology but different working hours.

We specify production functions of the service sectors in the two countries as follows

$$F_{s1}(t) = K_{s1}^{\alpha_1}(zN_{s1})^{\beta_1}, \quad F_{s2}(t) = K_{s2}^{\alpha_2}N_{s2}^{\beta_2},$$

$$\alpha_j + \beta_j = 1, \quad \alpha_j, \quad \beta_j > 0, \quad j = 1, 2 \qquad (10.1.2)$$

where α_j and β_j are parameters. It is assumed that the two countries have different production functions of services.

As services are consumed only by the country in which they are produced and services cannot be saved, the following equations are held

$$F_{sj} = C_{sj}, \quad j = 1, 2. \tag{10.1.3}$$

As both capital and labor force are assumed to be freely mobile from one sector to another and perfect competition is assumed in the domestic markets, the rate of interest is worldwide equal and wage rates are domestically equal. Maximizing profits of each sector in the system, we get the following marginal conditions

$$r = \frac{\alpha F_{ij}}{K_{ij}} = \frac{\alpha_j p_j F_{sj}}{K_{sj}}, \quad w_j = \frac{\beta F_{ij}}{N_{ij}} = \frac{\beta_j p_j F_{sj}}{N_{sj}}, \quad j = 1, 2. \tag{10.1.4}$$

Full employment of labor force and capital
Capital and labor force are assumed to be always fully employed in the two countries. This assumption is represented by the following equations

$$K_{i1} + K_{s1} - E = K_1, \quad K_{i2} + K_{s2} + E = K_2, \quad K_1 + K_2 = K,$$
$$N_{ij} + N_{sj} = N_j, \quad j = 1, 2. \tag{10.1.5}$$

Consumption and capital accumulation
It is assumed that the utility level that country j obtains is dependent on the consumption level $C_{ij}(t)$ of the commodity and the consumption level $C_{sj}(t)$ of services. For simplicity, the two countries' utility functions are specified as follows

$$U_j(t) = C_{ij}^{\xi_j} C_{sj}^{\gamma_j}, \quad \xi_j + \gamma_j = 1, \quad \xi_j, \gamma_j > 0. \tag{10.1.6}$$

The net income Y_j of country j is given by

$$Y_j = rK_j + w_j N_j, \quad j = 1, 2 \tag{10.1.7}$$

where rK_j is the income from the ownership of capital stocks and $w_j N_j$ is the wage income, respectively.

Each country chooses two variables, C_{sj} and C_{ij}, subject to the following budget constraint

$$p_j C_{sj} + C_{ij} = (1 - s_j)Y_j, \quad j = 1, 2 \tag{10.1.8}$$

where s_j is country j's fixed savings rate. Country j's households maximize $U_j(t)$ in (10.1.6) subject to (10.1.8). The optimal problem has the following unique solution

$$p_j C_{sj} = \gamma_j c_j Y_j, \quad C_{ij} = \xi_j c_j Y_j, \quad j = 1, 2 \tag{10.1.9}$$

where $c_j \equiv 1 - s_j$.

The capital accumulation of country j is given by

$$\frac{dK_j}{dt} = s_j Y_j - \delta_k K_j, \quad j = 1, 2 \tag{10.1.10}$$

where δ_k is the fixed depreciation rate of capital.

Since industrial output is used either for investment or consumption, we have

$$\sum_j F_{ij} = \sum_j (C_{ij} + s_j Y_j) \tag{10.1.11}$$

in which $\sum_j F_{ij}$ is the total output of the commodity in the world economy and $\sum_j (C_{ij} + s_j Y_j)$ is the sum of total consumption and total investment of the two countries.

We have thus competed building the trade model of endogenous accumulation of capital with international distribution of capital. The system consists of 28 endogenous variables, N_{ij}, N_{sj}, K_{ij}, K_{sj}, F_{ij}, F_{sj}, C_{ij}, C_{sj}, K_j, Y_j, U_j, p_j, w_j ($j = 1, 2$), r, and E.

10.2 The Dynamic Properties of the System

The system has 28 independent variables. Nevertheless, it contains only two-dimensional independent differential equations. We thus have to represent the dynamics in terms of two variables. In Appendix A.10.1, it is proved that the dynamics can be expressed in terms of $K_1(t)$ and $K_2(t)$.

Proposition 10.2.1.

The capital stocks, $K_1(t)$ and $K_2(t)$, owned by the two countries at any point of time are given by the following two dimensional dynamic system

$$\frac{dK_j}{dt} = s_j Y_j (K_1, K_2) - \delta_k K_j, \quad j = 1, 2 \tag{10.2.1}$$

where Y_j are functions only of K_1 and K_2 explicitly given in (10.A.1.12). All other variables in the system are uniquely determined as functions of $K_1(t)$ and $K_2(t)$ at any point of time by the following procedure: K_{ij} by (10.A.1.9) $\rightarrow$ K_{sj} by (10.A.1.4) $\rightarrow$ N_{ij} by (10.A.1.7) $\rightarrow$ N_{sj} by $N_{sj} = N_j - N_{ij} \rightarrow E$ by (10.A.1.5) $\rightarrow$ F_{ij} by (10.1.1) $\rightarrow$ F_{sj} by (10.1.2) $\rightarrow$ C_{sj} by (10.1.3) $\rightarrow r$, w_j and p_j by (10.1.4) $\rightarrow$ Y_j by (10.1.7) $\rightarrow$ C_{ij} by (10.1.9) $\rightarrow$ U_j by (10.1.6).

The above proposition is proved in Appendix A.10.1. The equations (10.2.1) determine the motion of $K_1(t)$ and $K_2(t)$. As all other variables are uniquely determined as functions of $K_1(t)$ and $K_2(t)$ at any point of time, it is sufficient to examine the dynamic properties of (10.2.1). It should be remarked that the values of variables so far are referred to their time-dependent values. In what follows, we refer variables to their equilibrium values.

Equilibrium of (10.2.1) is defined as a solution of

$$s_j Y_j = \delta_k K_j, \quad j = 1, 2. \tag{10.2.2}$$

It can be proved that (10.2.2) have solutions.

Proposition 10.2.2.

The dynamic system has equilibria. In particular, if $\alpha_0 + \alpha_1 \geq \alpha$, the system has a unique equilibrium. An equilibrium is stable (unstable) if $\Delta_2 \geq (<) 0$. Here, $\alpha_0 (> 0)$ and Δ_2 are parameters defined in Appendix A.10.2.

We will not interpret the conditions in detail as the parameters α_0 and Δ_2 are too complicated. It is noted that if $\alpha_1 \geq \alpha$, the system has a unique equilibrium.

Assumption 10.2.1.

We assume that $\alpha_0 + \alpha_1 \geq \alpha$ be held in the remainder of this chapter.

Under this assumption, the system has a unique equilibrium. From the discussion in Appendix A.10.2, it can be seen that when the above assumption is not satisfied, the system may have either a unique or multiple equilibria.

We now examine the direction of trade. From (10.A.1.5) and (10.A.1.9) in Appendix A.10.1, we have E as follows

$$E = (1 - \Lambda_0\Lambda)a_1 n_{12} K_2 \tag{10.2.3}$$

where

$$a_1 n_{12} K_2 > 0, \quad \Lambda \equiv \frac{K_1}{K_2}, \quad \Lambda_0 \equiv$$

$$\frac{1 - c_1\gamma_1 - g_{01}n_{11}}{g_{01}n_{12}} = \left(\frac{1 - c_1\gamma_1 + g_{01}c_1\gamma_1\alpha\beta_1/\beta}{1 - c_2\gamma_2 + g_{02}c_2\gamma_2\alpha\beta_2/\beta}\right)\frac{a_1 g_{02} N_2}{a_2 g_{01} z N_1} > 0,$$

$$a_j \equiv \frac{1}{1 - \beta_j c_j\gamma_j}, \quad g_{0j} \equiv 1 - c_j\gamma_j + \frac{a_j c_j\gamma_j}{\alpha} \tag{10.2.4}$$

and n_{jk} are defined in (10.A.1.10). The direction of trade is determined by $1 - \Lambda_0\Lambda$. If $\Lambda_0\Lambda > (<) 1$, $E < (>) 0$. The ratio Λ is uniquely determined by the equation, $\Phi(\Lambda) = 1$, in (10.A.2.1). From the definitions of Λ_0 and $\Phi(\Lambda)$, we see that it is not easy to generally determine whether $\Lambda_0\Lambda > 1$ or $\Lambda_0\Lambda < 1$. We now examine some special cases.

Under Assumption 10.2.1, $\Phi(\Lambda) = 1$ has a unique solution for $0 < \Lambda < \infty$ since $\Phi(0) - 1 > 0$ and $\Phi(\infty) - 1 < 0$. Moreover, the unique solution of $\Phi(\Lambda) = 1$ must be located in the interval $\Lambda \in (0, z)$ ($\Lambda \in (z, \infty)$) if $\Phi(z) - 1 < 0$ ($\Phi(z) - 1 > 0$).

From (10.A.2.2), we have

$$\Phi(z) = \left(\frac{1 - \alpha/g_2 a_2}{1 - \alpha z/g_1 a_1}\right)^\beta \left(\frac{g_1}{g_2}\right)^\alpha \frac{s_0}{z} \tag{10.2.5}$$

where

$$g_1 \equiv z\beta n_{11} + \beta n_{12} + \alpha > 0, \quad g_2 \equiv z\beta n_{21} + \beta n_{22} + \alpha > 0,$$

$$S_0 \equiv \left(\frac{zN_1}{N_2}\right)^\beta \left(\frac{a_1}{a_2}\right)^\alpha \frac{s_1}{s_2}.$$

From the definitions of n_{jk}, it can be shown that

$$\frac{g_1}{z} = \frac{-c_1\gamma_1}{g_{01}N_2}\beta znN_1 + \alpha\left(1 - \frac{\beta_1 c_1\gamma_1 g_{02}n}{g_{01}}\right)$$

$$+ \left(1 - c_2\gamma_2 + \frac{g_{02}c_2\gamma_2\alpha\beta_2}{\beta}\right)\frac{\beta a_2 nN_1}{a_1 g_{01}N_2},$$

$$g_2 = \left(\frac{1 - c_1\gamma_1}{g_{01}} + \frac{\alpha c_1\gamma_1\beta_1}{\beta}\right)\frac{a_1 nz\beta}{a_2} + \frac{1 - c_2\gamma_2}{g_{01}}\beta n$$

$$+ \alpha - \frac{\alpha c_2\gamma_2\beta_2 nzN_1}{N_2}. \tag{10.2.6}$$

The conditions are still too complicated. For analytical simplicity, we make the following assumption.

Assumption 10.2.2.
We assume: $N_1 = N_2$, $\alpha_1 = \alpha_2$ and $c_1\gamma_1 = c_2\gamma_2$.

The assumption means that the two countries have identical population (i.e., $N_1 = N_2$) and identical production function of the service sectors (i.e., $\alpha_1 = \alpha_2$). If country 1's savings rate is higher (lower) than that of country 2 (i.e., $s_1 > s_2$ ($s_1 < s_2$)), then country 1's propensity to consume services is higher (lower) than country 2 (i.e., $\gamma_1 > \gamma_2$ ($\gamma_1 < \gamma_2$)). Under this assumption, we have

$$a_1 = a_2, \ g_{01} = g_{02}, \ n = \frac{1}{1+z}.$$

From (10.2.6), we have

$$\Lambda_0 = \frac{1}{z}, \ \Phi(z) = \frac{s_1}{s_2} \tag{10.2.7}$$

where we use

$$\frac{g_1}{g_2} = z, \quad g_2 = \frac{1-c_1\gamma_1}{g_{01}}\beta + \alpha$$

which are obtained under Assumption 10.2.2. We see that if $s_1 \geq s_2$ ($s_1 < s_2$), the equilibrium value Λ of the ratio is not lower (lower) than the working time index z, i.e., $\Lambda \geq z$ ($\Lambda < z$). We thus have the following proposition.

Proposition 10.2.3.
Under Assumptions 10.2.1 and 10.2.2, we have the following results: Case I: if $s_1 > s_2$, then $K_1 / K_2 > z$ and $E < 0$; Case II: if $s_1 < s_2$, then $K_1 / K_2 < z$ and $E > 0$; and Case III: if $s_1 = s_2$, then $K_1 / K_2 = z$ and $E = 0$.

It is easy to interpret the above proposition. For instance, Case I simply states that if country 1's propensity to save is higher than that of country 2, then country 2 will utilize some of country 1's capital and the ratio of country 1's and country 2's capital stocks is larger than the working time difference.

In the remainder of this chapter, we will examine effects of changes in some parameters on the system. Assumptions 10.2.1 and 10.2.2 are accepted in the remainder of this chapter. It should be remarked that under Assumption 10.2.2, we have

$$\alpha_0 = \frac{1}{(1 + z)(1 - s_1)\gamma_1}.$$

Accordingly, Assumption 10.2.1 is given by

$$\frac{1}{\gamma_1(1 + z)(1 - s_1).} + \alpha_1 \geq \alpha$$

which is generally acceptable. As we have already explicitly solved the equilibrium problem, we can easily carry out comparative statics analysis under any meaningful combinations of the parameters. But we are only concerned with the above special cases as it is much more difficult to explicitly interpret analytical conclusions in other cases.

10.3 The Savings Rates and the World Economy

This section is concerned with the impact of changes in country 1's savings rate on the world economy. To keep the assumption, $c_1\gamma_1 = c_2\gamma_2$, satisfied, some other parameter (or parameters) in the equation have to be changed when s_1 is shifted. We assume that country 2's preference is fixed, i.e., s_2 and γ_2 being fixed. This implies: $d(c_1\gamma_1) = 0$, or

$$\frac{d\gamma_1}{ds_1} = \frac{\gamma_1}{c_1} \tag{10.3.1}$$

where we use $c_1 = 1 - s_1$. An increase in country 1's savings rate is associated with an increase in the country's propensity to consume services. By $\gamma_1 + \xi_1 = 1$, we have

$$\frac{d\xi_1}{d\gamma_1} = \frac{1 - \xi_1}{1 - \gamma_1}.$$

In the case that country 1's savings rate is increased, then the propensity to consume goods is decreased.

Taking derivatives of (10.A.2.2) with respect to s_1 yields

$$\Phi^* \frac{d\Lambda}{ds_1} = \frac{1}{s_1} > 0 \tag{10.3.2}$$

where Φ^* is a positive number (under Assumption 10.2.1) defined in (10.A.2.4). An increase in country 1's savings rate increases the ratio of capital stocks owned by the two countries. It should be remarked that we will not interpret the above equation in detail as this requires to follow how all the equations in the system are affected by a shift in country 1's savings rate.

From (10.A.2.7) and (10.3.2), we obtain the impact on the two countries' capital stocks as follows

$$\frac{\beta}{K_2}\frac{dK_2}{ds_1} = \frac{1}{s_1} + \left\{ \beta n_{11} + \alpha + \frac{(1 - \beta_1 c_1 \gamma_1)\beta^2 n_{12}}{\Phi_{12}} \right\} \frac{\alpha}{\Phi_{11}}\frac{d\Lambda}{ds_1} > 0,$$

$$\frac{1}{K_1}\frac{dK_1}{ds_1} = \frac{1}{K_2}\frac{dK_2}{ds_1} + \frac{1}{\Lambda}\frac{d\Lambda}{ds_1} > 0 \tag{10.3.3}$$

where Φ_{jk} are positive parameters defined in (10.A.2.2). In (10.3.3), we use (10.A.1.10) and (10.A.2.3) to judge the sign of dK_2 / ds_1. We see that in Case I (II), both countries' capital stocks are increased as country 1's savings rate is increased.

From $Y_j = \delta_k K_j / s_j$ and (10.3.3), we have

$$\frac{1}{Y_1}\frac{dY_1}{ds_1} = \frac{1}{K_2}\frac{dK_2}{ds_1} + \frac{1}{\Lambda}\frac{d\Lambda}{ds_1} - \frac{1}{s_1} > 0, \quad \frac{1}{Y_2}\frac{dY_2}{ds_1} = \frac{1}{K_2}\frac{dK_2}{ds_1} > 0.$$

(10.3.4)

The two countries' incomes are increased. We also directly have

$$\frac{Y_2}{Y_1}\frac{d(Y_1 / Y_2)}{ds_1} = \frac{1}{\Lambda}\frac{d\Lambda}{ds_1} - \frac{1}{s_1} > 0.$$

(10.3.5)

Country 1's income is increased more than country 2's income. Taking derivatives of (10.2.3) with respect to s_1 yields

$$\frac{1}{E}\frac{dE}{ds_1} = \frac{1}{K_2}\frac{dK_2}{ds_1} + \frac{1}{z - \Lambda}\frac{d\Lambda}{ds_1}.$$

(10.3.6)

In Case II in Proposition 10.2.3, as $E > 0$ and $z > \Lambda$, we have

$$\frac{dE}{ds_1} > 0.$$

As country 1's savings rate (and propensity to consume services) is increased, the trade gap E is expanded. From dK_2 / ds_1 in (10.3.3), we see that in Case I dE / ds_1 may be either positive or negative. Taking derivatives of (10.A.1.9), we obtain

$$\frac{1}{K_{i1}}\frac{dK_{i1}}{ds_1} = n_{11}\frac{dK_1}{ds_1} + n_{12}\frac{dK_2}{ds_1},$$

$$\frac{dK_{i2}}{ds_1} = (n_{22} + \Lambda)\frac{dK_2}{ds_1} + \frac{K_1}{\Lambda}\frac{d\Lambda}{ds_1}$$

(10.3.7)

in which n_{11} and n_{22} may be either positive or negative. If $n_{jj} \geq 0$, then $dK_{ij} / ds_1 > 0$. In the case of $n_{jj} < 0$, it is difficult to explicitly judge the sign of dK_{ij} / ds_1. Substituting (10.A.1.9) into (10.A.1.4) and then taking derivatives of the two equations with respect to s_1, we have

$$\frac{\beta K_{i1} + \alpha K_1}{K_{s1}} \frac{dK_{s1}}{ds_1} = (\alpha + \beta n_{11}) \frac{dK_1}{ds_1} + \beta n_{12} \frac{dK_2}{ds_1} > 0,$$

$$\frac{\beta K_{i2} + \alpha K_2}{K_{s2}} \frac{dK_{s2}}{ds_1} = \beta n_{21} \frac{dK_1}{ds_1} + (\alpha + \beta n_{22}) \frac{dK_2}{ds_1} > 0 \qquad (10.3.8)$$

where we use (10.A.1.10) and (10.A.2.3) to judge the signs. An increase in country 1's savings rate enlarges the capital stocks employed by the service sectors in the two countries.

From (10.A.1.7) we have

$$\frac{1}{N_{ij}} = \frac{\beta + \alpha \beta_1 c_1 \gamma_1 K_j / K_{ij}}{\beta N_1} a_1.$$

From this equation and (10.A.1.9), we obtain

$$\frac{dN_{i1}}{ds_1} = -\frac{\alpha \beta_1 c_1 \gamma_1 a_1 n_{12} N_{i1}^2}{(n_{11}\Lambda + n_{12})^2 \beta N_1} \frac{d\Lambda}{ds_1} < 0,$$

$$\frac{dN_{i2}}{ds_1} = \frac{\alpha \beta_1 c_1 \gamma_1 a_1 n_{21} N_{i2}^2}{(n_{21}\Lambda + n_{22})^2 \beta N_1} \frac{d\Lambda}{ds_1} > 0. \qquad (10.3.9)$$

As labor force is fixed and is fully employed within each country and there is no migration, from (10.3.9) we directly have

$$\frac{dN_{s1}}{ds_1} > 0, \quad \frac{dN_{s2}}{ds_1} < 0.$$

The employment of country 1's industrial (service) sector is reduced (increased); the employment of country 2's industrial (service) sector is expanded (reduced).

Taking derivatives of (10.1.1) and (10.1.2) with respect to F_{ij} and F_{sj} yields

$$\frac{1}{F_{ij}}\frac{dF_{ij}}{ds_1} = \frac{\alpha}{K_{ij}}\frac{dK_{ij}}{ds_1} + \frac{\beta}{N_{ij}}\frac{dN_{ij}}{ds_1},$$

$$\frac{1}{F_{sj}}\frac{dF_{sj}}{ds_1} = \frac{\alpha_1}{K_{sj}}\frac{dK_{sj}}{ds_1} + \frac{\beta_1}{N_{sj}}\frac{dN_{sj}}{ds_1}. \tag{10.3.10}$$

Country 1's service output is increased; but the output in the other sectors may be either increased or reduced. As $F_{sj} = C_{sj}$, we see that country 1's consumption level of services is increased, but country 2's may be either increased or decreased. From (10.1.9), we obtain

$$\frac{1}{C_{i1}}\frac{dC_{i1}}{ds_1} = \frac{1}{\Lambda}\frac{d\Lambda}{ds_1} + \frac{1}{K_2}\frac{dK_2}{ds_1} - \frac{1}{c_1 s_1}, \qquad \frac{1}{C_{i2}}\frac{dC_{i2}}{ds_1} = \frac{1}{Y_2}\frac{dY_2}{ds_1} > 0. \tag{10.3.11}$$

Country 2's consumption level of the commodity is increased. From (10.3.3) and the first equation in (10.3.11), we see that if $c_2 \geq \beta$, country 1's consumption level of the commodity is increased. In the case $c_2 < \beta$, dC_{i1}/ds_1 may be either positive or negative.

From $r = \alpha F_{ij}/K_{ij}$, $w_j = \beta F_{ij}/N_{ij}$ and (10.1.4), the effects on the wage rates and the rate of interest are given by

$$\frac{w_{01}}{\beta r}\frac{dr}{ds_1} = -\frac{w_{01}}{\alpha w_1}\frac{dw_1}{ds_1} = -(\beta n_{11} + \alpha\beta_1 c_1\gamma_1)\frac{dK_1}{ds_1} - \beta n_{12})\frac{dK_2}{ds_1} < 0,$$

$$\frac{w_{02}}{\alpha w_2}\frac{dw_2}{ds_1} = (\beta n_{22} + \alpha\beta_2 c_2\gamma_2)\frac{dK_2}{ds_1} + \beta n_{21}\frac{dK_1}{ds_1} > 0 \tag{10.3.12}$$

where $w_{0j} \equiv \beta K_{ij} + \alpha\beta_j c_j\gamma_j K_j > 0$. The rate of interest is reduced and the wage rates of the two countries are increased. From (10.1.9), (10.1.3) and $Y_j = \delta_k K_j/s_j$, we obtain

$$p_j = \frac{\delta_k c_j\gamma_j K_j}{s_j F_{sj}}.$$

Taking derivatives of these equations with respect to s_1 yields

$$\frac{1}{p_1}\frac{dp_1}{ds_1} = -\frac{1}{s_1} + \frac{1}{K_1}\frac{dK_1}{ds_1} - \frac{1}{F_{s1}}\frac{dF_{s1}}{ds_1},$$

$$\frac{1}{p_2}\frac{dp_2}{ds_1} = \frac{1}{K_2}\frac{dK_2}{ds_1} - \frac{1}{F_{s2}}\frac{dF_{s2}}{ds_1}. \qquad (10.3.13)$$

It is not easy to explicitly determine the signs of dp_j / ds_1.

It is not difficult to obtain effects of changes in s_1 on the ratios, C_{i1}/C_{i2}, C_{s1}/C_{s2}, F_{i1}/F_{i2}, F_{s1}/F_{s2}, w_1/w_2, and p_1/p_2. As it is not easy to explicitly judge the results, we omit further examination.

Appendix

A.10.1 Proving Proposition 10.2.1

First, from (10.1.4) we obtain

$$\frac{K_{sj}}{K_{ij}} = \frac{\beta\alpha_j N_{sj}}{\alpha\beta_j N_{ij}}, \quad \frac{F_{i1}}{K_{i1}} = \frac{F_{i2}}{K_{i2}}, \quad \frac{\alpha_1 p_1 F_{s1}}{K_{s1}} = \frac{\alpha_2 p_2 F_{s2}}{K_{s2}} \qquad (10.A.1.1)$$

which are held at any point of time.

From (10.1.4) and (10.1.7), we have

$$Y_j = \left(\frac{\alpha K_j}{K_{ij}} + \frac{\beta N_j}{N_{ij}}\right) F_{ij}. \qquad (10.A.1.2)$$

Using $N_j = N_{ij} + N_{sj}$, $N_{ij}/N_{sj} = \beta\alpha_j K_{ij}/\alpha\beta_j K_{sj}$ and (10.A.1.2), we obtain

$$Y_j = \left(\beta K_{ij} + \alpha K_j + \frac{\alpha\beta_j K_{sj}}{\alpha_j}\right)\frac{F_{ij}}{K_{ij}}. \qquad (10.A.1.3)$$

Substituting $p_j F_{sj} = \gamma_j c_j Y_j$ and (10.A.1.3) into $\alpha F_{ij}/K_{ij} = \alpha_j p_j F_{sj}/K_{sj}$ in (10.1.4) yields

$$K_{sj} = \frac{\beta K_{ij} + \alpha K_j}{\alpha} \alpha_j \gamma_j c_j a_j, \quad j = 1, 2 \qquad (10.A.1.4)$$

where $a_j \equiv 1 / (1 - \gamma_j c_j \beta_j)$. Substituting (10.A.1.4) into (10.1.5), we obtain

$$g_{01} a_1 K_{i1} = (1 - \gamma_1 c_1) a_1 K_1 + E,$$
$$g_{02} a_2 K_{i2} = (1 - \gamma_2 c_2) a_2 K_2 - E \qquad (10.A.1.5)$$

where

$$g_{0j} \equiv 1 - \gamma_j c_j - \frac{\gamma_j c_j a_j}{\alpha} > 0.$$

Adding the two equations in (10.A.1.5) yields

$$g_{01} a_1 K_{i1} = (1 - \gamma_1 c_1) a_1 K_1 - g_{02} a_2 K_{i2} + (1 - \gamma_2 c_2) a_2 K_2. \quad (10.A.1.6)$$

Substituting (10.A.1.4) and $N_j = N_{ij} + N_{sj}$ into

$$\frac{N_{ij}}{N_{sj}} = \frac{\beta \alpha_j K_{ij}}{\alpha \beta_j K_{sj}}$$

in (10.A.1.1), we obtain

$$\frac{N_{ij}}{K_{ij}} = \frac{\beta N_j}{(\beta K_{ij} + \alpha \beta_j c_j \gamma_j K_j) a_j}. \qquad (10.A.1.7)$$

Substituting (10.A.1.7) into $F_{i1} / K_{i1} = F_{i2} / K_{i2}$ in (10.A.1.1) yields

$$\beta a_1 K_{i1} + \alpha a_1 \beta_1 c_1 \gamma_1 K_1 = (\beta K_{i2} + \alpha \beta_2 c_2 \gamma_2 K_2) \frac{z a_2 N_1}{N_2}.$$

$$(10.A.1.8)$$

Substituting (10.A.1.6) into (10.A.1.8), we have

$$K_{ij} = n_{j1} K_1 + n_{j2} K_2 \qquad (10.A.1.9)$$

in which

$$n_{11} \equiv \left((1 - c_1 \gamma_1) \frac{zN_1}{N_2} - \frac{\alpha \beta_1 c_1 \gamma_1 g_{02}}{\beta} \right) \frac{n}{g_{01}},$$

$$n_{12} \equiv \left(1 - c_2 \gamma_2 + \frac{\alpha \beta_2 c_2 \gamma_2 g_{02}}{\beta} \right) \frac{a_2 z n N_1}{a_1 g_{01} N_2} > 0,$$

$$n_{21} \equiv \left(\frac{1 - c_1 \gamma_1}{g_{01}} + \frac{\alpha \beta_1 c_1 \gamma_1}{\beta} \right) \frac{a_1 n}{a_2} > 0,$$

$$n_{22} \equiv \frac{1 - c_2 \gamma_2}{g_{01}} n - \frac{\alpha \beta_2 c_2 \gamma_2 z n N_1}{\beta N_2}, \quad n \equiv \frac{1}{z N_1 / N_2 + g_{02} / g_{01}}.$$

$$\text{(10.A.1.10)}$$

It is important to note that n_{11} and n_{22} may be either positive or negative, and n_{12} and n_{21} are positive. This implies that an increase in capital stocks owned by country j will always increase the capital stocks employed by the other country's industrial sector but may either increase or decrease the capital stocks employed by country j's industrial sector.

For any given positive $K_1(t)$ and $K_2(t)$ at any point of time, $K_{i1}(t)$ and $K_{i2}(t)$ are uniquely determined by (10.A.1.9). It is easy to show that we can thus express all the variables in the system as unique functions of $K_1(t)$ and $K_2(t)$ at any point of time by the procedure given in Proposition 10.2.1.

We now explicitly express $Y_j(t)$, $j = 1, 2$, as functions of K_1 and K_2. From $p_j F_{sj} = \gamma_j c_j Y_j$ and $\alpha F_{ij} / K_{ij} = \alpha_j p_j F_{sj} / K_{sj}$, we have

$$Y_j = \frac{\alpha K_{sj} F_{ij}}{a_j \gamma_j c_j K_{ij}}.$$

Substituting K_{sj} in (10.A.1.4) into the above equation yields

$$Y_j = (\beta K_{ij} + \alpha K_j) \frac{a_j F_{ij}}{K_{ij}}. \qquad \text{(10.A.1.11)}$$

Using (10.1.1), (10.A.1.7), (10.A.1.9) and (10.A.1.11), we obtain $Y_j(K_1, K_2)$ as follows

$$Y_1(K_1, K_2) = \frac{a_1^\alpha (z\beta N_1)^\beta (\beta K_{i1} + \alpha K_1)}{(\beta K_{i1} + \alpha \beta_1 c_1 \gamma_1 K_1)^\beta},$$

$$Y_2(K_1, K_2) = \frac{a_2^\alpha (\beta N_2)^\beta (\beta K_{i2} + \alpha K_2)}{(\beta K_{i2} + \alpha \beta_2 c_2 \gamma_2 K_2)^\beta} \tag{10.A.1.12}$$

in which K_{ij} are functions of K_1 and K_2 defined in (10.A.1.9). From (10.1.10), we see that the dynamics are described by (10.2.1).

Appendix A.10.2 Proving Proposition 10.2.2

Dividing the two equations in (10.A.1.2), we have $s_1 Y_1 / s_2 Y_2 = K_1 / K_2$. Substituting (10.A.1.9) and (10.A.1.12) into this equation yields

$$\Phi(\Lambda) - 1 = 0 \tag{10.A.2.1}$$

where

$$\Phi(\Lambda) \equiv \frac{s_0 \Phi_{11} \Phi_{21}^\beta}{\Lambda \Phi_{22} \Phi_{12}^\beta}, \quad \Phi_{11} \equiv \beta n_{11} \Lambda + \alpha \Lambda + \beta n_{12},$$

$$\Phi_{12} \equiv \beta n_{11} \Lambda + \beta_1 \alpha c_1 \gamma_1 \Lambda + \beta n_{12},$$

$$\Phi_{21} \equiv \beta n_{21} \Lambda + \beta_2 \alpha c_2 \gamma_2 + \beta n_{22}, \quad \Phi_{22} \equiv \beta n_{21} \Lambda + \alpha + \beta n_{22}. \tag{10.A.2.2}$$

The equation (10.A.2.1) is only dependent on the ratio Λ of the capital stocks owned by the two countries. We now show that the equation, $\Phi(\Lambda) = 1$, $0 < \Lambda < \infty$, has at least one positive solution. First, we notice that n_{12} and n_{21} are positive but n_{11} and n_{22} may be either positive or negative. But from the definitions of n_{11} and n_{22} it is easy to check

$$\beta n_{11} + \alpha = (1 - c_1 \gamma_1) \frac{\beta n z N_1}{g_{01} N_2} + \left(1 - \frac{\beta_1 c_1 \gamma_1 n g_{02}}{g_{01}}\right) \alpha > 0,$$

$$\beta n_{11} + \alpha \beta_1 c_1 \gamma_1 = (1 - c_1 \gamma_1) \frac{\beta n z N_1}{g_{01} N_2} + \left(1 - \frac{n g_{02}}{g_{01}}\right) \alpha \beta_1 c_1 \gamma_1 > 0,$$

$$\beta n_{22} + \alpha = (1 - c_2\gamma_2)\frac{\beta n}{g_{01}} + \left(1 - \frac{\beta_2 c_2\gamma_2 nzN_1}{N_2}\right)\alpha > 0,$$

$$\beta n_{22} + \alpha\beta_2 c_2\gamma_2 = (1 - c_2\gamma_2)\frac{\beta n}{g_{01}} + \left(1 - \frac{nzN_1}{N_2}\right)\alpha\beta_2 c_2\gamma_2 > 0$$

$$\tag{10.A.2.3}$$

where we use

$$1 > c_j\gamma_j, \quad ng_{02} < g_{01}, \quad \frac{nzN_1}{N_2} < 1.$$

Using (10.A.2.3), we see that $\Phi_{jk}(\Lambda)$ are positive for any $\Lambda \geq 0$. We obtain

$$\Phi(0) - 1 > 0, \quad \Phi(\infty) - 1 < 0.$$

This implies that the equation, $\Phi(\Lambda) = 1$, $0 < \Lambda < \infty$, has at least one positive solution. Taking derivatives of $\Phi(\Lambda)$ with respect to Λ, we have

$$\Phi^* \equiv -\frac{1}{\Lambda}\frac{d\Phi}{d\Lambda} = \Phi_1 + \Phi_2 + \frac{\beta n_{21}}{\beta n_{21}\Lambda + \beta n_{22} + \alpha} \tag{10.A.2.4}$$

where

$$\Phi_1 \equiv \{\beta n_{12} + (\beta - b_1 c_1\gamma_1 - \beta n_{11})\Lambda\}\frac{\alpha\beta n_{12}}{\Phi_{12}\Phi_{11}\Lambda},$$

$$\Phi_2 \equiv \frac{\Lambda}{\beta} - \frac{\beta^2 n_{21}}{\Phi_{21}}. \tag{10.A.2.5}$$

If Φ^* is positive for any positive Λ, then $\Phi(\Lambda) = 1$ has a unique solution. As $\beta n_{21} / (\beta n_{21}\Lambda + \beta n_{22} + \alpha)$ is positive and $\Phi_2 > 0$, we see that if $\Phi_1 > 0$, Φ^* is positive. The sign of Φ_1 $(0 < \Lambda < \infty)$ is the same as that of $\beta n_{12} + (\beta - b_1 c_1\gamma_1 - \beta n_{11})\Lambda$, where $n_{12} > 0$. If the term

$$\beta - b_1 c_1\gamma_1 - \beta n_{11} = \frac{(\alpha_0 + \alpha_1 - \alpha)(1 - \beta_1 c_1\gamma_1)}{g_{01}}c_1\gamma_1 \tag{10.A.2.6}$$

where $\alpha_0 \equiv g_{02} n / c_1 \gamma_1 g_{01} > 0$ is positive, then $\Phi_1 > 0$. From (10.A.2.6), we see that $\Phi_1 > 0$, in the case of $\alpha_0 + \alpha_1 > \alpha$. In particular, $\Phi_1 > 0$ in the case of $\alpha_1 > \alpha$. It should be remarked that when $\alpha_0 + \alpha_1 > \alpha$ is not held, Φ^* may be either positive or negative. We have thus shown that if $\alpha_0 + \alpha_1 > \alpha$, then $\Phi(\Lambda) = 1$ has a unique positive solution.

As all the other variables can be expressed as functions of K_1 and K_2, the equilibrium of the system is determined if we can express K_1 and K_2 as functions of Λ. Substituting Y_1 in (10.A.1.12) into $Y_1 = \delta_k K_1 / s_1$ in (10.2.2), we determine K_1 and K_2 as functions of Λ as follows

$$
K_2 = a_1^{\alpha/\beta} \beta N_1 \frac{\Phi_{11}^{1/\beta}}{\Phi_{12}} \left(\frac{s_1}{\delta_k} \right)^{1/\beta} , \quad K_1 = \Lambda K_2 . \tag{10.A.2.7}
$$

It has thus been proved that the system has equilibria. In particular, if $\alpha_0 + \alpha_1 > \alpha$, the system has a unique equilibrium. We now provide stability conditions.

The Jacobian at equilibrium is given as follows

$$
J = \begin{bmatrix} s_1 \dfrac{\partial Y_1}{\partial K_1} - \delta_k & s_1 \dfrac{\partial Y_1}{\partial K_2} \\ s_2 \dfrac{\partial Y_2}{\partial K_1} & s_2 \dfrac{\partial Y_2}{\partial K_2} - \delta_k \end{bmatrix} \tag{10.A.2.8}
$$

where

$$
\frac{1}{Y_1} \frac{\partial Y_1}{\partial K_1} = \frac{\beta n_{11} + \alpha}{\beta K_{i1} + \alpha K_1} - \frac{\beta n_{11} + \alpha \beta_1 c_1 \gamma_1}{\beta K_{i1} + \alpha \beta_1 c_1 \gamma_1 K_1} \beta,
$$

$$
\frac{1}{Y_1} \frac{\partial Y_1}{\partial K_2} = - \frac{(1 - \beta_1 c_1 \gamma_1) \alpha \beta n_{12} K_1}{(\beta K_{i1} + \alpha \beta_1 c_1 \gamma_1 K_1)(\beta K_{i1} + \alpha K_1)} < 0,
$$

$$
\frac{1}{Y_2} \frac{\partial Y_2}{\partial K_2} = \frac{\beta n_{22} + \alpha}{\beta K_{i2} + \alpha K_2} - \frac{\beta n_{22} + \alpha \beta_2 c_2 \gamma_2}{\beta K_{i2} + \alpha \beta_2 c_2 \gamma_2 K_2} \beta,
$$

$$
\frac{1}{Y_2} \frac{\partial Y_2}{\partial K_1} = - \frac{(1 - \beta_2 c_2 \gamma_2) \alpha \beta n_{21} K_2}{(\beta K_{i2} + \alpha \beta_2 c_2 \gamma_2 K_2)(\beta K_{i2} + \alpha K_2)} < 0. \tag{10.A.2.9}
$$

We know that if

$$\Delta_1 = s_1 \frac{\partial Y_1}{\partial K_1} + s_2 \frac{\partial Y_2}{\partial K_2} - 2\delta_k < 0,$$

$$\Delta_2 = \left(s_1 \frac{\partial Y_1}{\partial K_1} - \delta_k \right) \left(s_2 \frac{\partial Y_2}{\partial K_2} - \delta_k \right) - s_1 s_2 \frac{\partial Y_2}{\partial K_1} \frac{\partial Y_1}{\partial K_2} > 0 \qquad (10.A.2.10)$$

then the equilibrium is stable. Substituting $\partial Y_1 / \partial K_1$ and $\partial Y_2 / \partial K_2$ in (10.A.2.9) into Δ_1 in (10.A.2.10), we obtain

$$\frac{\Delta_1}{\delta_k} = -\frac{\beta n_{12} K_2}{\beta K_{i1} + \alpha K_1} - \frac{\beta n_{11} + \alpha \beta_1 c_1 \gamma_1}{\beta K_{i1} + \alpha \beta_1 c_1 \gamma_1 K_1} \beta K_1 - \frac{\beta n_{21} K_1}{\beta K_{i2} + \alpha K_2}$$

$$- \frac{\beta n_{22} + \alpha \beta_2 c_2 \gamma_2}{\beta K_{i2} + \alpha \beta_2 c_2 \gamma_2 K_2} \beta K_2 < 0 \qquad (10.A.2.11)$$

where we use $s_j Y_j = \delta_k K_j$ and (10.A.2.3). The stability is determined by the sign of Δ_2. But it is not easy to explicitly determine the sign of Δ_2 as the expression is too complicated.

11 A Multi-Sector Trade Model with Endogenous Knowledge

The previous chapter proposed a trade model with economic structure and endogenous capital. We treated human capital as exogenous variables. This chapter is also concerned with trade and economic structures. We propose a dynamic two-country and multi-sector model with endogenous knowledge accumulation. The model describes a dynamic interdependence between knowledge utilization and creation, international division of labor, land rent and price structure over space under perfect competition. We examine how differences in knowledge utilization and creativity between the two countries may affect the economic geography. It is shown that the economic system may have either a unique or multiple equilibria and each equilibrium may be either stable or unstable, depending on the knowledge utilization and creativity of the production sectors in the two countries. We also examine effects of changes in some parameters on the economic geography.

The remainder of this chapter is organized as follows. Section 11.1 defines a two-country and multi-sector economic model with endogenous knowledge accumulation. Section 11.2 proves that the dynamic system may have either a unique or multiple equilibria. Section 11.3 examines the effects of changes in knowledge accumulation efficiency upon the equilibrium economic geography. Section 11.4 studies the impact of changes in preferences on trade patterns. Section 11.5 concludes the chapter. The appendix proves the main results of Section 11.2.

11.1 The Multi-Sector Model with Endogenous Knowledge

We consider that the world economy consists of two countries, indexed by 1 and 2, respectively. The system produces two commodities, indexed by 1 and 2, respectively. Each country is assumed to produce only one commodity. Each country has two production sectors, industry and service. Services are produced by combining knowledge, labor and land. Country j produces commodity j. It is assumed that each country's product is homogeneous. We assume a homogenous and fixed national labor force, N_j. We neglect any cost for migration and professional changes. We assume perfect competition in all markets. Each country has fixed land.

The land is distributed between the service sector and housing by perfect competition. We select commodity 1 to serve as numeraire, with all the other prices being measured relative to its price. For simplicity of analysis, we neglect transportation cost of commodities between and within countries. It can be shown that we may introduce transportation costs for commodities by taking Samuelson's "iceberg" form, in which transport costs are incurred in the good transported. It is noted that by adding transportation costs some of our results on geographical pattern formation may become stronger. As our model is already too complicated, we will accept zero transportation costs at this initial stage. The assumption of zero transportation cost of commodities implies price equality for any commodities between the two countries.

We introduce

i, s — subscript index for industry and services, respectively;

N_j and L_j — country j's fixed total population and territory size, $j = 1, 2$;

$F_{ij}(t)$ and $F_{sj}(t)$ — the output levels of country j's industrial and service sectors at time t, $j = 1, 2$;

$N_{ij}(t)$ and $N_{sj}(t)$ — the labor force employed by country j's industrial and the service sectors;

$L_{sj}(t)$ and $L_{hj}(t)$ (t) — the land size used by the service sector and for housing in country j;

$C_{kj}(t)$ — country j's consumption levels of commodity k, $j, k = 1, 2$;

$Z(t)$ — the knowledge stock of the global economy;

$p(t)$ and $p_j(t)$ — the price of commodity 2 and price of services in country j; and

$w_j(t)$ and $R_j(t)$ — country j's wage rate and land rent in country j.

Production sectors
First, we describe behavior of the production sectors in the system. We assume that service production is to combine knowledge, labor and land. We specify the production functions of the service sectors as follows

$$F_{sj} = Z^{m_{sj}} L_{sj}^{\alpha_j} N_{sj}^{\beta_j},$$
$$\alpha_j, \beta_j > 0, \quad \alpha_j + \beta_j = 1, \quad m_{sj} \geq 0, \quad j = 1, 2. \qquad (11.1.1)$$

The parameters m_{sj} describe knowledge utilization efficiency. We use m_{sj} to describe the knowledge utilization efficiency of country j's service sector. The marginal conditions of service production are given by

$$R_j = \frac{\alpha_j p_j F_{sj}}{L_{sj}}, \quad w_j = \frac{\beta_j p_j F_{sj}}{N_{sj}}, \quad j = 1, 2. \tag{11.1.2}$$

We specify the two countries' industrial production functions as follows

$$F_{ij} = Z^{m_{ij}} N_{ij}, \quad m_{ij} \geq 0, \quad j = 1, 2 \tag{11.1.3}$$

where m_{ij} are the knowledge utilization efficiency parameters of country j's industrial sector. The optimal conditions are given by

$$w_1 = Z^{m_{i1}}, \quad w_2 = pZ^{m_{i2}}, \quad j = 1, 2. \tag{11.1.4}$$

Consumers' behavior
We assume that a household's utility in a given country is dependent on his consumption levels of industrial commodities and housing conditions. We measure housing conditions by lot size (e.g., Alonso, 1964). The utility functions are specified as follows

$$U_j(t) = \frac{C_{sj}^{\gamma_j} C_{1j}^{\xi_{1j}} C_{2j}^{\xi_{2j}} L_{hj}^{\eta_j}}{N_j}, \quad \gamma_j, \xi_{1j}, \xi_{2j}, \eta_j > 0, \quad j = 1, 2 \tag{11.1.5}$$

in which $C_{sj}(t)$, $C_{1j}(t)$ and $C_{2j}(t)$ are respectively country j's consumption levels of services, commodity 1 and commodity 2 at time t.

Country j's income is given by

$$Y_j = w_j N_j + R_j L_j.$$

The consumer problem is defined by

$$\max U_j, \quad s.t.: p_j C_{sj} + C_{1j} + pC_{2j} + R_j L_{hj} = Y_j. \tag{11.1.6}$$

We have the following optimal solutions

$$C_{sj} = \frac{\gamma_j \rho_j p_j Y_j}{p_j}, \quad C_{1j} = \xi_{1j} \rho_j Y_j, \quad C_{2j} = \frac{\xi_{2j} \rho_j Y_j}{p},$$

$$L_{hj} = \frac{\eta_j \rho_j Y_j}{R_j}, \quad j = 1, 2 \tag{11.1.7}$$

where

$$\rho_j \equiv \frac{1}{\gamma_j + \xi_{1j} + \xi_{2j} + \eta_j}.$$

The balances of demand for and supply of commodities are given by

$$C_{j1} + C_{j2} = F_{ij}, \quad C_{sj} = F_{sj}, \quad j = 1, 2. \tag{11.1.8}$$

The trade balance condition is given

$$C_{12} = pC_{21}. \tag{11.1.9}$$

Full employment of labor and land
The assumption that labor force and land are fully employed is represented by

$$N_{ij}(t) + N_{sj}(t) = N_j, \quad L_{sj}(t) + L_{hj}(t) = L_j, \quad j = 1, 2. \tag{11.1.10}$$

Knowledge accumulation
We model knowledge accumulation as follows

$$\frac{dZ}{dt} = \sum_{j=1}^{2} \left(\frac{\tau_{sj} F_{sj}}{Z^{\varepsilon_{sj}}} + \frac{\tau_{ij} F_{ij}}{Z^{\varepsilon_{ij}}} \right) - \delta_z Z \tag{11.1.11}$$

in which δ_z is the fixed depreciation rate of knowledge, and τ_{sj} (≥ 0), τ_{ij} (≥ 0), ε_{sj} and ε_{ij}, $j = 1, 2$, are parameters. We take account of learning by doing effects in knowledge accumulation. As in Chapter 8, the term, $\tau_{i1} F_{i1} / Z^{\varepsilon_{i1}}$, for instance, implies that contribution of country 1's industrial sector to knowledge is positively related to its production scale, F_{i1}, and is dependent on the current level of knowledge stocks.

We have thus built the model. The system has 30 variables, N_{sj}, N_{ij}, L_{hj}, L_{sj}, F_{sj}, F_{ij}, C_{sj}, C_{1j}, C_{2j}, Y_j, U_j, w_j, p_j, R_j ($j = 1, 2$), p and Z. It contains the same number of independent equations. We now examine properties of the dynamic system.

11.2 Equilibria and Stability

This section is concerned with the conditions for existence of economic equilibria and stability. First, we show that for any given knowledge stock $Z(t)$ the division of labor and international trade patterns are uniquely determined at any point of time. The following proposition is proved in the appendix.

Proposition 11.2.1.

For any given level of knowledge $Z(t)$, all the other variables in the system are uniquely determined at any point of time. The values of the variables are given as functions of $Z(t)$ by the following procedure: N_{sj} and N_{ij} by (11.A.1.1) $\rightarrow L_{sj}$ and L_{ij} by (11.A.1.6) $\rightarrow p$ by (11.A.1.4) $\rightarrow w_j$, $j = 1, 2$, by (11.A.1.5) $\rightarrow F_{sj}$ by (11.1.1) $\rightarrow F_{ij}$ by (11.1.3) $\rightarrow p_j = w_j N_{sj} / \beta_j F_{sj}$ by (11.1.2) $\rightarrow R_j = \alpha_j p_j F_{sj} / L_{sj}$ by (11.1.3) $\rightarrow Y_j = w_j N_j + R_j L_j \rightarrow C_{sj}$, C_{1j}, and C_{2j} by (11.1.6) $\rightarrow U_j$ by (11.1.5).

The above proposition guarantees that if we can find knowledge $Z(t)$, we can explicitly solve all the other variables as functions of $Z(t)$ in the system at any point of time. Hence, to examine the dynamic properties of the system, it is sufficient to examine the dynamic properties of (11.1.11). From the above proposition, we know that we can explicitly express F_{ij} and F_{sj} as functions of Z. It is straightforward to show that substituting $F_{ij}(Z)$ and $F_{sj}(Z)$ into (11.1.11), we determine the knowledge accumulation dynamics $Z(t)$ as follows

$$\frac{dZ}{dt} = \sum_{j=1}^{2} \{\Phi_{sj}(Z) + \Phi_{ij}(Z)\}Z - \delta_z Z \tag{11.2.1}$$

where

$$\Phi_{sj} = \tau_{sj} L_{sj}^{\alpha_j} N_{sj}^{\beta_j} Z^{x_{sj}}, \quad \Phi_{ij} = \tau_{ij} N_{ij} Z^{x_{ij}}, \quad j = 1, 2 \tag{11.2.2}$$

in which

$$x_{sj} \equiv m_{sj} - \varepsilon_{sj} - 1, \quad x_{ij} \equiv m_{ij} - \varepsilon_{ij} - 1. \tag{11.2.3}$$

First, we notice that the dynamic properties of the system are basically determined by the combination of the parameters, x_{sj} and x_{ij}. It can be seen that these parameters may be either positive or negative. From $x_{i2} = m_{i2} - \varepsilon_{i2} - 1$, if country 2's industrial sector is effective in knowledge utilization (i.e., m_{i2} being large) and its contribution to knowledge exhibits increasing returns to scale (i.e., $\varepsilon_{i2} < 0$), then x_{i2} may be positive; if country 2's industrial sector is not effective in knowledge utilization and its contribution to knowledge exhibits decreasing returns to scale, then $x_{i2} < 0$. We can similarly discuss the other parameters. When $x_{ij} > (<) 0$, we say that country j's industrial sector exhibits increasing (decreasing) returns to scale in knowledge accumulation. Similarly, when $x_{sj} > (<) 0$, we say that country j's service sector exhibits increasing (decreasing) returns to scale in knowledge accumulation.

We can thus conclude that the parameters x_{ij} and x_{sj} may be either positive or negative, depending upon various combinations of knowledge utilization efficiency and creativity of different economic sectors in the two countries. The following proposition shows that the properties of our one-dimensional differential equation (11.2.1) are dependent on how these knowledge parameters are combined.

Proposition 11.2.2.

(i) If $x_{sj} > 0$, $x_{ij} > 0$, $j = 1, 2$, the system has a unique unstable equilibrium;

(ii) If $x_{ij} < 0$, $j = 1, 2$, the system has a unique stable equilibrium; and

(iii) In the remaining possible combinations of $x_{sj} < 0$ and $x_{ij} > 0$, the system has two equilibria - the one with higher value of knowledge is unstable and the other one is stable.

The above proposition is proved in the appendix. We interpreted the meanings of x_{sj} and x_{ij}. From these discussions we can directly interpret the conditions in the above proposition. The proposition implies that if the two countries exhibit increasing (decreasing) returns in knowledge accumulation, the system has a unstable (stable) unique equilibrium; if some sector(s) exhibits increasing returns in knowledge accumulation but the other(s) decreasing returns, the system has two equilibria.

In the remainder of this chapter, we will examine impact of changes in some parameters on the equilibrium structure of the economic geography.

11.3 The Impact of Knowledge Accumulation Efficiency

This section is concerned with the impact of changes in the knowledge accumulation efficiency parameters, τ_{sj} and τ_{ij}, $j = 1, 2$, of the industrial sector in country j on the system. Since the comparative static results will be similar for any of these parameters, it is sufficient to carry out the analysis with respect to, for instance, τ_{i1}.

Since we explicitly solved the equilibrium problem, it is straightforward to examine the impact of changes in any parameter. First, by (11.A.1.1) and (11.A.1.6), we see that a change in τ_{i1} have no impact on the land and labor distribution, N_{sj}, N_{ij}, L_{sj} and L_{ij}.

From (11.A.2.2) we get the impact of changes in τ_{i1} on Z as follows

$$- \Phi' \frac{dZ}{d\tau_{i1}} = \frac{\Phi_{i1}}{\tau_{i1}} > 0 \tag{11.3.1}$$

where $\Phi' = \sum_j (x_{sj}\Phi_{sj} + x_{ij}\Phi_{ij}) / Z$. The sign of Φ' may be either positive or negative, depending on the parameter values of x_{sj} and x_{ij}. It is easy to check that: (i) if $x_{is} > 0$ and $x_{ij} > 0$, $j = 1, 2$, $\Phi' > 0$ at the unique equilibrium; (ii) if $x_{sj} < 0$ and $x_{ij} < 0$, $j = 1, 2$, $\Phi' < 0$ at the unique equilibrium; (iii) in the remaining possible combinations of $x_{sj} <(>) 0$ and $x_{ij} > (<) 0$, $\Phi' > (<) 0$ at the equilibrium with the high (low) value of Z. We thus conclude that the sign of Φ' is dependent on whether each production sector exhibits increasing or decreasing returns. In case (i), we have $dZ / d\tau_{i1} < 0$. In case (ii), we have $dZ / d\tau_{i1} > 0$. In case (iii), we have $dZ / d\tau_{i1} <(>) 0$ at the equilibrium with high (low) values of Z. We see that an improvement in knowledge accumulation efficiency may either increase or decrease the equilibrium value of knowledge. For instance, in case (ii) which means that the four sectors exhibit decreasing returns, an improvement in knowledge accumulation efficiency of any country's production sector increases the equilibrium level of knowledge. In case (i), the impact in changes of knowledge accumulation efficiency is the opposite of that in the case of stability. We see that the effects of changes in the parameters on the system are significantly dependent upon the stability conditions. To explain how the new equilibrium given by (11.3.1) is achieved through a dynamic process, we have to examine all the relations connecting the 30 variables in the system. We omit the explanation of (11.3.1) in detail.

From (11.A.1.4) we directly have

$$\frac{1}{p}\frac{dp}{d\tau_{i1}} = \frac{m_i}{Z}\frac{dZ}{d\tau_{i1}}.$$ (11.3.2)

In case (i), we have: $dp / d\tau_{i1} > (<) 0$ if $m_{i1} < (>) m_{i2}$. In case (ii), the sign of $dp / d\tau_{i1}$ is the same as that of m_i. We see that the price of commodity may be either increased or decreasing depending on returns to scale as well as the difference of knowledge utilization efficiency between country 1's and country 2's industrial sectors. For instance, in the case that country 1's industrial sector utilizes knowledge more effectively than country 2's industrial sector, the price of commodity 2 will be reduced (increased) if the two countries' all sectors exhibit increasing (decreasing) returns to scale.

Taking derivatives of (11.A.1.5) with respect to τ_{i1} yields

$$\frac{1}{w_j}\frac{dw_j}{d\tau_{i1}} = \frac{m_{i1}}{Z}\frac{dZ}{d\tau_{i1}}.$$ (11.3.3)

The sign of $dw_j / d\tau_{i1}$ is the same as that of $dZ / d\tau_{i1}$. If knowledge is increased (reduced), then the two countries' wage rates are increased (reduced). By (11.1.1) and (11.1.3) we get

$$\frac{1}{F_{sj}}\frac{dF_{sj}}{d\tau_{i1}} = \frac{1}{C_{sj}}\frac{dC_{sj}}{d\tau_{i1}} = \frac{m_{sj}}{Z}\frac{dZ}{d\tau_{i1}}, \quad \frac{1}{F_{ij}}\frac{dF_{ij}}{d\tau_{i1}} = \frac{m_{ij}}{Z}\frac{dZ}{d\tau_{i1}}.$$ (11.3.4)

We see that the output levels of the production sectors are increased (decreased) when knowledge is increased (decreased). By (11.1.2), we have

$$\frac{1}{p_j}\frac{dp_j}{d\tau_{i1}} = \frac{m_{i1} - m_{sj}}{Z}\frac{dZ}{d\tau_{i1}}, \quad \frac{1}{R_j}\frac{dR_j}{d\tau_{i1}} = \frac{m_{i1}}{Z}\frac{dZ}{d\tau_{i1}}.$$ (11.3.5)

We see that country j's land rent is increased (reduced) as that knowledge is increased (reduced). In case (i), we have: $dp_j / d\tau_{i1} > (<) 0$ if $m_{i1} < (>) m_{sj}$. In case (ii), the sign of $dp_j / d\tau_{i1}$ is the same as that of $m_{j1} - m_{sj}$. We see that the price of each country's services may be either increased or decreasing depending on returns to scale as well as the difference of knowledge utilization efficiency between country 1's industrial sector and country j's industrial sector.

By $Y_j = L_{hj} R_j / \eta_j \rho_j$ in (11.1.7), we directly get

$$\frac{1}{Y_j} \frac{dY_j}{d\tau_{i1}} = \frac{m_{i1}}{Z} \frac{dZ}{d\tau_{i1}}. \tag{11.3.6}$$

By $C_{1j} = \xi_{1j} \rho_j Y_j$ and $C_{2j} = \xi_{2j} \rho_j Y_j / p$ in (11.1.7), we get

$$\frac{1}{C_{1j}} \frac{dC_{1j}}{d\tau_{i1}} = \frac{m_{i1}}{Z} \frac{dZ}{d\tau_{i1}}, \quad \frac{1}{C_{2j}} \frac{dC_{2j}}{d\tau_{i1}} = \frac{m_{i2}}{Z} \frac{dZ}{d\tau_{i1}}. \tag{11.3.7}$$

We got the impact of changes in τ_{i1} upon the equilibrium values of the variables in the system. It can be seen that the effects are very sensitive to how different values of the parameters are combined.

11.4 The Impact of the Preference for Foreign Goods

Taking derivatives of (11.A.1.1) and (11.A.1.6) with respect to ξ_{21}, we get the impact on the labor and land distribution as follows

$$\frac{dN_{s1}}{d\xi_{21}} = -\frac{dN_{i1}}{d\xi_{21}} = -\rho_1 N_{s1} < 0,$$

$$\frac{dN_{s2}}{d\xi_{21}} = \frac{dN_{i2}}{d\xi_{21}} = \frac{dL_{sj}}{d\xi_{21}} = \frac{dL_{ij}}{d\xi_{21}} = 0. \tag{11.4.1}$$

We see that as country 1's propensity to consume country 2's commodity is increased, some of country 1's labor force will be moved from service production to industrial production. Country 2's labor distribution and two countries' land distribution are not affected by change in ξ_{21}.

By (11.A.2.2) we get the impact of changes in ξ_{21} on Z as follows

$$-\Phi' \frac{dZ}{d\xi_{21}} = \left(-\beta_1 \Phi_{s1} + \frac{N_{s1} \Phi_{i1}}{N_{i1}} \right) \rho_1 \tag{11.4.2}$$

We thus conclude that the sign of Φ' is dependent on whether each production sector exhibits increasing or decreasing returns. For simplicity of discussion, we assume that contribution to knowledge accumulation by country 1's services sector is negligible, i.e., Φ_{s1} being small. Then, we have following conclusions. In case (i), we have $dZ / d\xi_{21} < 0$. In case (ii), we have $dZ / d\xi_{21} > 0$. In case (iii), we have $dZ / d\xi_{21} <(>) 0$ at the equilibrium with high (low) values of Z. We see that an increase in country 1's preference for country 2's commodity may either increase or decrease the equilibrium value of knowledge. For instance, in case (ii) which means that the four sectors exhibit decreasing returns, an increase in the preference increases the equilibrium level of knowledge. In case (i), the impact in changes of the preference is the opposite to the case of stability. We see that the effects of changes in the parameters on the system are significantly dependent upon the stability conditions and the 'relative contribution' to knowledge accumulation by different sectors. For instance, if we did not assume that the services sector's contribution is negligible, it is more complicated to explicitly judge the sign of $dZ / d\xi_{21}$.

Taking derivatives of (11.A.1.4) with respect to ξ_{21} yields

$$\frac{1}{p}\frac{dp}{d\xi_{21}} = \frac{m_i}{Z}\frac{dZ}{d\xi_{21}} + \frac{\xi_{11}}{\xi_{11}+\xi_{21}} - \frac{\rho_1 N_{s1}}{N_{i1}}. \tag{11.4.3}$$

The impact of change in ξ_{21} on the price of commodity 2 is ambiguous. By (11.A.1.5), we have

$$\frac{1}{w_1}\frac{dw_1}{d\xi_{21}} = \frac{m_{i1}}{Z}\frac{dZ}{d\xi_{21}}, \quad \frac{1}{w_2}\frac{dw_2}{d\xi_{21}} = \frac{m_{i1}}{Z}\frac{dZ}{d\xi_{21}} + \frac{\xi_{11}}{\xi_{11}+\xi_{21}} - \frac{\rho_1 N_{s1}}{N_{i1}}. \tag{11.4.4}$$

We see that the sign of $dw_1 / d\xi_{21}$ is the same as that of $dZ / d\xi_{21}$ and the sign of $dw_2 / d\xi_{21}$ is the same as that of $dp / d\xi_{21}$. We conclude that when country 1's wage rate is increased, country 2's wage rate may be either reduced or increased due to country 1's changed preference for country 2's exportable commodity.

By (11.1.1) and (11.1.3), we get the impact on the output levels

$$\frac{1}{F_{s1}}\frac{dF_{s1}}{d\xi_{21}} = \frac{1}{C_{s1}}\frac{dC_{s1}}{d\xi_{21}} = \frac{m_{s1}}{Z}\frac{dZ}{d\xi_{21}} - \frac{\rho_1 N_{s1}}{N_{i1}},$$

$$\frac{1}{F_{i1}}\frac{dF_{i1}}{d\xi_{21}} = \frac{m_{i1}}{Z}\frac{dZ}{d\xi_{21}} + \frac{\rho_1 N_{s1}}{N_{i1}}, \quad \frac{1}{F_{s2}}\frac{dF_{s2}}{d\xi_{21}} = \frac{1}{C_{sj}}\frac{dC_{s2}}{d\xi_{21}} = \frac{m_{s2}}{Z}\frac{dZ}{d\xi_{21}},$$

$$\frac{1}{F_{i2}}\frac{dF_{i2}}{d\xi_{21}} = \frac{m_{i2}}{Z}\frac{dZ}{d\xi_{21}}. \tag{11.4.5}$$

We see that the impact on country 2's output levels is in the same direction as the impact on knowledge. By (11.1.2), we have the impact on the prices of services and land rent in the two countries

$$\frac{1}{p_1}\frac{dp_1}{d\xi_{21}} = \frac{m_{i1} - m_{s1}}{Z}\frac{dZ}{d\xi_{21}} + \frac{\rho_1 N_{s1}}{N_{i1}} - \rho_1,$$

$$\frac{1}{p_2}\frac{dp_2}{d\xi_{21}} = \frac{m_{i1} - m_{s2}}{Z}\frac{dZ}{d\xi_{21}} + \frac{\xi_{11}}{\xi_{11} + \xi_{21}} - \frac{\rho_1 N_{s1}}{N_{i1}},$$

$$\frac{1}{R_1}\frac{dR_1}{d\xi_{21}} = \frac{m_{i1}}{Z}\frac{dZ}{d\xi_{21}} - \rho_1,$$

$$\frac{1}{R_2}\frac{dR_2}{d\xi_{21}} = \frac{m_{i1}}{Z}\frac{dZ}{d\xi_{21}} + \frac{\xi_{11}}{\xi_{11}+\xi_{21}} - \frac{\rho_1 N_{s1}}{N_{i1}}. \tag{11.4.6}$$

By (11.1.7), we directly get

$$\frac{1}{Y_1}\frac{dY_1}{d\xi_{21}} = \frac{m_{i1}}{Z}\frac{dZ}{d\xi_{21}}, \quad \frac{1}{Y_2}\frac{dY_2}{d\xi_{21}} = \frac{m_{i1}}{Z}\frac{dZ}{d\xi_{21}} + \frac{\xi_{11}}{\xi_{11} + \xi_{21}} - \frac{\rho_1 N_{s1}}{N_{i1}},$$

$$\frac{1}{C_{1j}}\frac{dC_{1j}}{d\xi_{21}} = \frac{m_{i1}}{Z}\frac{dZ}{d\xi_{21}}, \quad \frac{1}{C_{21}}\frac{dC_{21}}{d\xi_{21}} = \frac{m_{i2}}{Z}\frac{dZ}{d\xi_{21}} + \frac{1}{\xi_{21}} - \rho_1,$$

$$\frac{1}{C_{22}}\frac{dC_{22}}{d\xi_{21}} = \frac{m_{i2}}{Z}\frac{dZ}{d\xi_{21}}. \tag{11.4.7}$$

We see that it is complicated to judge the impact of changes in the preference.

Since we explicitly solved the equilibrium, it is straightforward to examine the impact of changes in other parameters on the system. For illustration we provide the impact of change in country 1's population on some variables as follows:

$$-\Phi'\frac{dZ}{dN_1} = \frac{-\beta_1 \Phi_{s1} + \Phi_{i1}}{N_1},$$

$$\frac{1}{w_1}\frac{dw_1}{dN_1} = \frac{m_{i1}}{Z}\frac{dZ}{dN_1}, \quad \frac{1}{w_2}\frac{dw_2}{dN_1} = \frac{m_{i1}}{Z}\frac{dZ}{dN_1} + \frac{1}{N_1},$$

$$\frac{1}{F_{s1}}\frac{dF_{s1}}{dN_1} = \frac{1}{C_{s1}}\frac{dC_{s1}}{dN_1} = \frac{m_{s1}}{Z}\frac{dZ}{dN_1} + \frac{1}{N_1},$$

$$\frac{1}{F_{i1}}\frac{dF_{i1}}{dN_1} = \frac{m_{i1}}{Z}\frac{dZ}{dN_1} + \frac{1}{N_1},$$

$$\frac{1}{F_{s2}}\frac{dF_{s2}}{dN_1} = \frac{1}{C_{s2}}\frac{dC_{s2}}{dN_1} = \frac{m_{s2}}{Z}\frac{dZ}{dN_1}, \quad \frac{1}{F_{i2}}\frac{dF_{i2}}{dN_1} = \frac{m_{i2}}{Z}\frac{dZ}{dN_1}. \quad (11.4.8)$$

It may be also be interesting to get the impact of changes in the preference for services on some variables

$$-\Phi'\frac{dZ}{d\gamma_1} = \left(\frac{\alpha_1\eta_1}{\alpha_1\gamma_1 + \eta_1} + \frac{\xi_{11} + \xi_{12} + \eta_1}{\gamma_1}\beta_1\rho_1\right)\Phi_{s1}$$

$$-\frac{(\xi_{11} + \xi_{12} + \eta_1)\rho_1 N_{s1}}{\gamma_1 N_{i1}}\Phi_{i1}, \quad \frac{1}{w_1}\frac{dw_1}{d\gamma_1} = \frac{m_{i1}}{Z}\frac{dZ}{d\gamma_1},$$

$$\frac{1}{w_2}\frac{dw_2}{d\gamma_1} = \frac{m_{i1}}{Z}\frac{dZ}{d\gamma_1} - \frac{\xi_{11} + \xi_{12} + \eta_1}{\gamma_1 N_{i1}}\rho_1 N_{s1},$$

$$\frac{1}{F_{s1}}\frac{dF_{s1}}{d\gamma_1} = \frac{1}{C_{s1}}\frac{dC_{s1}}{d\gamma_1} = \frac{m_{s1}}{Z}\frac{dZ}{d\gamma_1} + \frac{\alpha_1\eta_1}{\alpha_1\gamma_1 + \eta_1} +$$

$$\frac{\xi_{11} + \xi_{12} + \eta_1}{\gamma_1}\rho_1, \quad \frac{1}{F_{i1}}\frac{dF_{i1}}{d\gamma_1} = m_{i1}\frac{dZ}{d\gamma_1} - \frac{\eta_1 L_{s1}}{(\alpha_1\gamma_1 + \eta_1)L_{i1}},$$

$$\frac{1}{F_{s2}}\frac{dF_{s2}}{d\gamma_1} = \frac{m_{s2}}{Z}\frac{dZ}{d\gamma_1}, \quad \frac{1}{F_{i2}}\frac{dF_{i2}}{d\gamma_1} = \frac{m_{i2}}{Z}\frac{dZ}{d\gamma_1}. \quad (11.4.9)$$

We see that even in our very simplified global economy with endogenous knowledge it is quite complicated to judge the impact of changes in some parameters on the system.

Appendix

A.11.1 Proving Proposition 11.2.1

From $C_{sj} = F_{sj}$, (11.1.2), $N_{ij} + N_{sj} = N_j$ and $C_{sj} = \gamma_j\rho_j w_j N_j / p_j$, we have

$$N_{sj} = \gamma_j \rho_j \beta_j N_j, \quad N_{ij} = (1 - \gamma_j \rho_j \beta_j) N_j, \quad j = 1, 2. \qquad (11.A.1.1)$$

Substituting C_{12} and C_{21} in (11.1.7) into (11.1.9), we get

$$\frac{Y_1}{Y_2} = \frac{\xi_{12}\rho_2}{\xi_{21}\rho_1}. \qquad (11.A.1.2)$$

Substituting C_{ij} in (11.1.8) into $C_{j1} + C_{j2} = F_{ij}$ in (11.1.9) yields

$$\xi_{11}\rho_1 Y_1 + \xi_{12}\rho_2 Y_2 = F_{i1}, \quad \xi_{21}\rho_1 Y_1 + \xi_{22}\rho_2 Y_2 = pF_{i2}. \qquad (11.A.1.3)$$

Dividing the first equation by the second in (11.A.1.13), we get

$$p = aZ^{m_i}, \quad a \equiv \frac{(\xi_{12} + \xi_{22})\xi_{21} N_{i1}}{(\xi_{11} + \xi_{21})\xi_{12} N_{i2}}, \quad m_i \equiv m_{i1} - m_{i2} \qquad (11.A.1.4)$$

where we use (11.A.1.2) and (11.1.3). By (11.A.1.4) and (11.1.3), we get

$$w_1 = Z^{m_{i1}}, \quad w_2 = aZ^{m_{i1}}. \qquad (11.A.1.5)$$

By $C_{sj} = F_{sj}$ in (11.1.8), $R_j = \alpha_j p_j F_{sj} / L_{sj}$ in (11.1.2) and C_{sj} in (11.1.7), we get

$$L_{sj} = \frac{\alpha_j \gamma_j \rho_j Y_j}{R_j}.$$

From this equation and $L_{hj} = \eta_j \rho_j Y_j / R_j$ in (11.1.7), we get

$$\frac{L_{sj}}{L_{hj}} = \frac{\alpha_j \gamma_j}{\eta_j}.$$

With this equation and (11.1.10), we have

$$L_{hj} = \frac{\eta_j}{\alpha_j \gamma_j + \eta_j}, \quad L_{sj} = \frac{\alpha_j \gamma_j}{\alpha_j \gamma_j + \eta_j}. \qquad (11.A.1.6)$$

A.11.2 Proving Proposition 11.2.2

By (11.2.1) the knowledge accumulation is given by

$$\frac{dZ}{dt} = \sum_{j=1}^{2} \{\Phi_{sj}(Z) + \Phi_{ij}(Z)\}Z - \delta_z Z \equiv \Phi_0(Z). \tag{11.A.2.1}$$

We now examine properties of (11.A.2.1). Equilibrium is given as a solution of the following equation

$$\Phi(Z) \equiv \sum_{j=1}^{2} \{\Phi_{sj}(Z) + \Phi_{ij}(Z)\} - \delta_z = 0. \tag{11.A.2.2}$$

Our problem is whether or not $\Phi(Z) = 0$ has a positive solution.

In the case of $x_{sj} > 0$ and $x_{ij} > 0$, we have

$$\Phi(0) < 0, \quad \Phi(+\infty) > 0, \quad \Phi'(Z) > 0, \quad 0 < Z < +\infty.$$

Accordingly, there is a unique positive Z such that $\Phi(Z) = 0$. The stability is determined by the sign of $\Phi_0'(Z)$ at the equilibrium. If $\Phi_0'(Z) > 0$, the system is unstable; if $\Phi_0'(Z) < 0$, it is stable; and if $\Phi_0'(Z) = 0$, it is neutral. Taking derivatives of Φ with respect to Z yields

$$\Phi_0' = \sum_{j=1}^{2} \{x_{sj}\Phi_{sj}(Z) + x_{ij}\Phi_{ij}(Z)\} \tag{11.A.2.3}$$

which is evaluated at equilibrium. We thus conclude the system has a unique unstable equilibrium in this case.

In the case of $x_{sj} < 0$ and $x_{ij} < 0$, we have

$$\Phi(0) > 0, \quad \Phi(+\infty) < 0, \quad \Phi'(Z) < 0, \quad 0 < Z < +\infty.$$

We see that the system has a unique stable equilibrium in this case.

It is sufficient to check the case of $x_{i1} > 0$, $x_{i2} < 0$ and $x_{sj} < 0$ as the case $x_{i1} < 0$ and $x_{i2} > 0$ can be similarly proved. As $\Phi(0) > 0$ and $\Phi(+\infty) > 0$, the system has either no equilibrium or multiple ones. From

$$\Phi' = \sum_j \left(\frac{x_{sj}\Phi_{sj} + x_{ij}\Phi_{ij}}{Z} \right)$$

we see that $\Phi' = 0$ has a unique positive solution, denoted by Z_0. This implies that $\Phi(Z) = 0$ cannot have more than two solutions. When the system has two equilibria, the stability of each equilibrium is determined by the sign of $\Phi'_0(Z)$. It can be seen that if $Z < Z_0$, then $\Phi' < 0$ and if $Z > Z_0$, then $\Phi' > 0$. We thus proved the proposition.

12 Further Issues on International Trade

By working thus for a long time at one set of considerations, we get gradually nearer to those fundamental unites which are called nature's laws: we trace their action first singly, and then in combination; and thus make progress slowly but surely.

Marshall (1989)

Contemporary economic theory includes a number of separated sub-theories. It is more desirable to have one compact theoretical framework than multiple separate theories to explain various aspects of the reality. I have made efforts to examine various aspects of national economies with a few concepts within a single consistent framework (Zhang, 1999a). This book applied the basic concepts in my previous book *Capital and Knowledge* to explore complex interdependence between global economic growth, economic structures, sexual division of labor, and international trade. The national aspects in this book are not so complicated as in my previous book. As the introduction of international trade into the national models increases analytical complexity, it is necessary to simplify national economic structures in order to get explicit conclusions.

The purpose of this book is to explore complexity of global economic growth and international trade within a perfectly competitive framework. Our focus on perfect competition is different from the contemporary mainstream of formal trade theory (the new trade theory) that is mainly concerned with monopolistic competition in analyzing international goods production and flows. Our analysis has shown that our framework can be employed to explore the issues related to trade raised in the traditional trade theories as well as to provide insights into the issues related to interdependence between growth and international trade examined by the new trade theory.

This book has made attempts to provide a systematic treatment of international trade of real terms in a deterministic dynamic context. We have attempted to develop dynamic trade models to deal with issues about the relationship between knowledge, growth, economic structures, and trade patterns. The global economic growth within multi-country and multi-sector trade systems have been modeled. We showed that if we assume that economies are domestically and internationally perfectly competitive, free trade among nations may neither benefit knowledge growth nor the world economy from a long-run point of view. It should be remarked that the new trade theory gets a similar conclusion under the assumption that economies are not perfectly competitive within nations. We may conclude that the long-run impact of trade might be either beneficial or harmful, depending upon the cultural and economic characteristics of nations.

Our book is focused on dynamics of economic structures, capital, and knowledge, and human capital. It is not intended to be a comprehensive treatment of all the important issues related to international trades. We did not discuss issues such as monetary variables and the role of expectations. Moreover, this book does not represent any model of 'an open economy' which is often used in the literature of international trade. In fact, most of international economics deals with such economies (Fung and Ishikawa, 1992, Turnovsky, 1997). Our emphasis is much on the development of international trades among economies rather than the impact of the world on some small economies. We hold that models built upon the assumptions related to operation of small economies should be special cases of international trade models between 'equals'. Moreover, most of our investigations were limited to a two-country framework. It is important to examine trade patterns among multiple (at least three) countries when there are possible formations of trading blocks among some countries.

Since this book is based on a comprehensive system of national economies, it is conceptually easy to make further extensions of our international framework. We now mention a few directions of possible extensions of our work.

Scale effects of endogenous population
From the literature of classical economics we know at least four input factors which may exhibit increasing or decreasing returns to scale effects in economic dynamics: infrastructures (of transportation and communication systems), institutions, knowledge and population, (e.g., Malthus, 1933, Marshall, 1890, Haavelmo, 1954, Niehans, 1963, Zhang, 1999a). This book introduced endogenous knowledge and capital. It is not difficult to see that the impact of trade upon the long-run welfare of the world may be very complicated in economic systems with endogenous population. For instance, if we allow the world population to be affected by economic conditions, trade between countries is perhaps economically harmful to the world in the long term under certain circumstances.

Networks and infrastructures
In order to take infrastructure structures for transportation and communication into account, it is necessary to explicitly take account of space (Zhang, 1991a, 1991b). Channels, roads, railways and airline systems, which may be effectively treated as parameters in short-term analyses, determine the mobility and the costs associated with movements of people and goods. In a long-term analysis, it is necessary to examine decision-making processes involved in construction and maintenance of infrastructures.

Knowledge and human capital
We did not deal with economic evolution with knowledge in a comprehensive way because of analytical difficulties for obtaining explicit conclusions. Following the

modeling framework developed by Zhang (1999a), it is conceptually easy to introduce other aspects such as human capital structures and professional amenities into our framework.

It is worthwhile to point out that as far as I know, no theoretical model has been proposed to connect research amenity (in comparison to other jobs' amenities) and international trade within a compact framework. If sophisticated research is 'boring', a free society may not carry out sophisticated research when the research results have no immediate profitable markets. It is obvious that some professions are associated with more pleasures or less sufferings than others. People may get different levels of job amenity in doing science and working in a manufacturing factory. Wage rate is not a single factor that determines choice of profession. People may prefer a profession with low payment but high job amenity level to one with high payment but low job amenity level. It seems that the role of job amenity in affecting professional choice and labor distribution has increasingly become important in post-industrial societies. With many economies facing rapidly improved living conditions and rapid changes of attitudes towards various kinds of jobs, professional choice has increasingly become complicated. It may be argued that how people feel about doing science will strongly affect labor distribution between research and production. If to do science has no advantages in terms of social status and income, then only a few people may like to choose scientific research as career.

We were mainly concerned with knowledge creation and utilization. Another way to handle with knowledge utilization is to directly study human capital accumulation through learning by doing, learning through leisure or learning through education. The relationship of our approach to human capital approach in international trade may need a little more explanation. The concept of knowledge as an international public good is different from the concept of human capital which is widely used in the trade literature. We may consider that a person in society obtains certain objective knowledge. Indeed, one cannot master all the knowledge created by mankind. In an approximate sense, we may describe human capital as a function $g(Z)$ of knowledge Z. For an individual, $g(Z)$ is determined by culture, family background, social position, material conditions, education and other life experiences. Similarly, we may define a function $g(Z, N)$ as a measurement of a country j's human capital. According to this interpretation, we see that our concept of knowledge is identical to the concept of human capital (as far as production alone is concerned). Hence the human capital approach should not be considered to be in conflict with our approach. However, the concept of knowledge may be more convenient for some special problems. It is obvious that knowledge can be embodied both in capital and in humans. Similar to our preceding interpretation of human capital as a function of knowledge we may describe 'effective capital' by $f(Z, K)$ where K is some basic physical measurement of capital. For instance, we may have the same number of computers in two countries, but the quality of the computers may be different. Hence, by using the concept of knowledge we can introduce 'capital quality' into our approach. Indeed, when we should use concepts such as human capital, technology and knowledge when we study the impact of knowledge upon economic problems is dependent upon the issues under consideration.

Multiple kinds of capital, people and natural resources
It is not difficult to relax the assumption of a single kind of capital (Zhang, 1999a, Burmester and Dobell, 1970, Takayama, 1985). The introduction of multiple capital goods will cause analytical difficulties. It should be noted that the traditional neoclassical growth theory did not succeed in dealing with growth issues with multiple capital goods in the sense that the consumer behavior was not properly modeled (Zhang, 1999a).

Although we developed multi-group trade models, our classification of labor force was simplified. It should be noted that different kinds of labor force may enter production functions in different ways. We neglected issues related to natural resources and environment. The issues related to trade, resources and capital accumulation should be further examined.

Production sectors
We have used simple production functions in this book. In economics, it is common to use more general forms of production functions. Moreover, it is reasonable to introduce other factor inputs such as natural resources and infrastructures into production functions. We assumed perfect competition in domestic markets. But imperfect competition is important to describe the economic reality. If markets are not perfectly competitive, prices of goods and services may not be rapidly changed as we assumed in the dynamic models.

Preference structures
Utility functions may be taken on various forms. Except common issues related to forms of utility functions (Lancaster, 1966, 1971), we may also introduce preference change. For instance, when we write a utility function in the form of

$$U(t) = C^{\xi}(K + S - \delta_k K)^{\lambda}$$

we may introduce endogenous preference changes by allowing ξ and λ to be changeable in the long term (Zhang, 1999a). Furthermore, it should be remarked that Dixit and Stiglitz (1977) have emphasized the implications of the endogenization of the number of goods for productivity progress and R&D. In general this idea can be taken into account by assuming that knowledge affects the parameters in the utility and production functions.

Government policy
Governments may intervene economic systems in different ways even within freely competitive economic systems. It is important to examine the impact of various government interventions on trade patterns. For instance, economic issues related to regional integration and block formation are currently important issues in trade theory.

Various possible taxes on imports and exports are important for analyzing trade flows and global economic growth (Jones and Kenen, 1984, Neary, 1995a, 1995b).

Full employment of production factors
We assumed that production factors such as labor force, capital and land are always fully employed. These assumptions should be relaxed in order to analyze modern economies. In particular, one of the central topics in trade theory is related to the impact of trade on unemployment. This issue can be handled according to the model with unemployment suggested in Zhang (1999a).

Conditions of Capital mobility and migration
We assumed that perfect competition of the international capital market makes the interest rates identical across the world economy. But due to factors such as transaction costs, risks and institutions, rates of interest may not be equalized among nations. It is necessary to specify some principles of capital mobility among nations.

How migration is endogenously determined is a complicated issue. We were concerned only with a single case in which there are no social or institutional limitations on migration. There are many possibilities of migration patterns, some of them might be very important in analyzing trade patterns. We may also introduce international tourism (i.e., the utilization of the service sectors by foreigners) into our modeling framework.

Dynamics of monetary variables
We assume that trade takes place in the form of barter; in other words, money is treated as a veil which has no impact on the underlying variables but serves as a reference unit, the *numeraire*. This book is not concerned with important issues such as the balance-of-payments adjustment processes under fixed or varying exchange rates. This omission of monetary aspects does not mean that we consider it unimportant to integrate international monetary economics with our approach. We assumed that monetary variables are fast in the sense that their values are determined by their marginal values at any point of time. In reality, monetary variables may seldom be adjusted so quickly. We may generally denote monetary dynamics in the following general form

$$\frac{dp}{dt} = \varepsilon G(p, K)$$

where p is a vector of monetary variables such as money, exchange rates and prices of goods and ε is the adjustment speed vector. Different theories can be applied to specify functional forms of $G(p, K, Z)$ (e.g., Jones and Kenen, 1985, Friedman and Hahn, 1990, Gandolfo, 1994b,).

Bibliography

Aghion, P., Howitt, P. (1992): A Model of Growth through Creative Destruction. Econometrica 60, 323-351

Aghion, P., Howitt, P. (1998): Endogenous Growth Theory. Mass., Cambridge: The MIT Press

Alonso, W. (1964): Location and Land Use. MA., Cambridge: Harvard University Press

Arrow, K.J. (1962): The Economic Implications of Learning by Doing. Review of Economic Studies 29: 155-173

Arthur, W.B., Landesmann, M., Scazzieri, R. (1991): Dynamics and Structures. Structural Change and Economic Dynamics 2, 1-7

Ashenfelter, O., Layard, R. (Eds.) (1992): Handbook of Labor Economics, Volume I. Amsterdam: North-Holland

Auerbach, A.J., Feldetein, M. (Eds.) (1990): Handbook of Public Economics, Volume I. Amsterdam: North-Holland

Auerbach, A.J., Feldetein, M. (Eds.) (1991): Handbook of Public Economics, Volume II. Amsterdam: North-Holland

Baldwin, R.E. (1992): Are Economists' Traditional Trade Policy Views Still Valid?. Journal of Economic Literature XXX, 804-832

Bardhan, P.K. (1965): Optimum Capital Accumulation and International Trade. Review of Economic Studies 32, 241-244

Barro, R.J., Sala-i-Martin, X. (1995): Economic Growth. New York: McGraw-Hill, Inc

Becker, G.S. (1957): The Economics of Discrimination. Chicago: The University of Chicago Press

Becker, G.S. (1965): A Theory of the Allocation of Time. Economic Journal 75, 493-517

Becker, G.S. (1975): Human Capital, 2nd edition. New York: National Bureau of Economic Research

Becker, G.S. (1976): The Economic Approach to Human Behavior. Chicago: The University of Chicago Press

Becker, G.S. (1981): A Treatise on the Family. Mass., Cambridge: Harvard University Press

Becker, G.S. (1985): Human Capital, Effort, and the Sexy Division of Labor. Journal of Labor Economics 3, S34-58

Bhagwati, J.N. (1976): The International Brain Drain and Taxation: A Survey of Issues. In Bhagwati, J.N. (Ed.): The Brain Drain and Taxation, 3-27. Amsterdam: North-Holland

Bhagwati, J.N. (Ed.) (1991): International Trade - Selected Readings, 2nd edition. Mass., Cambridge: The MIT Press

Bhagwati, J.N., Hamada, K. (1974): The Brain Drain, International Integration of Markets for Professionals and Unemployment: A Theoretical Analysis. Journal of Development Economics 1, 19-42

Bhagwati, J.N., Srinivasan, T.N. (1983): On the Choice between Capital and Labor Mobility. Journal of International Economics 14, 209-221

Brody, A. (1970): Proportions, Prices and Planning, A Mathematical Restatement of the Labour Theory of Value. Amsterdam: North-Holland Publishing Company

Bruce, N. (1977): The Effects of Trade Taxes in a Two-Sector Model of Capital Accumulation. Journal of International Economics 7, 283-294

Burmeister, E., Dobell, A.R. (1970): Mathematical Theories of Economic Growth. London: Collier Macmillan Publishers

Cain, G.G. (1986): The Economic Analysis of Labor Market Discrimination: A Survey. In Ashenfelter, O.C., Layard, R. (Eds.): Handbook of Labor Economics. Amsterdam: North-Holland

Chamberlin, E. (1933): The Theory of Monopolistic Competition. Cambridge: Harvard University Press

Chiang, A.C. (1973): A Simple Generalization of the Kaldor-Pasinetti Theory of Profit Rate and Income Distribution. Economica XL, 311-13

Chiappori, P.A. (1988): Rational Household Labor Supply. Econometrica 51, 63-89

Chiappori, P.A. (1992): Collective Labor Supply and Welfare. Journal of Political Economy 100, 438-467

Chipman, J.S. (1965a): A Survey of the Theory of International Trade, Part 1. Econometrica 33, 477-519

Chipman, J.S. (1965b): A Survey of the Theory of International Trade, Part 2. Econometrica 33, 685-760

Cole, H.L., Mailath, G.J., Postlewaite, A. (1992): Social Norms, Savings Behavior, and Growth. Journal of Political Economy 100, 1092-125

Deardorff, A.V. (1973): The Gains from Trade in and out of Steady State Growth. Oxford Economic Papers 25, 173-91

Devereux, M.B., Shi, S. (1991): Capital Accumulation and the Current Account in a Two-Country Model. Journal of International Economics 30, 1-25

Dixit, A.K., Norman, V. (1980): Theory of International Trade. Cambridge: Cambridge University Press

Dixit, A.K., Stiglitz, J.E. (1977): Monopolistic Competition and Optimum Product Diversity. American Economic Review 67, 297-308

Dixon, H.D., Rankin, N. (1994): Imperfect Competition and Macroeconomics: A Survey. Oxford Economic Papers 46, 171-199

Djajic, S., Milbourne, R. (1988): A General Equilibrium Model of Guest-Worker Migration - The Source-Country Perspective. Journal of International Economics 25, 335-251

Dollar, D. (1986): Technological Innovation, Capital Mobility, and the Product Cycle in the North-South Trade. American Economic Review 76, 177-190

Dosi, G., Pavitt, K., Soete, L. (1990): The Economics of Technical Change and International Trade. New York: Harvester Whertsheaf

Drandakis, E., Phelps, E.S. (1966): A Model of Induced Invention, Growth and Distribution. Economic Journal LXXVI, 823-40

Duchin, F. (1989): An Input-Output Approach to Analyzing the Future Economic Implications of Technological Change. In Miller, R.E., Polenske, K.R., Rose, A.Z. (Eds.): Frontiers in Input-Output Analysis. Oxford: Oxford University Press

Eaton, J. (1987): A Dynamic Specific-Factors Model of International Trade. Review of Economic Studies 54, 325-338

Eaton, J., Panagariya, A. (1979): Gains from Trade under Variable Returns to Scale, Commodity Taxation, Tariffs and Factor Market Distortions. Journal of International Economics 9, 481-502

Ethier, W.J. (1974): Some of the Theorems of International Trade with Many Goods and Factors. Journal of International Economics 4, 199-206

Ethier, W.J. (1979): Internationally Decreasing Costs and World Trade. Journal of International Economics 9, 1-24

Ethier, W.J. (1982): National and International Returns to Scale in the Modern Theory of International Trade. American Economic Review 72, 389-405

Ethier, W.J. (1982a): Decreasing Costs in International Trade and Frank Graham's Argument for Protection. Econometrica 50

Ethier, W.J., Svensson, L.E.O. (1986): The Theorems of International Trade with Factor Mobility. Journal of International Economics 20, 21-42

Fei, J.C.H., Ranis, G., Kuo, S.W.Y. (1978): Growth and the Family Distribution of Income by Factor Components. Quarterly Journal of Economics XCII, 17-53

Fershtman, C., Weiss, Y. (1993): Social Status, Culture and Economic Performance. The Economic Journal 103, 946-959

Findlay, R. (1978): Relative Backwardness, Direct Foreign Investment and Transfer of Technology. Quarterly Journal of Economics 92, 1-16

Findlay, R. (1984): Growth and Development in Trade Models. In Jones, R.W., Kenen, R.B. (Eds.): Handbook of International Economics. Amsterdam: North-Holland

Fischer, S., Frenkel, J.A. (1972): Investment, the Two-Sector Model and Trade in Debt and Capital Goods. Journal of International Economics 2, 211-233

Folbre, N. (1986): Cleaning House - New Perspectives on Households and Economic Development. Journal of Economic Development 22, 5-40

Frenkel, J.A., Razin, A. (1987): Fiscal Policy and the World Economy. MA., Cambridge: MIT Press

Francois, J.F. (1994): Global Production and Trade: Factor Migration and Commercial Policy with International Scale Economies. International Economic Review 35, 565-581

Friedman, B.M., Hahn, F.H. (Eds.) (1990): Handbook of Monetary Economics, Volumes I, II. Amsterdam: North-Holland

Fung, K.M., Ishikawa, J. (1992): Dynamic Increasing Returns, Technology and Economic Growth in a Small Open Economy. Journal of Development Economics 35, 63-87

Gandolfo, G. (1994a): International Economics I - The Pure Theory of International Trade, 2nd edition. Berlin: Spriner-Verlag

Gandolfo, G. (1994b): International Economics II - International Monetary Theory and Open-Economy Macroeconomics, 2nd edition. Berlin: Spriner-Verlag

Gersovitz, M. (1988): Saving and Development. In Chenery, H., Srinivasan, T.N. (Eds.): Handbook of Development Economics, Volume I. Amsterdam: North Holland

Graham, F.D. (1923): Some Aspects of Protection Further Considered. Quarterly Journal of Economics 37, 199-227

Grinols, E.L. (1992): Increasing Returns and the Gains From Trade. International Economic Review 32, 973-984

Grossman, G.M., Helpman, E. (1991): Innovation and Growth in the Global Economy. Mass., Cambridge: The MIT Press

Haavelmo, T. (1954): A Study in the Theory of Economic Evolution. Amsterdam: North-Holland

Heckman, J.J., Macurdy, T.E. (1980): A Life Cycle Model of Labor Supply. Review of Economic Studies 47, 47-74

Heckscher, E. (1919): The Effect of Foreign Trade on the Distribution of Income. Ekonomisk Tidskrift, 497-512

Helpman, E., Krugman, P. R. (1985): Market Structure and Foreign Trade. Cambridge: MIT Press

Ikeda, S., Ono, Y. (1992): Macroeconomic Dynamics in a Multi-Country Economy - A Dynamic Optimization Approach. International Economic Review 33, 629-644

Isard, W. (1956): Location and Space Economy. MA., Cambridge: MIT Press

Ishikawa, J. (1992): Trade Patterns and Gains from Trade with an Intermediate Good Produced under Increasing Returns to Scale. Journal of International Economics 32, 57-81

Jensen, B.S. (1994): The Dynamic Systems of Basic Economic Growth Models. Dordrecht: Kluwer Academic

Jensen, B.S., Wong, K.Y. (Eds.) (1998): Dynamics, Economic Growth, and International Trade. Ann Arbor: The University of Michigan Press

Johnson, H.G. (1971): Trade and Growth: A Geometric Exposition. Journal of International Economics I, 83-101

Jones, R.W. (1971): A Three-Factor Model in Theory, Trade and History. In Bhagwati, J.N., et al. (Eds.): Trade, Balance of Payments and Growth. Amsterdam: North-Holland

Jones, R.W. (1979): International Trade: Essays in Theory. Amsterdam: North-Holland Publishing Company

Jones, R.W., Kenen, P.B. (Eds.) (1984): Handbook of International Economics - International Trade. Amsterdam: North-Holland

Jones, R.W., Kenen, P.B. (Eds.) (1985): Handbook of International Economics - International Monetary Economics and Finance. Amsterdam: North-Holland

Jones, R.W., Neary, J.P. (1984): The Positive Theory of International Trade. In Jones, R.W., Kenen, P.B. (Eds.) (1985): 1-62

Kaldor, N. (1955): Alternative Theories of Distribution. Review of Economic Studies 23, 83-100

Kaldor, N. (1956): Alternative Theories of Distribution. Review of Economic Studies XXIII, 83-100

Kaldor, N. (1961): Capital Accumulation and Economic Growth. In Lutz, F.A. (Ed.): The Theory of Capital. London: Macmillan

Kaldor, N., Mirrlees, J.A. (1962): A New Model of Economic Growth. Review of Economic Studies XXIX, 174-92

Kemp, M.C. (1961): Foreign Investment and National Advantage. Economic Record 28, 56-62

Kemp, M.C., Negishi, T. (1970): Variable Returns to Scale, Commodity Taxes, Factor Market Distortions, and Implications for Trade Gains. Swedish Journal of Economics 72, 1-11

Kennedy, C. (1964): Induced Bias in Innovation and the Theory of Distribution. Economic Journal LXXIV, September

Knight, F.H. (1924): Some Fallacies in the Interpretation of Social Costs. Quarterly Journal of Economics 38, 582-606

Krugman, P.R.   (1989): Increasing Returns, Monopolistic Competition, and International Trade. Journal of International Economics 9, 469-479

Krugman, P.R. (1990): Rethinking International Trade. Mass., Cambridge: The MIT Press

Krugman, P.R. (1991): Increasing Returns and Economic Geography. Journal of Political Economy 99, 483-499

Kuznets, S. (1963): Quantitative Aspects of the Economic Growth of Nations. Economic Development and Cultural Change XI, 1-80

Kuznets, S. (1966): Modern Economic Growth - Rate, Structure, and Spread. London: Yale University Press

Lancaster, K. (1966): A New Approach to Consumer Theory. Journal of Political Economy 74, 132-157

Lancaster, K. (1971): Consumer Demand. New York: Columbia University Press

Lazear, E.P., Rosen, S. (1990): Male-Female Wage Differentials in Job Ladders. Journal of Labor Economics 8, S106-23

Leontief, W.W. (1941): The Structure of American Economy, 1919-1939. New York: Oxford University Press

Leontief, W.W. (1949): The Structure of American Economy, 1919-1939. London: Oxford University Press

Leontief, W.W. (1966): Input-Output Economics. London: Oxford University Press

Lerner, A.P. (1952): Factor Prices and International Trade. Economica 19: 1-15

Lewis, W.A. (1955): The Theory of Economic Growth. London: Allen & Unwin

Lucas, R.E. (1988): On the Mechanics of Economic Development. Journal of Monetary Economics 22, 3-42

MacDougall, G.D.A. (1960): The Benefits and Costs of Private Investment from Abroad: A Theoretical Approach. Economic Record 27, 13-15

Malthus, T.R. (1933): An Essay on Population. London: J.D. Deut

Marglin, S.A. (1984): Growth, Distribution, and Prices. Cambridge: Harvard University Press

Markusen, J.R., Melvin, J.R. (1984): The Gains from Trade Theorem with Increasing Returns to Scale. In Kierzkowski, H. (Ed.): Monopolistic Competition and International Trade. Oxford: Clarendon Press

Marshall, A. (1890): Principles of Economics, 1990. London: Macmillan

Matsuyama, K. (1991): Increasing Returns, Industrialization, and Indeterminacy of Equilibrium. Quarterly Journal of Economics 106, 617-650

Matthews, R.C.O. (1949): Reciprocal Demand and Increasing Returns. Review of Economic Studies 37, 149-158

Maurer, R. (1998): Economic Growth and International Trade with Capital Goods – Theories and Empirical Goods. Tübingen: Mohr Siebeck

Mincer, J. (1962): Labor Force Participation of Married Woman: A Study of Labor Supply. Lewis, H.G. (Ed.): Aspects of Labor Economics. Princeton: Princeton University Press

Mill, J.S. (1848): Principles of Political Economy. 1970. London: Penguin

Mills, E.S., Hamilton, B.W. (1985): Urban Economics. London: Foresman and Company

Modigliani, F. (1986): Life Cycle, Individual Thrift and the Wealth of Nations. American Economic Review 76, 297-313

Morishima, M. (1964): Equilibrium, Stability, and Growth. Oxford: Claredon Press

Morishima, M. (1969): Theory of Economic Growth. Oxford: Clarendon Press

Morishima, M. (1989): Ricardo's Economics - A General Equilibrium Theory of Distribution and Growth. Cambridge: Cambridge University Press

Mussa, M. (1974): Tariffs and the Distribution of Income: The Importance of Factor Specificity, Substitutability, and Intensity in the Short and Long Run. Journal of Political Economy 82, 1191-1203

Neary, J.P. (1995a): International Trade – Welfare and Trade Policy. Aldershot: Edward Elgar Publishing Limited

Neary, J.P. (1995b): International Trade – Production Structure, Trade and Growth. Aldershot: Edward Elgar Publishing Limited

Negishi, T. (1972): General Equilibrium and International Trade. Amsterdam: North-Holland Publishing Company

Nelson, R.R., Winter, S.G. (1982): An Evolutionary Theory of Economic Change. MA., Cambridge: Harvard University Press

Niehans, J. (1963): Economic Growth with Two Endogenous Factors. Quarterly Journal of Economics 77

Nikaido, H. (1968): Convex Structures and Economic Theory. New York: Academic Press

Obstfeld, M. (1981): Capital Mobility and Devaluation in an Optimizing Model with Rational Expectations. American Economic Review 71, 217-221

Ohlin, B. (1933): Interregional and International Trade. Cambridge: Harvard University Press

Oniki, H., Uzawa, H. (1965): Patterns of Trade and Investment in a Dynamic Model of International Trade. Review of Economic Studies XXXII, 15-38

Panico, C., Salvadori, N. (Eds.) (1993): Post Keynesian Theory of Growth and Distribution. Vermont: Elward Elgar Publishing Limited

Pasinetti, L.L. (1974): Growth and Income Distribution - Essays in Economic Theory. Cambridge: Cambridge University Press

Pasinetti, L.L. (1981): Structural Change and Economic Growth - A Theoretical Essay on the Dynamics of the Wealth of Nations. Cambridge: Cambridge University Press

Pasinetti, L.L. (1993): Structural Economic Dynamics - A Theory of the Economic Consequences of Human Learning. Cambridge: Cambridge University Press

Persson, I., Jonung, C. (Eds.) (1997): Economics of the Family and Family Policies. London: Routledge

Persson, I., Jonung, C. (Eds.) (1998.): Women's Work and Wages. London: Routledge

Phelps, E.S. (1966): Models of Technical Progress and the Golden Rule of Research. Review of Economic Studies XXXIII, 133-45

Ram, R. (1982): Dependency Rates and Aggregate Savings: A New International Cross-section Study. American Economic Review 72, 537-44

Ramsey, F. (1928): A Mathematical Theory of Saving. Economic Journal 38, 543-559.

Rauch, J.E. (1991a): Reconciling the Pattern of Trade with the Pattern of Migration. The American Economic Review 81, 775-796

Rauch, J.E. (1991b): Comparative Advantage, Geographic Advantage and the Volume of Trade. The Economic Journal 101, 1230-1244

Ricardo, D. (1817): On the Principles of Political Economy and Taxation, 1987. London: Everyone's Library

Rivera-Batiz, L.A., Romer, P.M. (1991): Economic Integration and Endogenous Growth. Quarterly Journal of Economics 106, 531-556

Robson, A.J. (1980): Costly Innovation and Natural Resources. International Economic Review 21, 17-30

Rodriguez, C.A. (1975): Brain Drain and Economic Growth - a Dynamic Model. Journal of Development Economics 2, 223-247

Romer, P.M. (1986): Increasing Returns and Long-Run Growth. Journal of Political Economy 94, 1002-1037

Rostow, W.W. (1960): The Stages of Economic Growth. Cambridge: Cambridge University Press

Ruffin, R.J. (1979): Growth and the Long-Run Theory of International Capital Movements. American Economic Review 69, 832-842

Rybczynski, T.M. (1955): Factor Endowments and Relative Commodity Prices. Economica 22: 336-341

Ryder, H.E. (1967): Optimal Accumulation and Trade in an Open Economy of Moderate Size. In Shell, K. (Ed.): Essays on the Theory of Optimal Growth. Mass., Cambridge: M.I.T. Press

Salvadori, N. (1991): Post-Keynesian Theory of Distribution in the Long Run. In Nell, E.J., Semmler, W. (Eds.): Nicholas Kaldor and Mainstream Economics - Confrontation or Convergence?. London: Macmillan

Samuelson, P.A. (1948): International Trade and Equalisation of Factor Prices. Economic Journal 58, 163-184

Samuelson, P.A. (1949): International Factor-Price Equalisation Once Again. Economic Journal 59, 181-197

Samuelson, P.A. (1958): An Exact Consumption Loan Model of Interest with or without the Social Contrivance of Money. Journal of Political Economy 66, 467-482

Samuelson, P.A. (1965): A Theory of Induced Innovation Along Kennedy-Weizsäcker Lines. Review of Economics and Statistics XLVII, 343-56

Samuelson, P.A. (1971): Ohlin Was Right. Swedish Journal of Economics 73, 365-384

Samuelson, P.A., Modigliani, F. (1966): The Pasinetti Paradox in Neo-Classical and More General Models. Review of Economic Studies XXXIII, 269-301

Sato, R., Tsutsui, S. (1984): Technical Progress, the Schumpeterian Hypothesis and Market Structure. Journal of Economics S4, 1-37

Schultz, T.W. (1981): Investing in People - The Economics of Population Quality. Berkeley: University of California Press

Smith, A. (1776): An Inquiry into the Nature and Causes of the Wealth of Nations, edited by E. Cannan, 1976. Chicago: The University of Chicago Press

Smith, A. (1984): Capital Theory and Trade Theory. In Jones, R.W., Kenen, P.B. (Eds.): Handbook of International Economics, Vol. I. Amsterdam: North-Holland

Smith, J. (1977): Family Labor Supply over the Life Cycle. Explorations in Economic Research 4, 205-276

Solow, R. (1956): A Contribution to the Theory of Growth. Quarterly Journal of Economics 70, 65-94

Sraffa, P. (1960): Production of Commodities by Means of Commodities: Prelude to a Critique of Economic Theory. Cambridge: Cambridge University Press

Stokey, N.L. (1991): The Volume and Composition of Trade Between Rich and Poor Countries. Review of Economic Studies 58, 63-80

Stolper, W., Samuelson, P.A. (1941): Protection and Real Wages. Review of Economic Studies 9, 58-73

Swan, T.W. (1956): Economic Growth and Capital Accumulation. Economic Record XXXII, 334-61

Takayama, A. (1985): Mathematical Economics, 2nd edition. Cambridge: Cambridge University Press

Turnovsky, S.J. (1997): International Macroeocnomic Dynamics. Mass., Cambridge: The MIT Press

Uzawa, H. (1965): Optimal Technical Change in an Aggregative Model of Economic Growth. International Economic Review 6: 18-31

Valdés, B. (1999): Economic Growth – Theory, Empirics and Policy. Cheltenham: Edward Elgar

Wang, J.Y. (1990): Growth, Technology Transfer, and the Long-Run Theory of International Capital Movements. Journal of International Economics 29, 255-271

Wang, J.Y., Blomström, M. (1992): Foreign Investment and Technology Transfer - A Simple Model. European Economic Review 36, 137-155

Weiss, Y., Willis, R.J. (1985): Children as Collective Goods and Divorce Settlements. Journal of Labor Economics 3, 268-292

Weizsäcker, C.C. (1966): Tentative Notes on a Two-Sector Model with Induced Technical Progress. Review of Economic Studies XXXIII, 245-51

Wong, K.Y. (1995): International Trade in Goods and Factor Mobility. Mass., Cambridge: MIT Press

Zhang, W.B. (1989): Cyclical Economic Development with International Noninstantaneous Transfer of Technical Knowledge. International Journal of Systems Science 20, 311-321

Zhang, W.B. (1990): Economic Dynamics - Growth and Development. Heidelberg: Springer-Verlag

188   Bibliography

Zhang, W.B. (1990): Brain Drain and Economic Cycles with International Migration: A Case of Minimum Wage in the Unskilled Sector. Journal of Development Economics 32, 191-203

Zhang, W.B. (1990): Economic Growth and Technological Change. International Journal of Systems Science 21, 1933-1949

Zhang, W.B. (1991a): Regional Dynamics with Creativity and Knowledge Diffusion. The Annals of Regional Science 25, 179-191

Zhang, W.B. (1991b): Economic Development with Creativity and Knowledge Diffusion. Socio-Spatial Dynamics 2, 19-30

Zhang, W.B. (1992a): A Two-Country Growth Model - Knowledge Accumulation with International Interactions. Journal of Scientific & Industrial Research 31, 187-194

Zhang, W.B. (1992b): Trade and World Economic Growth - Differences in Knowledge Utilization and Creativity. Economic Letters 39, 199-206

Zhang, W.B. (1993a): Trade, Knowledge and Government Research Policy. International Review of Economics and Finance 2, 103-114

Zhang, W.B. (1993b): Knowledge, Economic Structure and Growth. Technological Forecasting and Social Change 43, 63-74

Zhang, W.B. (1993c): Woman's Labor Participation and Economic Growth - Creativity, Knowledge Utilization and Family Preference. Economics Letters 42, 105-110

Zhang, W.B. (1994a): A Multi-Country Free Trade Model With Capital Accumulation. International Economic Journal 8, 53-66

Zhang, W.B. (1994b): Knowledge, Growth and Patterns of Trade. The Annals of Regional Science 28, 285-303

Zhang, W.B. (1994c): Dynamics of Economic Geography with Return to Scale. Working Paper of CERUM, University of Umeå, CWP-1994:2

Zhang, W.B. (1995a): Leisure Time, Savings and Trade Patterns - A Two-Country Growth Model. Economic Modelling 12, 425-434

Zhang, W.B. (1995b): A Two-Country Dynamic Trade Model With Multiple Groups. International Economic Journal 9, 67-80

Zhang, W.B. (1996a): Knowledge and Value - Economic Structures with Time and Space. Uemå: Umeå Economic Studies of Umeå University

Zhang, W.B. (1996b): Growth, Trade and Land Values. Working Paper 96-1, Dept. of Social Systems Eng., Tottori University, Japan

Zhang, W.B. (1997): A Two-Region Model With Endogenous Capital and Knowledge - Locational Amenities and Preferences. International Review of Economics and Finance 6, 1-16

Zhang, W.B. (1998a): Japan versus China in the Industrial Race. London: Macmillan

Zhang, W.B. (1998b): Economic Geography with Two Regions - Capital Accumulation and Economic Structure. Australian Economic Papers 35, 225-35

Zhang, W.B. (1998c): A Two-Region Growth Model - Competition, References, Resources, and Amenities. Papers in Regional Science 77, 173-188

Zhang, W.B. (1999a): Capital and Knowledge - Dynamics of Economic Structures with Non-Constant Returns. Heidelberg: Springer

Zhang, W.B. (1999b): Confucianism and Modernization - Industrialization and Democratization of the Confucian Regions. London: Macmillan

Zhang, W.B (2000): Adam Smith and Confucius - *The Theory of Moral Sentiments* and *The Analects* (forthcoming)

Name Index

Aghion, P. 15, 109
Alonso, W. 162
Arrow, K.J. 15, 97
Arthur, W.B. 141
Ashenfelter, O. 53
Auerbach, A.J. 67

Baldwin, R.E. 108
Bardhan, P.K. 10
Barro, R.J. 98
Becker, G.S. 53, 54
Bhagwati, J.N. 9, 42, 80
Blomström, M. 16
Brody, A. 124, 141
Bruce, N. 10
Burmeister, E. 23, 24, 178

Cain, G.G. 53
Chamberlin, E. 13
Chiang, A.C. 42
Chiappori, P.A. 53
Chipman, J.S. 5, 11
Cole, H.L. 26

Deardorff, A.V. 23
Devereux, M.B. 11
Dixit, A.K. 4, 13, 17, 178
Dixon, H.D. 16
Djajic, S. 80
Dobell, A.R. 23, 24, 178
Dollar, D. 98
Domar, E.D. 23
Dosi, G. 97
Drandakis, E. 97
Duchin, F. 124

Eaton, J. 10, 12, 23, 42, 140
Edgeworth, F.Y. 9
Ethier, W.J. 8, 9, 12, 14

Fei, J.C.H. 53

Feldetein, M. 67
Fershtman, C. 26
Findlay, R. 9, 16, 23, 42
Fischer, S. 10
Folbre, N. 53
Francois, J.F. 14
Frenkel, J.A. 10, 23
Friedman, B.M. 179
Fung, K.M. 175

Gandolfo, G. 3, 8, 179
Gersovitz, M. 26
Graham, F.D. 12, 13
Grinols, E.L. 13
Grossman, G.M. 15, 98, 109

Haavelmo, T. 176
Hahn, F.H. 179
Hamada, K. 80
Hamilton, B.W. 53
Harrod, R.F. 23, 42
Heckman, J.J. 53
Heckscher, E. 8
Helpman, E. 13, 15, 17, 98, 109
Howitt, P. 15, 109

Ikeda, S. 23
Isard, W. 124
Ishikawa, J. 15, 175

Jensen, B.S. 15, 109
Johnson, H.G. 10
Jones, R.W. 3, 4, 9, 10, 42, 179
Jonung, C. 54

Kaldor, N. 42
Kemp, M.C. 10, 13
Kenen, P.B. 9, 179
Kennedy, C. 97
Keynes, J.M. 42
Knight, F.H. 12

Krugman, P.R. 13, 17, 98
Kuo, S.W.Y. 54
Kuznets, S. 141

Lancaster, K. 53, 178
Landesmann, M. 141
Layard, R. 53
Lazear, E.P. 53
Leontief, W.W. 124, 141
Lerner, A P. 8
Lewis, W.A. 141
Lucas, R.E. 45

MacDougall, G.D.A. 10
Macurdy, T.E. 53
Mailath, G.J. 26
Malthus, T.R. 176
Marglin, S.A. 42
Markusen, J.R. 13
Marshall, A. 4, 9, 12, 175, 176
Marx, K. 14, 18, 41
Matsuyama, K. 16
Matthews, R.C.O. 13
Maurer, R. 15
Melvin, J.R. 13
Milbourne, R. 80
Mincer, J. 53
Mill, J.S. 4, 5, 9
Mills, E.S. 53
Mirrlees, J.A. 42
Modigliani, F. 26, 42
Morishima, M. 1, 125, 141
Mussa, M. 10

Neary, J.P. 3, 179
Negishi, T. 4, 5, 13
Nelson, R.R. 15, 97
Niehans, J. 176
Nikaido, H. 141
Norman, V. 4

Obstfeld, M. 10
Ohlin, B. 8, 13
Oniki, H. 10, 23
Ono, Y. 23

Panagariya, A. 13
Panico, C. 42
Pasinetti, L.L. 42, 124, 141
Pavitt, K. 97
Persson, I. 53

Phelps, E.S. 15, 97
Postlewaite, A. 26

Ram, R. 26
Ramsey, F. 28
Ranis, G. 53
Rankin, N. 16
Rauch, J.E. 80, 98
Razin, A. 23
Ricardo, D. 1, 2, 18, 41
Rivera-Batiz, L.A. 16
Robson, A.J. 15
Rodriguez, C.A. 80
Romer, P.M. 15, 16, 97
Rosen, S. 54
Rostow, W.W. 141
Ruffin, R.J. 23, 42
Rybczynski, T.M. 8
Ryder, H.E. 10

Sala-i-Martin, X. 98
Salvadori, N. 42
Samuelson, P.A. 8, 10, 42, 97
Sato, R. 15, 97
Scazzieri, R. 141
Schultz, T.W. 97
Schumpeter, J.A. 14
Shi, S. 11
Smith, A. 1, 12, 14
Smith, A. 23
Smith, J. 54
Soete, L. 97
Solow, R. 23
Sraffa, P. 124, 141
Srinivasan, T.N. 42, 80
Stiglitz, J.E. 13, 17, 178
Stokey, N.L. 98
Stolper, W. 8
Svensson, L.E.O. 9
Swan, T.W. 23

Takayama, A. 178
Tsutsui, S. 15, 97
Turnovsky, S.J. 176

Uzawa, H. 10, 15, 23, 97

Valdés, B. 15

Wang, J.Y. 16, 23, 97
Weiss, Y. 26, 54

Weizsäcker, C.C. 97
Willis, R.J. 54
Winter, S.G. 15, 97
Wong, K.Y. 9, 15, 109

Zhang, W.B. 10, 11, 15, 17, 23, 24, 26,
  41-3, 80, 112, 175-9

Lecture Notes in Economics and Mathematical Systems

For information about Vols. 1–295
please contact your bookseller or Springer-Verlag

Vol. 296: A. Börsch-Supan, Econometric Analysis of Discrete Choice. VIII, 211 pages. 1987.

Vol. 297: V. Fedorov, H. Läuter (Eds.), Model-Oriented Data Analysis. Proceedings, 1987. VI, 239 pages. 1988.

Vol. 298: S.H. Chew, Q. Zheng, Integral Global Optimization. VII, 179 pages. 1988.

Vol. 299: K. Marti, Descent Directions and Efficient Solutions in Discretely Distributed Stochastic Programs. XIV, 178 pages. 1988.

Vol. 300: U. Derigs, Programming in Networks and Graphs. XI, 315 pages. 1988.

Vol. 301: J. Kacprzyk, M. Roubens (Eds.), Non-Conventional Preference Relations in Decision Making. VII, 155 pages. 1988.

Vol. 302: H.A. Eiselt, G. Pederzoli (Eds.), Advances in Optimization and Control. Proceedings, 1986. VIII, 372 pages. 1988.

Vol. 303: F.X. Diebold, Empirical Modeling of Exchange Rate Dynamics. VII, 143 pages. 1988.

Vol. 304: A. Kurzhanski, K. Neumann, D. Pallaschke (Eds.), Optimization, Parallel Processing and Applications. Proceedings, 1987. VI, 292 pages. 1988.

Vol. 305: G.-J.C.Th. van Schijndel, Dynamic Firm and Investor Behaviour under Progressive Personal Taxation. X, 215 pages.1988.

Vol. 306: Ch. Klein, A Static Microeconomic Model of Pure Competition. VIII, 139 pages. 1988.

Vol. 307: T.K. Dijkstra (Ed.), On Model Uncertainty and its Statistical Implications. VII, 138 pages. 1988.

Vol. 308: J.R. Daduna, A. Wren (Eds.), Computer-Aided Transit Scheduling. VIII, 339 pages. 1988.

Vol. 309: G. Ricci, K. Velupillai (Eds.), Growth Cycles and Multisectoral Economics: The Goodwin Tradition. III, 126 pages. 1988.

Vol. 310: J. Kacprzyk, M. Fedrizzi (Eds.), Combining Fuzzy Imprecision with Probabilistic Uncertainty in Decision Making. IX, 399 pages. 1988.

Vol. 311: R. Färe, Fundamentals of Production Theory. IX, 163 pages. 1988.

Vol. 312: J. Krishnakumar, Estimation of Simultaneous Equation Models with Error Components Structure. X, 357 pages. 1988.

Vol. 313: W. Jammernegg, Sequential Binary Investment Decisions. VI, 156 pages. 1988.

Vol. 314: R. Tietz, W. Albers, R. Selten (Eds.), Bounded Rational Behavior in Experimental Games and Markets. VI, 368 pages. 1988.

Vol. 315: I. Orishimo, G.J.D. Hewings, P. Nijkamp (Eds), Information Technology: Social and Spatial Perspectives. Proceedings 1986. VI, 268 pages 1988.

Vol. 316: R.L. Basmann, D.J. Slottje, K. Hayes, J.D. Johnson, D.J. Molina, The Generalized Fechner-Thurstone Direct Utility Function and Some of its Uses. VIII, 159 pages. 1988.

Vol. 317: L. Bianco, A. La Bella (Eds.), Freight Transport Planning and Logistics. Proceedings, 1987. X, 568 pages. 1988.

Vol. 318: T. Doup, Simplicial Algorithms on the Simplotope. VIII, 262 pages. 1988.

Vol. 319: D.T. Luc, Theory of Vector Optimization. VIII, 173 pages. 1989.

Vol. 320: D. van der Wijst, Financial Structure in Small Business. VII, 181 pages. 1989.

Vol. 321: M. Di Matteo, R.M. Goodwin, A. Vercelli (Eds.), Technological and Social Factors in Long Term Fluctuations. Proceedings. IX, 442 pages. 1989.

Vol. 322: T. Kollintzas (Ed.), The Rational Expectations Equilibrium Inventory Model. XI, 269 pages. 1989.

Vol. 323: M.B.M. de Koster, Capacity Oriented Analysis and Design of Production Systems. XII, 245 pages. 1989.

Vol. 324: I.M. Bomze, B.M. Pötscher, Game Theoretical Foundations of Evolutionary Stability. VI, 145 pages. 1989.

Vol. 325: P. Ferri, E. Greenberg, The Labor Market and Business Cycle Theories. X, 183 pages. 1989.

Vol. 326: Ch. Sauer, Alternative Theories of Output, Unemployment, and Inflation in Germany: 1960–1985. XIII, 206 pages. 1989.

Vol. 327: M. Tawada, Production Structure and International Trade. V, 132 pages. 1989.

Vol. 328: W. Güth, B. Kalkofen, Unique Solutions for Strategic Games. VII, 200 pages. 1989.

Vol. 329: G. Tillmann, Equity, Incentives, and Taxation. VI, 132 pages. 1989.

Vol. 330: P.M. Kort, Optimal Dynamic Investment Policies of a Value Maximizing Firm. VII, 185 pages. 1989.

Vol. 331: A. Lewandowski, A.P. Wierzbicki (Eds.), Aspiration Based Decision Support Systems. X, 400 pages. 1989.

Vol. 332: T.R. Gulledge, Jr., L.A. Litteral (Eds.), Cost Analysis Applications of Economics and Operations Research. Proceedings. VII, 422 pages. 1989.

Vol. 333: N. Dellaert, Production to Order. VII, 158 pages. 1989.

Vol. 334: H.-W. Lorenz, Nonlinear Dynamical Economics and Chaotic Motion. XI, 248 pages. 1989.

Vol. 335: A.G. Lockett, G. Islei (Eds.), Improving Decision Making in Organisations. Proceedings. IX, 606 pages. 1989.

Vol. 336: T. Puu, Nonlinear Economic Dynamics. VII, 119 pages. 1989.

Vol. 337: A. Lewandowski, I. Stanchev (Eds.), Methodology and Software for Interactive Decision Support. VIII, 309 pages. 1989.

Vol. 338: J.K. Ho, R.P. Sundarraj, DECOMP: An Implementation of Dantzig-Wolfe Decomposition for Linear Programming. VI, 206 pages.

Vol. 339: J. Terceiro Lomba, Estimation of Dynamic Econometric Models with Errors in Variables. VIII, 116 pages. 1990.

Vol. 340: T. Vasko, R. Ayres, L. Fontvieille (Eds.), Life Cycles and Long Waves. XIV, 293 pages. 1990.

Vol. 341: G.R. Uhlich, Descriptive Theories of Bargaining. IX, 165 pages. 1990.

Vol. 342: K. Okuguchi, F. Szidarovszky, The Theory of Oligopoly with Multi-Product Firms. V, 167 pages. 1990.

Vol. 343: C. Chiarella, The Elements of a Nonlinear Theory of Economic Dynamics. IX, 149 pages. 1990.

Vol. 344: K. Neumann, Stochastic Project Networks. XI, 237 pages. 1990.

Vol. 345: A. Cambini, E. Castagnoli, L. Martein, P Mazzoleni, S. Schaible (Eds.), Generalized Convexity and Fractional Programming with Economic Applications. Proceedings, 1988. VII, 361 pages. 1990.

Vol. 346: R. von Randow (Ed.), Integer Programming and Related Areas. A Classified Bibliography 1984–1987. XIII, 514 pages. 1990.

Vol. 347: D. Ríos Insua, Sensitivity Analysis in Multiobjective Decision Making. XI, 193 pages. 1990.

Vol. 348: H. Störmer, Binary Functions and their Applications. VIII, 151 pages. 1990.

Vol. 349: G.A. Pfann, Dynamic Modelling of Stochastic Demand for Manufacturing Employment. VI, 158 pages. 1990.

Vol. 350: W.-B. Zhang, Economic Dynamics. X, 232 pages. 1990.

Vol. 351: A. Lewandowski, V. Volkovich (Eds.), Multiobjective Problems of Mathematical Programming. Proceedings, 1988. VII, 315 pages. 1991.

Vol. 352: O. van Hilten, Optimal Firm Behaviour in the Context of Technological Progress and a Business Cycle. XII, 229 pages. 1991.

Vol. 353: G. Ricci (Ed.), Decision Processes in Economics. Proceedings, 1989. III, 209 pages 1991.

Vol. 354: M. Ivaldi, A Structural Analysis of Expectation Formation. XII, 230 pages. 1991.

Vol. 355: M. Salomon. Deterministic Lotsizing Models for Production Planning. VII, 158 pages. 1991.

Vol. 356: P. Korhonen, A. Lewandowski, J . Wallenius (Eds.), Multiple Criteria Decision Support. Proceedings, 1989. XII, 393 pages. 1991.

Vol. 357: P. Zörnig, Degeneracy Graphs and Simplex Cycling. XV, 194 pages. 1991.

Vol. 358: P. Knottnerus, Linear Models with Correlated Disturbances. VIII, 196 pages. 1991.

Vol. 359: E. de Jong, Exchange Rate Determination and Optimal Economic Policy Under Various Exchange Rate Regimes. VII, 270 pages. 1991.

Vol. 360: P. Stalder, Regime Translations, Spillovers and Buffer Stocks. VI, 193 pages . 1991.

Vol. 361: C. F. Daganzo, Logistics Systems Analysis. X, 321 pages. 1991.

Vol. 362: F. Gehrels, Essays in Macroeconomics of an Open Economy. VII, 183 pages. 1991.

Vol. 363: C. Puppe, Distorted Probabilities and Choice under Risk. VIII, 100 pages . 1991

Vol. 364: B. Horvath, Are Policy Variables Exogenous? XII, 162 pages. 1991.

Vol. 365: G. A. Heuer, U. Leopold-Wildburger. Balanced Silverman Games on General Discrete Sets. V, 140 pages. 1991.

Vol. 366: J. Gruber (Ed.), Econometric Decision Models. Proceedings, 1989. VIII, 636 pages. 1991.

Vol. 367: M. Grauer, D. B. Pressmar (Eds.), Parallel Computing and Mathematical Optimization. Proceedings. V, 208 pages. 1991.

Vol. 368: M. Fedrizzi, J. Kacprzyk, M. Roubens (Eds.), Interactive Fuzzy Optimization. VII, 216 pages. 1991.

Vol. 369: R. Koblo, The Visible Hand. VIII, 131 pages.1991.

Vol. 370: M. J. Beckmann, M. N. Gopalan, R. Subramanian (Eds.), Stochastic Processes and their Applications. Proceedings, 1990. XLI, 292 pages. 1991.

Vol. 371: A. Schmutzler, Flexibility and Adjustment to Information in Sequential Decision Problems. VIII, 198 pages. 1991.

Vol. 372: J. Esteban, The Social Viability of Money. X, 202 pages. 1991.

Vol. 373: A. Billot, Economic Theory of Fuzzy Equilibria. XIII, 164 pages. 1992.

Vol. 374: G. Pflug, U. Dieter (Eds.), Simulation and Optimization. Proceedings, 1990. X, 162 pages. 1992.

Vol. 375: S.-J. Chen, Ch.-L. Hwang, Fuzzy Multiple Attribute Decision Making. XII, 536 pages. 1992.

Vol. 376: K.-H. Jöckel, G. Rothe, W. Sendler (Eds.), Bootstrapping and Related Techniques. Proceedings, 1990. VIII, 247 pages. 1992.

Vol. 377: A. Villar, Operator Theorems with Applications to Distributive Problems and Equilibrium Models. XVI, 160 pages. 1992.

Vol. 378: W. Krabs, J. Zowe (Eds.), Modern Methods of Optimization. Proceedings, 1990. VIII, 348 pages. 1992.

Vol. 379: K. Marti (Ed.), Stochastic Optimization. Proceedings, 1990. VII, 182 pages. 1992.

Vol. 380: J. Odelstad, Invariance and Structural Dependence. XII, 245 pages. 1992.

Vol. 381: C. Giannini, Topics in Structural VAR Econometrics. XI, 131 pages. 1992.

Vol. 382: W. Oettli, D. Pallaschke (Eds.), Advances in Optimization. Proceedings, 1991. X, 527 pages. 1992.

Vol. 383: J. Vartiainen, Capital Accumulation in a Corporatist Economy. VII, 177 pages. 1992.

Vol. 384: A. Martina, Lectures on the Economic Theory of Taxation. XII, 313 pages. 1992.

Vol. 385: J. Gardeazabal, M. Regúlez, The Monetary Model of Exchange Rates and Cointegration. X, 194 pages. 1992.

Vol. 386: M. Desrochers, J.-M. Rousseau (Eds.), Computer-Aided Transit Scheduling. Proceedings, 1990. XIII, 432 pages. 1992.

Vol. 387: W. Gaertner, M. Klemisch-Ahlert, Social Choice and Bargaining Perspectives on Distributive Justice. VIII, 131 pages. 1992.

Vol. 388: D. Bartmann, M. J. Beckmann, Inventory Control. XV, 252 pages. 1992.

Vol. 389: B. Dutta, D. Mookherjee, T. Parthasarathy, T. Raghavan, D. Ray, S. Tijs (Eds.), Game Theory and Economic Applications. Proceedings, 1990. IX, 454 pages. 1992.

Vol. 390: G. Sorger, Minimum Impatience Theorem for Recursive Economic Models. X, 162 pages. 1992.

Vol. 391: C. Keser, Experimental Duopoly Markets with Demand Inertia. X, 150 pages. 1992.

Vol. 392: K. Frauendorfer, Stochastic Two-Stage Programming. VIII, 228 pages. 1992.

Vol. 393: B. Lucke, Price Stabilization on World Agricultural Markets. XI, 274 pages. 1992.

Vol. 394: Y.-J. Lai, C.-L. Hwang, Fuzzy Mathematical Programming. XIII, 301 pages. 1992.

Vol. 395: G. Haag, U. Mueller, K. G. Troitzsch (Eds.), Economic Evolution and Demographic Change. XVI, 409 pages. 1992.

Vol. 396: R. V. V. Vidal (Ed.), Applied Simulated Annealing. VIII, 358 pages. 1992.

Vol. 397: J. Wessels, A. P. Wierzbicki (Eds.), User-Oriented Methodology and Techniques of Decision Analysis and Support. Proceedings, 1991. XII, 295 pages. 1993.

Vol. 398: J.-P. Urbain, Exogeneity in Error Correction Models. XI, 189 pages. 1993.

Vol. 399: F. Gori, L. Geronazzo, M. Galeotti (Eds.), Nonlinear Dynamics in Economics and Social Sciences. Proceedings, 1991. VIII, 367 pages. 1993.

Vol. 400: H. Tanizaki, Nonlinear Filters. XII, 203 pages. 1993.

Vol. 401: K. Mosler, M. Scarsini, Stochastic Orders and Applications. V, 379 pages. 1993.

Vol. 402: A. van den Elzen, Adjustment Processes for Exchange Economies and Noncooperative Games. VII, 146 pages. 1993.

Vol. 403: G. Brennscheidt, Predictive Behavior. VI, 227 pages. 1993.

Vol. 404: Y.-J. Lai, Ch.-L. Hwang, Fuzzy Multiple Objective Decision Making. XIV, 475 pages. 1994.

Vol. 405: S. Komlósi, T. Rapcsák, S. Schaible (Eds.), Generalized Convexity. Proceedings, 1992. VIII, 404 pages. 1994.

Vol. 406: N. M. Hung, N. V. Quyen, Dynamic Timing Decisions Under Uncertainty. X, 194 pages. 1994.

Vol. 407: M. Ooms, Empirical Vector Autoregressive Modeling. XIII, 380 pages. 1994.

Vol. 408: K. Haase, Lotsizing and Scheduling for Production Planning. VIII, 118 pages. 1994.

Vol. 409: A. Sprecher, Resource-Constrained Project Scheduling. XII, 142 pages. 1994.

Vol. 410: R. Winkelmann, Count Data Models. XI, 213 pages. 1994.

Vol. 411: S. Dauzère-Péres, J.-B. Lasserre, An Integrated Approach in Production Planning and Scheduling. XVI, 137 pages. 1994.

Vol. 412: B. Kuon, Two-Person Bargaining Experiments with Incomplete Information. IX, 293 pages. 1994.

Vol. 413: R. Fiorito (Ed.), Inventory, Business Cycles and Monetary Transmission. VI, 287 pages. 1994.

Vol. 414: Y. Crama, A. Oerlemans, F. Spieksma, Production Planning in Automated Manufacturing. X, 210 pages. 1994.

Vol. 415: P. C. Nicola, Imperfect General Equilibrium. XI, 167 pages. 1994.

Vol. 416: H. S. J. Cesar, Control and Game Models of the Greenhouse Effect. XI, 225 pages. 1994.

Vol. 417: B. Ran, D. E. Boyce, Dynamic Urban Transportation Network Models. XV, 391 pages. 1994.

Vol. 418: P. Bogetoft, Non-Cooperative Planning Theory. XI, 309 pages. 1994.

Vol. 419: T. Maruyama, W. Takahashi (Eds.), Nonlinear and Convex Analysis in Economic Theory. VIII, 306 pages. 1995.

Vol. 420: M. Peeters, Time-To-Build. Interrelated Investment and Labour Demand Modelling. With Applications to Six OECD Countries. IX, 204 pages. 1995.

Vol. 421: C. Dang, Triangulations and Simplicial Methods. IX, 196 pages. 1995.

Vol. 422: D. S. Bridges, G. B. Mehta, Representations of Preference Orderings. X, 165 pages. 1995.

Vol. 423: K. Marti, P. Kall (Eds.), Stochastic Programming. Numerical Techniques and Engineering Applications. VIII, 351 pages. 1995.

Vol. 424: G. A. Heuer, U. Leopold-Wildburger, Silverman's Game. X, 283 pages. 1995.

Vol. 425: J. Kohlas, P.-A. Monney, A Mathematical Theory of Hints. XIII, 419 pages, 1995.

Vol. 426: B. Finkenstädt, Nonlinear Dynamics in Economics. IX, 156 pages. 1995.

Vol. 427: F. W. van Tongeren, Microsimulation Modelling of the Corporate Firm. XVII, 275 pages. 1995.

Vol. 428: A. A. Powell, Ch. W. Murphy, Inside a Modern Macroeconometric Model. XVIII, 424 pages. 1995.

Vol. 429: R. Durier, C. Michelot, Recent Developments in Optimization. VIII, 356 pages. 1995.

Vol. 430: J. R. Daduna, I. Branco, J. M. Pinto Paixão (Eds.), Computer-Aided Transit Scheduling. XIV, 374 pages. 1995.

Vol. 431: A. Aulin, Causal and Stochastic Elements in Business Cycles. XI, 116 pages. 1996.

Vol. 432: M. Tamiz (Ed.), Multi-Objective Programming and Goal Programming. VI, 359 pages. 1996.

Vol. 433: J. Menon, Exchange Rates and Prices. XIV, 313 pages. 1996.

Vol. 434: M. W. J. Blok, Dynamic Models of the Firm. VII, 193 pages. 1996.

Vol. 435: L. Chen, Interest Rate Dynamics, Derivatives Pricing, and Risk Management. XII, 149 pages. 1996.

Vol. 436: M. Klemisch-Ahlert, Bargaining in Economic and Ethical Environments. IX, 155 pages. 1996.

Vol. 437: C. Jordan, Batching and Scheduling. IX, 178 pages. 1996.

Vol. 438: A. Villar, General Equilibrium with Increasing Returns. XIII, 164 pages. 1996.

Vol. 439: M. Zenner, Learning to Become Rational. VII, 201 pages. 1996.

Vol. 440: W. Ryll, Litigation and Settlement in a Game with Incomplete Information. VIII, 174 pages. 1996.

Vol. 441: H. Dawid, Adaptive Learning by Genetic Algorithms. IX, 166 pages.1996.

Vol. 442: L. Corchón, Theories of Imperfectly Competitive Markets. XIII, 163 pages. 1996.

Vol. 443: G. Lang, On Overlapping Generations Models with Productive Capital. X, 98 pages. 1996.

Vol. 444: S. Jørgensen, G. Zaccour (Eds.), Dynamic Competitive Analysis in Marketing. X, 285 pages. 1996.

Vol. 445: A. H. Christer, S. Osaki, L. C. Thomas (Eds.), Stochastic Modelling in Innovative Manufactoring. X, 361 pages. 1997.

Vol. 446: G. Dhaene, Encompassing. X, 160 pages. 1997.

Vol. 447: A. Artale, Rings in Auctions. X, 172 pages. 1997.

Vol. 448: G. Fandel, T. Gal (Eds.), Multiple Criteria Decision Making. XII, 678 pages. 1997.

Vol. 449: F. Fang, M. Sanglier (Eds.), Complexity and Self-Organization in Social and Economic Systems. IX, 317 pages, 1997.

Vol. 450: P. M. Pardalos, D. W. Hearn, W. W. Hager, (Eds.), Network Optimization. VIII, 485 pages, 1997.

Vol. 451: M. Salge, Rational Bubbles. Theoretical Basis, Economic Relevance, and Empirical Evidence with a Special Emphasis on the German Stock Market.IX, 265 pages. 1997.

Vol. 452: P. Gritzmann, R. Horst, E. Sachs, R. Tichatschke (Eds.), Recent Advances in Optimization. VIII, 379 pages. 1997.

Vol. 453: A. S. Tangian, J. Gruber (Eds.), Constructing Scalar-Valued Objective Functions. VIII, 298 pages. 1997.

Vol. 454: H.-M. Krolzig, Markov-Switching Vector Auto-regressions. XIV, 358 pages. 1997.

Vol. 455: R. Caballero, F. Ruiz, R. E. Steuer (Eds.), Advances in Multiple Objective and Goal Programming. VIII, 391 pages. 1997.

Vol. 456: R. Conte, R. Hegselmann, P. Terna (Eds.), Simulating Social Phenomena. VIII, 536 pages. 1997.

Vol. 457: C. Hsu, Volume and the Nonlinear Dynamics of Stock Returns. VIII, 133 pages. 1998.

Vol. 458: K. Marti, P. Kall (Eds.), Stochastic Programming Methods and Technical Applications. X, 437 pages. 1998.

Vol. 459: H. K. Ryu, D. J. Slottje, Measuring Trends in U.S. Income Inequality. XI, 195 pages. 1998.

Vol. 460: B. Fleischmann, J. A. E. E. van Nunen, M. G. Speranza, P. Stähly, Advances in Distribution Logistic. XI, 535 pages. 1998.

Vol. 461: U. Schmidt, Axiomatic Utility Theory under Risk. XV, 201 pages. 1998.

Vol. 462: L. von Auer, Dynamic Preferences, Choice Mechanisms, and Welfare. XII, 226 pages. 1998.

Vol. 463: G. Abraham-Frois (Ed.), Non-Linear Dynamics and Endogenous Cycles. VI, 204 pages. 1998.

Vol. 464: A. Aulin, The Impact of Science on Economic Growth and its Cycles. IX, 204 pages. 1998.

Vol. 465: T. J. Stewart, R. C. van den Honert (Eds.), Trends in Multicriteria Decision Making. X, 448 pages. 1998.

Vol. 466: A. Sadrieh, The Alternating Double Auction Market. VII, 350 pages. 1998.

Vol. 467: H. Hennig-Schmidt, Bargaining in a Video Experiment. Determinants of Boundedly Rational Behavior. XII, 221 pages. 1999.

Vol. 468: A. Ziegler, A Game Theory Analysis of Options. XIV, 145 pages. 1999.

Vol. 469: M. P. Vogel, Environmental Kuznets Curves. XIII, 197 pages. 1999.

Vol. 470: M. Ammann, Pricing Derivative Credit Risk. XII, 228 pages. 1999.

Vol. 471: N. H. M. Wilson (Ed.), Computer-Aided Transit Scheduling. XI, 444 pages. 1999.

Vol. 472: J.-R. Tyran, Money Illusion and Strategic Complementarity as Causes of Monetary Non-Neutrality. X, 228 pages. 1999.

Vol. 473: S. Helber, Performance Analysis of Flow Lines with Non-Linear Flow of Material. IX, 280 pages. 1999.

Vol. 474: U. Schwalbe, The Core of Economies with Asymmetric Information. IX, 141 pages. 1999.

Vol. 475: L. Kaas, Dynamic Macroelectronics with Imperfect Competition. XI, 155 pages. 1999.

Vol. 476: R. Demel, Fiscal Policy, Public Debt and the Term Structure of Interest Rates. X, 279 pages. 1999.

Vol. 477: M. Théra, R. Tichatschke (Eds.), Ill-posed Variational Problems and Regularization Techniques. VIII, 274 pages. 1999.

Vol. 478: S. Hartmann, Project Scheduling under Limited Resources. XII, 221 pages. 1999.

Vol. 479: L. v. Thadden, Money, Inflation, and Capital Formation. IX, 192 pages. 1999.

Vol. 480: M. Grazia Speranza, P. Stähly (Eds.), New Trends in Distribution Logistics. X, 336 pages. 1999.

Vol. 481: V. H. Nguyen, J. J. Strodiot, P. Tossings (Eds.). Optimations. IX, 498 pages. 2000.

Vol. 482: W. B. Zhang, A Theory of International Trade. XI, 192 pages. 2000.